LATIN
FOR THE ILLITERATI

LATIN
FOR THE ILLITERATI

Exorcizing the Ghosts of a Dead Language

Jon R. Stone

ROUTLEDGE
New York & London

Published in 1996 by

Routledge
29 West 35th Street
New York, NY 10001

Published in Great Britain in 1996 by

Routledge
11 New Fetter Lane
London EC4P 4EE

Copyright © 1996 by Jon R. Stone

Printed in the United States of America
Design: Mary Neal Meador
Typography: Jack Donner

All rights reserved. No part of this book may be reprinted or reproduced or utilized in any form or by any electronic, mechanical, or other means, now known or hereafter invented, including photocopying and recording, or in any information storage or retrieval system without permission in writing from the publishers.

Library of Congress Cataloging-in-Publication Data

Stone, Jon R., 1959–
   Latin for the illiterati : exorcizing the ghosts of a dead language / Jon R. Stone.
       p.   cm.
   Includes bibliographical references (p.   ).
   ISBN 0–415–91774–3 (alk. paper). — ISBN 0–415–91775–1 (pbk. : alk. paper)
   1. Latin language—Dictionaries—English. 2. Latin language—Terms and phrases. I. Title.
PA2365.E5S76 1996
473'.21—dc20
                                                                                                 95–47985
                                                                                                      CIP

CONTENTS

Preface	ix
References	xiii
Pronunciation Guide	xv
Latin for the Illiterati	
Verba (Common Words and Expressions)	1
Dicta (Common Phrases and Familiar Sayings)	103
Abbreviations	153
Miscellaneous	165
English-Latin Index	173

To my mother
Bobbie Jean Stone
who taught me my first Latin words:
Amo, Amas, Amat

PREFACE

A decade ago, while in my first years of graduate study, I was taking a seminar in which my fellow graduate students and I were required to read standard theoretical works in the History of Religions. Among the books on that long list of dry academic tomes were several titles in the philosophy of religion, including Rudolf Otto's neo-Kantian work, *The Idea of the Holy* (or *Das Heilige*). It was here that I came face-to-face with the ghosts of a dead language: Latin.

Though as an undergraduate I had encountered the usual "i.e.s" and "e.g.s," along with the periodic "cogito ergo sums" and "et tu, Brutes," Otto presented a nearly insurmountable challenge to a boy who had studied German and Greek. Indeed, the proliferation of Latin words and quotations began to haunt me as I struggled through Otto's work. What was one to make of such things as the "numinous" experience (from the word "numen") with its characteristic religious feelings of awful dread and awe-inspiring fascination that Otto called "mysterium tremendum" and "mysterium fascinosum?" Worse still were the seemingly innumerable phrases that came with no corresponding English translation, leaving me to ward off these menacing spirits as best I could with a moldy old Latin dictionary I had found for half a dollar in a downtown used book store.

To help exorcize these daemons, I began keeping lists of the Latin words and phrases I continuously encountered in my reading. These lists began to grow over my several years of graduate study to the point that they filled a section of the weather-worn notebook I had used during my college days. It was at that point that I decided to type these lists into a handy reference book, not simply for my use but for the use of others likewise haunted. While I would not claim to have rid myself of these ghosts altogether—I still keep lists—I have become fairly comfortable with their presence in my life. What is more, one happy and incidental result of the struggle to deliver myself from my ignorance was a genuine love of Latin and an appreciation of its remarkable influence in the development of Western philosophical and cultural thought. But of greater importance, what I have learned over the past ten years is that one need not be haunted by the specter of Latin.

Latin forms an integral part of our daily lives and its use is foundational to our major branches of knowledge from law and medicine to literature and commerce. To deal adequately with its ubiquitous presence, it is necessary to have access to helpful reference tools. Unfortunately, few reference works exist that focus on remedying the challenges faced by the modern reader whose educational experience—even at the college level—is not firmly grounded in the so-called Classical tradition. Sadly, most of the books that are available to the general reader, while sometimes amusing, are really of no practical value (for instance, few of us have the occasion—or the inclination—to give a toast or recite the Gettysburg Address in Latin; and fewer still have an audience of relatives or interested business associates willing to endure such novelty). This book seeks to correct this deficiency by giving the student and general reader a helpful and practical reference guide. Here, then, is a fairly comprehensive compendium of nearly 6,000 Latin words, phrases, and standard abbreviations taken from the world of art, music, law, philosophy, theology, medicine and the theater as well as miscellaneous remarks and sagely advice from ancient writers such as Virgil, Ovid, Cicero, Terence, Juvenal, Seneca, and others, a *vade mecum* of sorts, that is meant to guide its users as well as instruct them.

Because the specific aim of this book is not to teach Latin but to help the modern reader exorcize the ghosts of this ancient and influential tongue, the various sections are arranged in alphabetical order, giving first the Latin word or phrase and then its common or usual meaning. In some cases, a literal translation of the word or phrase in brackets [ ] is given, followed by its more specialized meaning. An explanation of its origins or usage is sometimes given in parentheses. While most of the translations are not mine *per se*, having been culled from reference books and dictionaries over the years, many of the bracketed translations and most of the parenthetical remarks are my own, with the aid, that is, of *Cassell's Concise Latin Dictionary*. Although I have carefully checked and rechecked both the spellings and tenses of words, I fear that inadvertent errors may still have crept into this text. If mistakes exist beyond the rare editorial lapses, they are my own fault (*mea culpa, mea culpa, mea culpa*).

In addition, I have attempted to be gender-inclusive and gender-neutral

PREFACE

wherever possible and whenever such modifications did not compromise grammatical integrity too greatly or run counter to the spirit of a word's or phrase's meaning. I must also point out that on occasion the reader may spot a Greek word or two. As with most languages, foreign words also crept into Latin as the Roman Empire began to expand its territories through conquest. Many of those listed in this work became fairly standard by the Christian era, including such words as logos (word), sophia (wisdom), soter (savior), hippodromos (race track), margarita (pearl), and sarcophagus (coffin).

Finally, let me say a word or two about the insensitive or prejudicial sayings that occasionally appear in this work. In truth, I cringe at some of the phrases in the popular Roman "body of knowledge" that reveal a flagrant disregard of and disrespect for human cultural differences. However, in partial defense of the Romans, I think it is foolish for us moderns, with our greater historical and cultural perspective, to condemn a people who could not escape their own peculiar world with its illiberal views of women and its hostility towards all things foreign. We moderns certainly "know better" than the ancients did, though it did take us nearly two millennia to liberate ourselves from our unenlightened view of the world. Having said this, it must be remembered that, in the end, this book is a reference work, not an apology for Western Roman culture. Though we cannot erase our cruel and ignorantly insensitive past, we can certainly learn from it and endeavor to live above and beyond it.

Valeat Quantum Valere Potest.

Jon R. Stone
University of California, Santa Barbara
February 1995

REFERENCES

Angeles, Peter A. *Dictionary of Christian Theology*. NY: Harper & Row, 1985.
———. *Dictionary of Philosophy*. NY: Barnes & Noble Books, 1981.
Anon. *Latin for Lawyers* (2nd ed.). London: Sweet and Maxwell, LTD, 1937.
Cassell's Concise Latin-English/English-Latin Dictionary (compiled by D.P. Simpson). NY: MacMillan Publishing Co., 1977.
Hines, Sister Therese and Rev. Edward J. Welch, S.J. *Our Latin Heritage*. NY: Harcourt, Brace & World, 1966.
Horn, Annabel, John F. Gummere, and Margaret M. Forbes. *Using Latin*. Glenview, IL: Scott, Foresman and Co., 1961.
Koller, Hermann. *Orbis Pictus Latinus* (3rd ed.) Zürich: Artemis Verlag, 1983.
Mawson, C.O. Sylvester and Charles Berlitz (eds.). *Dictionary of Foreign Terms* (2nd ed.). NY: Barnes & Noble Books, 1979.
Meissner, C. *Latin Phrase-Book* (H.W. Auden, trans.). London: McMillan & Co., 1938.
Moreland, Floyd L. and Rita M. Fleischer. *Latin: An Intensive Course*. Berkeley: University of California Press, 1977.
Novum Testamentum Latine: Textum Vaticanum (11th edition, Eberhard Nestle, ed.). Stuttgart: Württembergische Bibelanstalt, 1971.
Reese, W. L. (ed.). *Dictionary of Philosophy and Religion: Eastern and Western Thought*. Atlantic Highlands, NJ: Humanities Press, 1980.
Webster's II: New Riverside University Dictionary. Boston: Houghton Mifflin Co., 1984.
Webster's New World Dictionary (3rd College Edition). NY: Prentice Hall, 1988.
Wheelock, Frederick M. *Latin* (College Outline Series). NY: Barnes & Noble Books, 1962.

PRONUNCIATION GUIDE

Pronouncing Latin words can seem mystifying at first, even daunting, but one need not utter Latin words and phrases with such tongue-tied trepidation. Most Latin sounds have corresponding English sounds, following the same rules for short and long pronunciation of vowels. For example, the long *a* in *father* is the same sound as the long *a* in the Latin word *pater*. The short *a* in the English words *par* and *far* are very similar in sound to that of the Latin words *pax* and *fax*. The short *e* in *pet* is similar in sound to the Latin *et*, as is the short *i* in *twig* the same as the *i* in the Latin word *signum*. The long *o* in *Ohio* sounds very much like the *o* in the Latin word *dolor*. In the same way, the short *o* in *pot* is pronounced similarly to the short *o* in *populas*. Likewise, the Latin *u* in *runa* and *pudicus*, one long and the other short, sound the same as the long and short *u* vowels in *rude* and *put*.

With respect to Latin consonants, one should nearly always pronounce them as those in English (e.g., **b** = b, **d** = d, **f** = f, **l** = l, **m** = m, **n** = n, **p** = p, **r** = r, **s** = s, **t** = t, etc.), with the exception of **c**, **g**, **h**, **i-j**, and **v**, which are always pronounced like **k** (as in kirk), **g** (as in give, gave, and go), **h** (as in hard), **y** (as in you, yam, and use), and **w** (as in we and was) respectively (though, I must confess, I have never heard William F. Buckley, Jr., quote Julius Caesar as having declared before the Roman Senate: "weenie, weedie, weekie" [i.e., "I came, I saw, I conquered"]. I suspect that most *literati* shy away from such ridiculous and silly sounding pronunciations as this one).

Vowel diphthongs are another matter. Most Classical Latin linguists prefer to pronounce **ae** as if it were a long *i* (as in pine), **oe** as *oi* (as in boy), **au** as *ou* or *ow* (as in bough or now), **ei** as a long *a* (as in weight), **eu** as *eu* (as in feud), **ui** as *wee* (as in the French *oui*).

XV

VERBA
Common Words and Expressions

A

a bene placito: at pleasure
a capite ad calcem [from head to heel]: from head to toe (i.e., completely or entirely)
a cuspide corona [from the spear a crown]: honor for military exploits
a dato: from date
a dextra: on the right
a die: from that day
a fortiori [with greater force]: more conclusively; in logic, an argument made from the lesser to the greater
a latere: from the side
a maximis ad minima: from the greatest to the least
a mensa et toro (or **thoro**) [from table and bed]: (leg.) from bed and board
a mille passibus: a mile away
a minori ad majus: from the lesser to the greater
a posse ad esse: from possibility to realization or reality
a posteriori [from after]: reasoning from specific instances to general conclusions (i.e., inductive or empirical knowledge)
a primo: from the first
a principio: from the beginning
a priori [from before]: reasoning from premise to logical conclusion (i.e., deductive or presumptive knowledge)
a pueris or **a puero:** from boyhood
a quo: from which (opposite of **ad quem**)
a sinistra: on the left
a teneris annis [from tender years]: from childhood or youth
a tergo [in the rear]: behind
a verbis ad verbera: from words to blows
a vinculo matrimonii [from the bonds of marriage]: an absolute divorce
ab: from
ab absurdo: from the absurd
ab aeterno: from the beginning of time
ab asino lanam [wool from an ass]: blood from a stone
ab epistulis [of letters]: secretarial matters
ab extra [from without]: from the outside
ab imo pectore: from the bottom of the heart

ab inconvenienti [from the inconvenience (involved)]: usually designating a law which should not be passed due to certain hardships or inconveniences it would create

ab incunabulis [from the cradle]: from childhood

ab infima ara: from the bottom of the altar

ab initio (ab init.): from the beginning

ab integro: anew

ab intra: from within

ab invito: unwillingly

ab irato [from an angry man]: in a fit of anger (i.e., not to be taken too seriously)

ab origine: from the origin or beginning

ab ovo [from the egg]: from the beginning

ab uno ad omnes: from one to all

ab urbe condita (A.U.C.): from the founding of the city (i.e., Rome)

abacus [a square board]: a hand-held calculating table

abest (pl. **absunt**): he/she is absent

abiit ad plures or **majores** (pl. **abierunt**): he/she has gone to the majority (i.e., is dead)

abnormis sapiens [unconventionally wise]: a natural-born philosopher

abscissio infiniti [cutting off the infinite or negative part]: in logic, the process by which the true conclusion is reached by a systematic comparison and rejection of hypotheses

absente reo (abs. re.): (leg.) the defendant being absent

absit invidia [let there be no ill-will]: no offense intended

absit omen: may the omen augur no evil

absolvo: I absolve

absonus: out of tune

absque [but for]: without

absque hoc [without this]: a legal term used in a special traverse or formal denial

abusque ulla nota: without any mark

abusus non tollit usum [abuse does not take away use]: (leg.) abuse is no argument against use

abyssus abyssum invocat: deep calls unto deep

Academia: The Academy (i.e., the grove near Athens where Plato taught his disciples)

accedas ad curiam [you may approach the court]: in English law, a common law writ to remove a case to a higher court

accentus: part of a church service chanted or sung by the priest and his/her assistant at the altar, distinguished from **concentus** which is sung by the congregation or choir

accepta [receipts]: credits

accessio initium regni: ascension to the throne

accessit (pl. **accesserunt**) [he/she came near]: "honorable mention" in a contest

accessus et recessus: ebb and flow

acerbus et ingens: fierce and mighty
acervatim [in heaps]: summarily
acta sanctorum: holy deeds of the martyred saints
actum agere: to do what has already been done
actum est: it is all over
actus: an act in a play
actus: an action or an actuality
actus Dei: an act of God
actus purus [pure act]: (theo.) a reference to God as a complete and perfect being
actus reus: (leg.) a criminal act
acus: a needle
ad: to or at; (med.) up to
ad absurdum [to what is absurd]: an argument which demonstrates the absurdity of an opponent's proposition
ad amussim [according to a rule]: accurately or exactly
ad annum: a year from now
ad aperturam libri [at the opening of the book]: wherever the book opens (a reference to a certain type of prognostication)
ad arbitrium: at will
ad arma concurrere: to rush to arms
ad astra [to the stars]: to an exalted place or to high renown
ad baculum [to the rod]: an argument or appeal which resorts to force rather than reason
ad captandum: an argument or appeal which is presented for the sake of pleasing the audience
ad captandum vulgus [to catch or attract the crowd]: to please the rabble
ad clerum: to the clergy
ad crumenam [to the purse]: an argument or appeal to one's personal interests
ad eundem gradum (ad eund.): to the same degree or standing
ad exiguum tempus: for a short time
ad extra: in an outward direction
ad extremum [to the extreme]: to the last or to the end
ad extremum tumulum: on the edge of the hill
ad filum aquae: (leg.) to the center of the stream
ad filum viae: to the center of the road
ad finem (ad fin.) [to or at the end]: finally
ad finem fidelis: faithful to the end
ad gloriam: for glory
ad gustum [to taste]: to one's taste
ad hanc vocem (a.h.v.): at this word
ad hoc [to this]: an action taken for a specific purpose, case, or situation
ad hominem [at the man]: an argument which appeals to personal prejudice or emotions rather than reason
ad horam compositam: at the agreed hour

ad hunc locum (a.h.l.): at this place

ad idem: to the same point

ad ignorantiam [to ignorance]: an argument or appeal that is ignorant of the needed facts

ad inferos descendere: to descend into the lower world

ad infinitum (ad inf. or **ad infin.)** [to infinity]: endless, limitless, or forever

ad initium (ad init.): at the beginning

ad instar [after the fashion of]: like

ad interim (ad int.): in the meantime

ad internecionem: to the point of extermination

ad invidiam [to envy]: an argument which appeals to prejudice or envy

ad judicium [to judgment]: an argument which appeals to common sense

ad libitum (ad lib.) [at pleasure]: in music, used as a direction to musicians to improvise a certain number of measures

ad limina apostolorum or **ad limina** [to the threshold of the Apostles]: to the highest authority

ad lineam: in a straight line or perpendicularly

ad litem: (leg.) for the suit or action

ad litteram or **ad literam** [to the letter]: literally

ad locum (ad loc.): to or at the place

ad lunam: by moonlight

ad manum [at hand]: in readiness

ad me: to my house

ad meridiem: southward

ad misericordiam [to pity]: an argument which appeals to pity

ad modum [in or after the manner of]: like

ad multam noctem: until late at night

ad multum diem: until late in the day

ad multus annos: for many years

ad nauseam [to nausea]: to the point of disgust

ad occasum: westward

ad occidentem: westward

ad ostium ecclesiae [at the church door]: at the marriage

ad patres [to the fathers]: dead or passed away

ad paucos dies: for a few days

ad perpendiculum: in a straight line or perpendicularly

ad perpetuitatem: forever

ad populum [to the people]: an argument which appeals to people's prejudices or passions

ad postremum: for the last time

ad quem: at or to which (the opposite of **a quo**)

ad quod damnum: (leg.) to what dammage

ad referendum [for reference]: for further consideration or for the approval of a superior

ad rem [to the matter]: a legal term denoting something relevant to the point at issue
ad sectam (**ads.**): (leg.) at the suit of
ad summam [on the whole]: in general or in short
ad summum: to the highest point or amount
ad tempus [at the right time]: in due time or according to the circumstances
ad ultimum: to the last
ad unguem [to a fingernail]: to a T (i.e., perfectly)
ad unum omnes [all to a one]: everyone without exception (i.e., unanimously)
ad usum (**ad us.**): according to custom
ad usum Delphini [for the Dauphin's use]: a work expurgated to avoid offending a prince or other high official
ad utrumque paratus [prepared for either event]: prepared for the worst
ad valorem (**ad val.**): according to the value
ad verbum [word for word]: literally or to the letter
ad verecundiam [to modesty]: an argument which appeals to modesty
ad vicem: in place of or instead of
ad vitam: for life
ad vitam aeternam [for eternal life]: for all time
ad vitam aut culpam [for life or until misbehavior]: during good behavior
ad vivum [to the life]: lifelike
adde (**add.**): (med.) let there be added (i.e., add)
adde huc (or **adde eo**) [add to this]: consider this as well
addendum (pl. **addenda**): an attachment to the end of a manuscript indicating the words to be added or corrections to be made
additum (pl. **addita**): something added
ades dum or **adesdum:** come hither
Adeste Fideles: O Come, All Ye Faithful
adfatim: sufficiently
adhuc sub judice lis est: (leg.) the case is still before the court
adiectivum or **adjectivum** (**adi.** or **adj.**): an adjective
adiratum (pl. **adirata**): (leg.) lost or strayed
adscriptus glebae (pl. **adscripti glebae**) [bound to the soil]: a serf
adsum [I am present]: here!
adsumptio: in logic, the minor premise of a syllogism
adumbratio: a sketch
adversa: things noted
adversaria [written observations]: a diary or journal
adverso colle or **adversus collem:** uphill
adverso flumine: against the stream
adversus (**adv.**): against
advocatus diaboli: the Devil's advocate (opposite of **promotor fidei** in an ecclesiastical argument in favor of the beatification of a person)
aeger [sick]: a medical excuse

aeger amore: love sick
aegis [a shield]: sponsorship or protection
aegra amans [lover's disease]: love sick
aegri somnia [a sick person's dreams]: hallucination
aegris oculis: with envious eyes
aegrotat (pl. **aegrotant**) [he/she is ill]: a medical excuse
aenigma: a riddle
aequabiliter et diligenter: uniformly and diligently
aequam servare mentem: to keep one's cool
aequanimiter [with equanimity]: with composure
aequi iniqui: friend and foe
aequinoctium autumnale: the autumnal equinox
aequinoctium vernum: the vernal equinox
aequo animo [with an equal spirit]: with equanimity or resignation (i.e., calmly)
aequo marte: a draw (i.e., an indecisive match)
aequum est: it is just
aere perennius [more lasting than bronze]: everlasting
aes alienum [money belonging to another]: debt or debts
aes publicum: a public inscription
aes signatum: coined money
aes triplex [triple brass]: a strong defense
aestas: summer
aestu incitato: at high tide
aetate progrediente: with advancing years
aetatis (**aet.** or **aetat.**): of the age or of one's lifetime
aetatis suae (**A.S.**): of his/her age or lifetime
aeternum vale: farewell forever
afflatus [breath or breeze]: poetic inspiration
afflatus montium: mountain air
Africus: the southwest wind (properly, **ventus Africus**)
age dum: come now
ager publicus: public land
agita (**agit.**): (med.) shake
agmen novissimum or **agmen extremum:** the rear guard
agmen primum: the vanguard
Agnus Dei [Lamb of God]: an appelation of Christ and a section of the Latin Mass
albae gallinae filius [a son of a white hen]: a fortunate son
albo lapillo notare diem [to mark a day with a white stone]: a red letter day
alere flammam: to feed the flame
alias dictus [otherwise called]: an alias
alibi: at another place
alieni appetens [eager for another's property]: covetous
alieni generis: of a different kind

alieni juris: (leg.) subject to the authority of another
alio intuitu: from another point of view
alio pacto: in another way
aliqua: in some way
aliud ex alio: one thing after another
aliunde [from another source]: from elsewhere
alius alias: one now, another later
alius alio: in various directions
alius aliter: in different ways
alma mater [fostering mother]: a university or other institution where a person has been educated
alter ego [one's other self]: a best friend or a bosom buddy
alter idem [another of the same kind]: a second self
alternis annis: every other year
alternis diebus: every other day
alternus: one after the other
alterum tantum [as much again]: twice as much
alteruter: one of two
altum silentium: deep silence or silence from on high
alumna [foster daughter]: a female graduate
alumnus [foster son]: a male graduate
amabo te or **amabo:** please
amantium irae: a lovers' quarrels
amari aliquid [something bitter]: a touch of bitterness
ambigendi locus: room for doubt
ambo [two together]: both
ambrosia: the food or nectar of the gods
amicissimus meus or **amicissimus mihi:** my best friend
amiciter: in a friendly way
amicitia sine fraude: friendship without deceit
amicus curiae [a friend of the court]: a disinterested advisor
amicus humani generis: a friend of the human race
amor habendi: love of possessing
amor nummi: love of money
amor patriae: love of country (i.e., patriotism)
amor proximi: love of one's neighbor
amor sui: self-love
amplissimi viri: men of the highest position
ancilla theologiae [the handmaid of theology]: philosophy
ancora: an anchor
anguis in herba [a snake in the grass]: an unsuspected danger
aniles fabellae: "old wives'" tales
anima bruta [the brute soul]: the vital principle of lower animals

anima divina: the divine soul
anima humana: the human soul
anima mundi [the spirit of the universe]: the creative and energizing force that permeates all nature
anima or **animus** (pl. **animae**): breath, soul, or spirit
animal disputans: an argumentative person
animal rationale: a reasoning person
animo aeger: (med.) heart-sick physically
animo et facto: (leg.) in intention and fact
animo fractus: heartbroken
animo furandi: (leg.) with the intention to steal
animo testandi: (leg.) with the intention of making a will
animus angustus: narrow-minded
animus capiendi: (leg.) the intention of taking
animus furandi: (leg.) the intention of stealing
animus gratus: thankfulness
annales (ann.): records or chronicles
annis tribus: three years ago (properly **abhinc annis tribus**)
anniversarius: yearly
anno aetatis suae (A.A.S.): in the year of his/her age
anno Christi: in the year of Christ
anno Domini (A.D.): in the year of our Lord
anno Hebraico (A.H.): in the Hebrew year (see also **anno mundi**)
anno Hejirae or **Hegirae (A.H.):** in the year of the Hegira (the Prophet Muhammad's flight from Mecca to Medina & the first year of the Muslim era, 622 C.E.)
anno humanae salutis (A.H.S.): in the year of man's redemption
anno interiecto: after the interval of a year
anno mundi (A.M.): in the year of the world since its creation (see also **anno Hebraico**)
anno post Christum natum (A.P.C.N.): in the year after the birth of Christ
anno post Roman conditam (A.P.R.C.): in the year after the building of Rome (ca. 753 B.C.E.)
anno regni (A.R.): in the year of the reign
anno salutis (A.S.): in the year of redemption
anno urbis conditae (A.U.C.): in the year of the founded city (i.e., Rome, ca. 753 B.C.E.)
anno vertente: in the course of the year
annos prope XL natus: almost forty years old
annos tres: three years ago (properly **abhinc annos tres**)
annos vixit (a.v.): he/she lived (so many years)
annua pecunia: an annuity
annus (pl. **anni**): year
annus bisextus: leap-year
annus luctus: year of mourning

annus magnus [great year]: the Platonic year; in astronomy, the year in which the celestial bodies make a complete cycle (about 26,000 years)

annus mirabilis [wonderful year]: a year of wonders (a reference especially to the year 1666 C.E., when the Great Fire ravaged most of London)

ante: before

ante bellum [before the war]: before the American Civil War

ante Christum (A.C.): before Christ

ante Christum natus (A.Ch.N.): before Christ's birth

ante cibum (a.c.): (med.) before meals

ante diem (a.d.): before the day

antehac [before this time]: formerly

ante litem motam: (leg.) before litigation has begun

ante lucem: before daybreak

ante meridiem or **ante meridianus (A.M.** or **a.m.):** before noon

ante mortem: before death

ante omnia [before all things]: in the first place

ante partum or **antepartum** [before birth]: before childbirth

ante tempus [too soon]: before its time

ante urbem conditam: before the founding of the city (i.e., Rome)

antecepta informatio: an innate idea

antenna: a sail yard (i.e., the cross piece of a ship's mast from which a sail hangs)

antiquitatis memoria: ancient history

anxius: uneasy

aper: a wild boar

apis: a bee

apologia pro vita sua: a defense or justification of the conduct of one's life

apotheca: a wine cellar or storage room

apotheosis [deification]: the transformation of a mortal into a deity at death

apparatus belli: munitions or materiel of war

apparatus criticus [critical apparatus]: reference texts used in scholarly work

apparet: it is clear

apricatio: sun-bathing

apricus: sunny

apud [according to]: in the writings of

apud Ciceronem: in the works of Cicero

apud me: at my house

apud patres: in the time of our fathers

aqua (aq.): water

aqua bulliens (aq. bull.): boiling water

aqua caelestis [celestial water]: pure rain water; also, a cordial

aqua destillata (aq. dest.): distilled water

aqua et igni interdictus [forbidden water and fire]: banished

aqua et ignis [water and fire]: the necessary things of life

aqua fontana: spring water
aqua fortis [strong water]: nitric acid
aqua mirabilis [wonderful water]: (pharm.) an aromatic cordial
aqua pura [pure water]: distilled water
aqua regia [royal water]: a mixture of nitric and hydrocloric acids
aqua saliens: a jet of water
aqua tofana [Tofana's water]: a poison made by a certain Tofana, a 17th century Sicilian woman infamous for its use
aqua vitae [water of life]: alcohol (i.e., whiskey or brandy)
aquarius: a water-carrier
aquilo: the north wind
ara: an altar
aranea: a spider
aratrum: a plow
arbiter bibendi [the judge of the drinking]: master of the feast (i.e., a toastmaster)
arbiter elegantiae or **elegantiarum** [a judge of elegance]: a judge in matters of taste
arbitrio suo: (leg.) under his own control
arbor infelix [infelicitous tree]: the gallows
arbor novella: a seedling
Arcades ambo [Arcadians both]: two persons of similar tastes or two simpletons; two of a kind (Virgil)
arcana caelestia [heavenly secrets]: celestial mysteries
arcana imperii: state secrets
arcanum arcanorum [secret of secrets]: a reference to the hidden keys that unlock the secrets of nature underlying alchemy, astrology, and magic
arcanus: secret or esoteric
arcus: a bow
arcus pluvius: a rainbow
ardentia verba [words that burn]: glowing words
ardor: a flame or heat from a flame
area [an open or level space]: a courtyard
arena sine calce [sand without lime]: an incoherent speech (Suetonius)
argentum (ag.): silver
argentum signatum: coined silver
argentum vivum: mercury
argumentum [argument]: a proof
argumentum ab auctoritate: in logic, a proof derived from authority
argumentum ab inconvenienti: in logic, an appeal to hardship or inconvenience
argumentum ad absurdum: in logic, an argument to prove the absurdity of an opponent's argument
argumentum ad baculum: in logic, an appeal to force or the threat of force (also **argumentum baculinum**)
argumentum ad captandum: in logic, an appeal made by arousing popular passions

argumentum ad crumenam [an argument to the purse]: in logic, an appeal to a person's interests

argumentum ad hominem: in logic, an evasive argument relying on attack of opponent's character

argumentum ad ignorantiam: in logic, an argument based on an opponent's ignorance of the facts or on his or her inability to prove the opposite

argumentum ad invidiam: in logic, an appeal to prejudices or base passions

argumentum ad judicium: in logic, an appeal to judgment or common sense

argumentum ad misericordiam: in logic, an appeal to pity

argumentum ad populum [argument to the people]: in logic, an appeal to people's lower nature rather than to their intellect

argumentum ad rem: in logic, a proper argument that bears on the real point of the issue at hand

argumentum ad verecundiam [also **ipse dixit**, or argument from authority]: in logic, an appeal to modesty or to a person's sense of reverence (e.g., a reliance on the prestige of a great or respected person rather than on the independent consideration of the question itself)

argumentum baculinum or **ad baculum:** in logic, an appeal to force or the threat of force

argumentum ex concesso [argument from concession]: an argument based on points already held by one's opponent

aries: a ram

arma accipere [to receive arms]: to be made a knight

arrectus auribus [with ears pricked up]: on the alert

ars amandi [the art of loving]: the art of love

ars artium [art of arts]: philosophical logic

ars artium omnium conservatrix [the art which preserves all arts]: printing

ars dicendi [the art of speaking]: oratory

ars fingendi: the art of sculpture

ars ludicra: the art of drama

ars magica: sorcery

ars moriendi: the art of dying

ars navigandi: seamanship

ars poetica: the art of poetry

ars Punica [the Punic art]: treachery

arteria: a blood vessel

artes ingenuae: the fine arts

artes liberales: the liberal arts

artes perditae: lost arts

arthriticus: pain in the joints of the body (i.e., arthritis)

articulorum dolor: (med.) a form of gout

Artium Baccalaureus (A.B. or **B.A.):** Bachelor of Arts

Artium Magister (A.M. or **M.A.):** Master of Arts

asinus: a jackass

asperges [thou shalt sprinkle]: the sprinkling with holy water at the beginning of the High Mass

assensio mentium [a meeting of the minds]: (leg.) mutual consent

Assensus [assent]: an essential item in Medieval Christian faith (together with **Fiducia** and **Notitia**)

assignatus utitur jure auctoris: (leg.) the assignee is possessed of the rights of the one he or she represents

assumpsit [he undertook]: (leg.) a suit to recover damages for breach of a contract or actionable promise, either expressed or implied

astrum: a star or constellation

atra cura [black care]: (fig.) in mourning

atrium: a hall

auctor ignotus: an unknown author

aucupia verborum: quibbling

audita querela [the complaint having been heard]: (leg.) a common law writ giving the defendant opportunity to appeal

augustus: majestic

aura (pl. **aurae**): wind, air, or breeze

aura popularis [the popular breeze]: popular favor (Cicero)

aurea mediocritas [the golden mean]: moderation in all things (Horace)

auris: the ear

auritus [long-eared]: attentive

aurora: dawn or the break of day

aurora australis [southern dawn]: the southern lights

aurora borealis [northern dawn]: the northern lights

aurum (au.): gold

auspex: an augar who observed the behavior of animals to foretell the future

auster: the south wind

australis: south

ave! [hail!]: Greetings!

Ave Maria: Hail Mary (salutation to the Virgin Mary)

Ave Regina Caelorum: Hail, Queen of Heaven (salutation to the Virgin Mary)

avis: a bird

avunculus [mother's brother]: an uncle (also **patruus**, father's brother)

B

babae!: wonderful!

baccalaris: a young nobleman seeking knighthood

baculum: a staff or walking stick

Bancus Communium Placitorum: (leg.) Court of Common Pleas

Bancus Regis: (leg.) King's Bench

Beata Maria or **Beata Virgo** (**B.M.** or **B.V.**): the Blessed Virgin

Beata Virgo Maria: the Blessed Virgin Mary
beata vita: happiness or bliss
beatae memoriae (B.M.): of blessed memory
beati possidentes [happy are those who possess]: possession is nine-tenths of the law
beatus [blessed]: a candidate for beatification in the Roman Catholic Church
belli denuntiatio: a declaration of war
belli ratio: (mil.) battle tactics
bellicum: (mil.) the signal for march or attack
bellum atrocissimum: a war of atrocities
bellum civile: civil war
bellum domesticum: civil war
bellum internecinum [internecine war]: a war of extermination
bellum intestinum: civil war
bellum lethale: deadly war
bellum omnium in omnes: a war of all against all
bellus: pretty
bene: well or good
bene!: excellent!
bene decessit [he died well]: he died naturally
bene esse: well-being
bene est: it is well
bene exeat [let him/her go forth well]: a certificate of good character
bene facis [I am obliged to you]: much obliged
bene facta: good deeds
bene habet: all right
bene merenti (pl. **merentibus**): to the well-deserving
bene meritus (pl. **meriti**): having well deserved
bene tibi or **bene te:** your health!
bene vale (b.v.): farewell
bene vale vobis [farewell to you]: good luck
benedicite!: bless you!
Benedictus qui venit in nomine Domini [Blessed is he who comes in the name of the Lord]: a section of the Latin Mass
beneficium [kindness or favor]: a benefice
benevolentia: good-will
benigne dicis [much obliged]: thank you or no thank you
benigno numine: by the favor of heaven
bes: two-thirds
bestia: a beast
bibliopola: a bookseller
bibliotheca: a library
biduum: a period of two days
biennium: a period of two years

bifariam: in two parts
bifurcus: having two forks or prongs
bilibra: two pounds weight
billa vera: (leg.) true bill
bimulus: two years old
bimus: lasting two years
bini [twofold]: a pair
bis [twice]: in music, to be repeated
bis bina [twice two]: two pairs
bis in die (b.i.d.): (med.) twice a day
bona: (leg.) property
bona aetas: youth
bona fide [in good faith]: sincerely or genuinely
bona fides [good faith]: honest intention
bona fiscalia: (leg.) fiscal or public property
bona gratia: in all kindness
bona mixta malis: a mixture of good and evil
bona mobilia: (leg.) movable goods
bona notabilia: (leg.) noteworthy things
bona pars: a considerable amount
bona peritura: (leg.) perishable goods
bona vacantia: (leg.) unclaimed goods
bona verba: words of good omen
bonae artes: good qualities
bonae memoriae: of happy memory
bonae notae: meritorious
bonis avibus [with good birds]: under favorable auspices
bono animo esse: to be of good cheer
bonum diffusivium sui [diffusing his goodness]: (theo.) a reference to the inherent goodness of the divine creation
bonum omen: a good omen
bonum publicum (b.p.): the common good
Boreas: the north wind
bos in lingua [an ox on the tongue]: speechless or silent
brevi praecidam: to put it briefly
breviarium [summary or abridgement]: a medieval devotional book containing the Psalms and other sacred writings
bruma: the winter solstice
brutum fulmen (pl. **bruta fulmina**) [a harmless thunderbolt]: an empty threat
bucina: a curved trumpet
bulla [a seal]: a papal encyclical or declaration

C

cacoëthes: a bad habit, an irrepressible desire or a mania
cacoëthes carpendi: a tendency to find fault
cacoëthes loquendi: a tendency to talk
cacoëthes scribendi: an itch for writing or scribbling
cadaver: a corpse
cadit quaestio [the question falls on the ground]: the discussion has come to an end
caduceus: a prophet's or messenger's staff
caelum: the heavens
calculus [a pebble]: a checker piece, voting pebble, or a counting piece
calidus: hot
caligo [fog or darkness]: mental darkness
callida junctura [skillful joining]: craftsmanship (Horace)
calvaria: the human skull
calvus: bald
calx: the heel
calx [limestone or chalk]: a goal marked with chalk (i.e., a finish line)
calx viva: quicklime
Camera Stellata [Star Chamber]: a tribunal or inquisitorial council; (fig.) a severe and arbitrary court
camera: a vaulted chamber or room
Campus Martius [Field of Mars]: a field used for military exercises
campus: a field or plain
cancer: a crab
candelabrum: a candlestick
candida Pax: white-robed Peace (Ovid)
candidatus [white-robed]: the traditional Roman dress of applicants for public office
candor [bright white]: (fig.) sincere
Canis Major [Greater Dog]: a constellation containing Sirius, the Dog Star
Canis Minor [Lesser Dog]: a constellation to the east of Orion
canis in praesepi [dog in a manger]: someone who keeps others from enjoying the use of what he or she is not using him or herself
Cantabrigiensis (Cantab.): of Cambridge
cantate Domino: sing unto the Lord
cantillatio: chanted portions of a religious service, as in the Mass
cantio or **cantus:** a song
cantor: a singer
cantoris: to be sung by the cantorial side of the antiphonal
cantus firmus [fixed song]: Gregorian melody
cantus planus [plain song]: Gregorian chant
caper: a he-goat
capiat (cap.): (med.) take

17

capillus: head of hair
capra: a she-goat
capricornus: a horned goat
capsa acuum: a box or container in which to hold pins or needles
captatio benevolentiae: reaching after or currying favor
caput (pl. **capita**): head
caput cenae: the main dish
caput lupinum [wolf's head]: an outlaw or fugitive from the law
caput mortuum [dead head]: worthless residue
caput mundi [capital of the world]: Rome
cardo: the north-south axis of an area divided into four sections by a crossroads
cardo duplex [a double hinge]: a cardinal point; the ends of the earth's axis (i.e., the poles)
caritas: love or charity
Carmen Christi [hymn of Christ]: (theo.) referring to the Pauline hymn to the incarnation of Christ (Philippians 2:5-11)
carmen epicum: epic poetry
carmen triumphale: a triumphal song
casa: a cottage
cassetur billa: (leg.) let the bill be set aside or tabled
casus [a falling or fall]: an occasion, event, or occurrence
casus belli: a cause justifying war
casus conscientiae: a case of conscience
casus foederis [a case of the treaty]: a case within the stipulations of a treaty
casus fortuitus [a fortunate fall]: a chance happening
casus omissus: (leg.) a case omitted or unprovided for
Caurus or **Corus:** the northwest wind
causa: a cause
causa causans [the cause that causes all things]: the Great First Cause; the cause of an action
causa causata [the cause resulting from a previous cause]: an effect
causa cognoscendi: cause of knowledge
causa essendi: cause of being
causa fiendi: cause of becoming
causa finalis: final cause
causa immanens [immanent cause]: change produced from within
causa latentis: hidden cause
causa mali [an evil cause]: a cause of mischief
causa privata: (leg.) a civil case
causa proxima: immediate cause
causa publica: (leg.) a criminal case
causa remota: remote cause
causa secunda: secondary cause

causa sine qua non: an indispensible condition (also **sine qua non**)
causa transiens [cause from beyond]: change imposed from without
causa vera: a true cause
cautim [cautiously]: with security or foresight
caveat [let him beware]: a warning or caution
Cena Domini: the Lord's Supper
cena: dinner
cenatus: after dinner
censor morum: a censor of morals
centum (cent.): a hundred
centum anni [a hundred years]: a century
centuplex: a hundred-fold
cera: wax
cerebrum: the brain
certamina divitiarum [struggles of riches]: strivings after wealth
certiorari [to be certified]: (leg.) a writ calling up the records of a lower court
certitudo salutis: (theo.) assurance of salvation
certo [certainly]: yes
cervix: the back of the neck
cessio bonorum: (leg.) a surrender of goods
cetera or **caetera desunt:** the rest are lacking
ceteris or **caeteris paribus (cet. par.):** other things being equal
ceteris rebus: as regards the rest
charismata: (theo.) spiritual gifts
chimaera: a mythical fire-breathing creature usually depicted with the head of a lion, the body of a goat, and whose tail is that of a serpent
chorea scriptorum: writer's cramp
chorus [to dance in a circle]: in theater, a troop of person's singing and dancing
Christianus: a Christian
Christus: Christ
cibus delicatus: delicacies
cicatrix manet: the scar remains
cingulum Veneris: the girdle of Venus
circa (c. or **ca.):** about, near, or around
circiter (c. or **circ.):** about
circuitus verborum [a circuit of words]: circumlocution
circulus in definiendo [a circle in defining]: a type of circular reasoning (i.e., a vicious cycle)
circulus in probando [a circle in proving]: a type of circular reasoning (i.e., a vicious circle)
circulus vitiosus [a vicious cycle]: circular reasoning
circum (c. or **circ.):** around or about
citato equo: at full gallop

civica corona [civic crown]: an award in recognition for those who had saved the life of a Roman in war

civis bonus [a good citizen]: a patriot

Civitas Dei: the City of God in opposition to the Earthly City (St. Augustine)

Civitas Terrena: the Earthly City in opposition to the City of God (St. Augustine)

clamor bellicus: a war-cry

classicum: a trumpet call

clava: a club

clavis (pl. **claves**) [key]: a glossary

clepsydra: a water clock used to measure the time allotted to orators

cochleare (coch.): (med.) a spoonful

cochleare magnum (coch. mag.): a tablespoonful

cochleare parvum (coch. parv.): a teaspoonful

codex: a book

codex rescriptus: a palimpsest

coelum: the heavens

cognati [connected by blood]: (leg.) relations on the mother's side

cognatus: related by birth

cognitus: known or proven

cognomen: a surname or family name

cognovit or **cognovit actionem** [he has acknowledged the action]: (leg.) the defendant's acknowledgement of the plaintiff's claim

cohors: a battalion

coitus interruptus [interrupted intercourse]: a method of natural birth control

collato pede: hand to hand fighting

collectanea: a miscellany or an anthology

collegium (pl. **collegia**) [a college]: a body or society of persons with common interests or pursuits

collis [high ground]: a hill

collum or **collus:** the neck

colluvies vitiorum [a collection of filthy vices]: a den of iniquity

collyrium: (med.) an eyewash

columna Herculis: the Pillars of Hercules

columna rostrata: a pillar in the Forum decorated with ships' prows

comata silva: in full leaf

comitas inter gentes [comity of nations]: civility among peaceful nations

comitia curiata: the original assembly of the Roman people

commentarii diurni: a diary

commisce: mix together

commodum: at the right or at a suitable time

commune bonum: the common good

communi consensu: by common consent

communibus annis: in common or average years

communicatio essentiae [communication of essence]: (theo.) a doctrine which teaches that Christ the Son receives his divine essence from God the Father

communicatio idiomatum [communication of similarities]: (theo) the transference of divine qualities to humans

communio sanctorum: communion of the saints

communitas: community or fellowship

complexio: in logic, the statement of a syllogism

complexus [an embracing]: an aggregate of parts or a complicated whole

componere lites: to settle disputes

compos mentis [sound of mind]: in one's right mind

compos sui: master of himself

compos voti: having obtained one's wish

concedo [I admit]: I grant (i.e., a concession made in an argument)

concentus [concord or harmony]: part of the church service sung or chanted by the congregation or choir, distinguished from **accentus,** which is sung by the priest and his/her assistant at the altar

concha: a seashell

conchylium: a type of shellfish from which purple dye is extracted

conciliatrix: a procuress

concio ad clerum: discourse to the clergy

concordia: harmony

concordia discors: discordant harmony

concubia nocte: at dead of night

condimentum: seasoning

condiscipulus [fellow student]: a classmate

conditio sine qua non: an indispensible condition

confer (cf.): compare

confessio: the tomb of a martyred saint

confiteor [I confess]: a prayer of public confession

congius (c.): (med.) a gallon

congressio or **congressus:** a meeting, an association, or a social encounter

conjunctis viribus [with united powers]: a confederation or an alliance

conjunx or **conjux (con.):** a marriage partner

conlegium: a guild

conlibitum est: it pleases or it is agreeable

connubium: intermarriage

consanguinitas: related by blood

conscientia mala: a bad conscience

conscientia recta: a good conscience

consensus: agreement

consensus audacium [agreement of the rash]: a conspiracy

consensus gentium: consent of the nations

consensus omnium: universal consent

consilium: a council or assembly

consortium: participation or a partnership

constat: it is agreed

consuetudo pro lege servatur [custom is held as law]: (leg.) where there are no specific laws, the issue should be decided by custom

consul designatus: a consul-elect

conterminus: bordering upon

continuetur remedia: (med.) let the cure be continued

contra (con.) [opposite]: against or on the opposite side (i.e., on the contrary)

contra bonos mores (cont. bon. mor.): contrary to good manners

contra formam statuti [against the form of the statute]: (leg.) against the letter of the law

contra jus fasque: (leg.) against all law, human and divine

contra jus gentium: (leg.) against the law of nations

contra legem: (leg.) illegally

contra mundum: against the world

contra pacem: (leg.) against the peace

contra rem publica: to the disadvantage of the state

contradictio in adjecto: a contradiction in terms

contraria contrariis curantur [opposites are cured by opposites]: the principle of allopathy

convenit [it is fitting]: it is agreed

converso ad occidens: facing west

conviva: a party guest

convivium: a feast or banquet

copia fandi: a great flow or abundance of talk

copia verborum [abundance of words]: prolixity

copula [a link or connection]: in logic, a form of the verb "to be" linking the subject and predicate terms of a proposition

cor: heart

coram: [before]: face to face or in the presence of

coram domine rege: before the lord our king

coram judice: (leg.) before a judge

coram nobis [before us]: (leg.) in the court of King's Bench

coram non judice [before a judge without jurisdiction]: (leg.) before one not the proper judge

coram paribus [before equals]: before one's peers

coram populo [in public]: in the sight of spectators

cordi est: I like it

cornu: a horn

cornu copiae: the horn of plenty (symbol of abundance)

corona: a crown or garland

corona lucis [crown of light]: a circular chandelier hung from the central interior roof of a church or cathedral

Corpus Christi [body of Christ]: Christian festival in honor of the Holy Eucharist
Corpus Juris Canonici: the body of canon law
Corpus Juris Civilis: the body of civil or Roman law
corpus [body or corpse]: a body or collection of writings
corpus delicti [the body of the crime]: the substance or fundamental facts of a crime
corpus humanum: the human body
corpus juris [body of law]: a collection of laws of a country or jurisdiction
corpus omnis Romani juris: compendium of all Roman law
corpus sine pectore: a body without a soul
corpus vile: a worthless matter
corrigendum (pl. **corrigenda**) [to be corrected]: corrections to be made in a book manuscript before publication
cortina Phoebi: the oracle of Apollo
cos ingeniorum: a whetstone for the wits
cras: tomorrow
cras mane: tomorrow morning
cras mane summendus: (med.) to be taken the next morning
cras mihi: my turn tomorrow
cras nocte: tomorrow night
cras vespere: tomorrow evening
crassa neglegentia or **crassa negligentia:** (leg.) gross negligence
crastinus: on the morrow
creatio ex nihil [creation from nothing]: (theo.) the belief that God created the world from absolute nothingness
crede Deo: trust God
credendum (pl. **credenda**) [a thing to be believed]: an article of faith
creditum: a loan
Credo in unum Deum [I believe in one God]: a section of the Latin Mass
credo [I believe]: a creed
crepusculum: twilight or dusk
crescens luna: a crescent moon
cribrum: a sieve
crimen (pl. **crimina**): (leg.) a crime
crimen falsi: the crime or charge of perjury
crimen laesae majestatis: the crime or charge of high treason
cruciatus tormentorum: the pains of torture
crucis supplicium: crucifixion
crus: a leg or shank
crustum: bread, cake, or pie
Crux: the Southern Cross
crux [cross]: a puzzle or a perplexing problem
crux ansata: the Egyptian ankh
crux commissa: the tau (T) cross

crux criticorum: the crux or puzzle of critics
crux decussata: the chi (X) cross of St. Andrew or St. Patrick
crux medicorum: the crux or puzzle of doctors
crux stellata: a type of cross in which its arms extend into stars
cubitum: the elbow
cui bono? or **cui bono fuisset?** [for whose advantage?]: to what end?
cui fuisset bono?: for whose advantage?
cui malo?: whom will it harm?
cuique suum: to each his own
cuius or **cujus (cuj.):** of which or whose
culmina Alpium: the Alpine summits
culpa: (leg.) fault or negligence
culpa lata: (leg.) gross negligence
culpa levis [a slight fault]: (leg.) excusable negligence
cultus animi [care of the soul]: education
cultus dei: worship of the gods
cultus deorum [care of the gods]: reverence or divine service
cum (c̄): with
cum bona venia: with your good favor
cum eo quod: on that condition
cum grano salis [with a grain of salt]: with reservation
cum imperio esse [to be vested with *imperium*]: to have unlimited power
cum laude [with praise]: with distinction
cum maxime: precisely
cum multis aliis: with many others
cum nimbo [with a cloud]: the halo surrounding the head of saints in sacred art
cum notis variorum: with the notes of various commentators
cum onere: (leg.) with the burden of proof
cum privilegio: with privilege
cum telo: armed
cum uxoribus et liberis: with wife and child
cumulus nimbus [a cloud heap]: rain clouds
cunabula: a craddle
cunae: a bird's nest
cuniculus: a rabbit
cupido: longing or desire
curatius: more carefully
curia advisari vult (cur. adv. vult or **c.a.v.):** (leg.) the court wishes to be advised or to consider the matter
currente calamo [with a running pen]: fluently; offhandedly
curriculum vitae (c.v.) [course of life]: a résumé (also **vitae curriculum**)
cursor [runner]: a messenger or courier
cursus curiae est lex curiae: (leg.) the practice of the court is the law of the court

custodia legis: (leg.) in the custody of the law
custodia libera: (leg.) house-arrest
custos: a custodian or guardian
custos morum: a custodian of morals
custos rotulorum (C.R.) [custodian of rolls]: the principle justice of the peace in an English county
cutis anserina [goose flesh]: goose bumps or goose pimples
cutis capitis: the scalp
cyathus [a ladle used for filling wine glasses]: a fluid measure (i.e., a cupful)
cyathus vinosus: a cupful of wine
cyma recta: a type of arch
cyma reversa: a type of arch

D

da (d.): (med.) give
damnosa haereditas [a damaging inheritance]: an inheritance that entails loss
damnum (pl. **damna**) [damage]: physical harm or material loss
damnum absque injuria [loss without injury]: (leg.) loss due to lawful competition
dante Deo: by the gift of God
dapes inemptae [unbought feasts]: home-made products
data et accepta [things given and received]: expenditures and receipts
datio [giving]: (leg.) the right of alienation
de auditu: from hearsay
de bonis asportatis: (leg.) of goods carried away
de bonis non administratis: (leg.) of the goods not yet administered
de bonis propriis [out of his own goods]: (leg.) out of one's own pocket
de bono et malo [of good and bad]: for better or for worse
de claro die: by the light of day
de die: while still day
de die in diem (de d. in d.): from day to day
de facto [in fact]: in reality or actually the case
de fide [of the faith]: (theo.) required as an article of faith
de fide et officio judicis non recipitur quaestio: (leg.) concerning the good faith and duty of the judge, no quesion can be allowed
de gratia: (leg.) by favor
de industria: intentionally
de integro: afresh or anew
de jure [by right]: (leg.) rightful or rightfully
de lana caprina [about goat's wool]: a non-existent or worthless thing
de lunatico inquirendo: (leg.) a writ to inquire into the sanity of a person
de monte alto: from the high mountain

de more: habitually
de nocte: while still night
de novo: anew or afresh
de pilo pendet [it hangs by a hair]: a precarious situation
de plano [with ease]: easily; (leg.) clearly, patently
de plebe: one of the people
de praesenti: of or for the present
de profundis: out of the depths (Psalm 130:1)
de proprio motu [of its own motion]: spontaneously
de tenero ungui: from childhood
de verbo in verbum or **de verbo** [word for word]: literally
dea: a goddess
debitum (pl. **debita**): (leg.) a debt
debitum naturae [the debt of nature]: death
Decalogus: the Ten Commandments
decani: in music, to be sung by the decanal side of the antiphonal
decanta: pour off
decanus [leader of ten]: a dean
decem anni: a decade
deceptio visus: an optical illusion
decessit sine prole (d.s.p.): died without issue
decet [it is fitting]: it is proper, either morally or physically
decor: grace or beauty
decretum (d.): a decree or an ordinance
decuma (or **decima**) [a tenth part]: a tithe
decumanus: the east-west axis of an area divided into four sections by a crossroads
dedita opera: intentionally
dediticii [those having surrendered]: subjects of Rome without rights
defectio lunae: a lunar eclipse
defectio solis: a solar eclipse
defectus sanguinis: (leg.) failure of issue
definiendum [that which is defined]: in definitions, the term that is to be defined
definiens [that which does the defining]: the definition of a term
definitum: a defined thing
Dei judicium [judgement of God]: trial by ordeal
Dei propitii: the favor of heaven
delenda: things to be deleted
delictum (pl. **delicta**) [fault or crime]: (leg.) an offense or misdemeanor
delineavit (del.): he or she drew it
delirium tremens (D.T.) [trembling delirium]: mental delusions caused by alcohol poisoning
dementia: insanity
dementia a potu [insanity from drinking]: delirium tremens

dementia praecox: (med.) a form of early insanity
deminutio capitis: loss of civil rights
demissi capilli: hair growing long
demonstratio: a type of oratory concerned with praise and censure
demortuus: the late (i.e., deceased)
denarius: a Roman siver coin
dens (pl. **dentis**): a tooth
descendere ex equo: to dismount a horse
desertus: a solitary place
desideratum: something desired (also **desiderium:** a yearning or desire for something)
desilio ad pedes: to dismount
desuetudo: disuse
desunt caetera or **desunt cetera:** the rest is wanting (e.g., the missing part of a quotation)
desunt multa: many things are wanting
detur [let it be given]: a book prize given to undergraduates at Harvard
Deus absconditus [the hidden God]: (theo.) the doctrine that God's nature is not fully revealed to humanity, even after the advent of Christ (Martin Luther)
Deus ignotus: an unknown or ignorant god
Deus pro nobis [God for us]: (theo.) those aspects and manifestations of God open to the finite human mind; God's direct relation to humans through Christ
deus: a god
deus ex machina [a god from a machine]: providential intervention, esp. in a play or a novel
deus incognitus: the unknown, unknowable God
deus mobilis: a changing or changeable god
deus philosophorum: the god of the philosophers (Lactantius)
deverticula flexionesque: twists and turns
dextimus: on the right hand or side
dextra: the right hand
dextras dare [to give right hands]: to shake hands as a pledge of good faith
dextro tempore [at the right time]: at the opportune moment
di or **dii majores** [the greater gods]: men of outstanding merit
di or **dii minores** [the lesser gods]: men of lesser merit
di or **dii penates:** household gods
diabolus: a devil
dic bona fide: tell me in good faith (Plautus)
dic quid sentias: give me your opinion
dicis causa or **dicis gratia** [for form's sake]: for the sake of appearances
dicitur [it is said]: they say
dictum (pl. **dicta**) [a word or speech]: a truism or witty sayings
dictum de dicto [report upon hearsay]: second-hand story
dictum factum: said and done

diebus alternis: every other day
diebus tertiis: every third day
diem ex die: from day to day
Dies Irae [day of wrath]: Day of Judgment (a hymn sung during the requiem mass)
dies: daytime or day
dies datus [a day given]: (leg.) a day appointed for hearing a lawsuit
dies dominicus: the Lord's day (i.e., Sunday)
dies faustus or **fasti:** a lucky day (i.e., the days on which the praetor could administer justice)
dies festus: a festival or holiday
dies infaustus: an unlucky day (inauspicious days for civic affairs or for court judgments)
dies juridicus: (leg.) a day on which the court sits
dies natalis: a birthday
dies nefasti or **nefasti** [forbidden days]: days on which no public business is transacted
dies non juridicus or **dies non:** (leg.) a day on which the court does not sit
dies profesti [common days]: week days (i.e., non-holy days)
difficiles nugae: hard-earned trifles
digitale: a thimble
digito monstrari [be pointed out with the finger]: to be famous
digitulus [little finger]: the touch of a finger
digitus [finger]: a finger's breadth (i.e., one inch)
digitus anularius: the ring finger
digitus auricularis: the little finger
digitus index: the index finger
digitus medius: the middle finger
digitus pollex: the thumb or big toe
dignus vindice nodus [a knot worthy of a liberator]: a difficulty needing divine intervention
diluculo: in the morning twilight
diluculum: dawn or daybreak
dilue (dil.): (med.) dilute or dissolve
diluvium: a flood or deluge
dimidia pars: half
dimidio minus [less by half]: half as much
dimissio: dismissal
dirae: bad omens
disciplina arcana [secret teaching]: rituals and doctrines known only to those fully initiated into a religion
discursus: running to and fro
disjecta membra: scattered parts or remains (i.e., fragments)
disparatum: in rhetoric, the contradictory proposition
dispendia morae: loss of time

dispudet: it is a great shame
dissolutio criminum: a refutation
dissolutio naturae: death
dissolutio navigii: shipwreck
diverbium: in theater, dialogue on the stage
divina particula aurae [divine particle of light]: the divine spirit in the human person
divinatio: (leg.) the selection of a prosecutor by the court
divinitas [divinity]: the power of prophecy or divination
Divinitatis Baccalaureus (D.B.): Bachelor of Divinity
Divinitatis Doctor (D.D.): Doctor of Divinity (an honorary degree)
divinitatis sensus: (theo.) an awareness of the divine presence in the world
divinus: superhuman or divine
dixi: I have spoken
do ut des [I give that you may give]: (leg.) a form of commutative contract
do ut facias [I give that you may do]: (leg.) a form of commutative contract
doctor utriusque legis: doctor of both Canon and Civil laws
doctrina: teaching or instruction
doctus cum libro [learned with a book]: a person who lacks practical knowledge
dodrans: three fourths in length (i.e., nine inches of a standard foot)
dogma: a philosophical doctrine
dolor: pain or sorrow
dolor artuum: (med.) gout
dolus: (leg.) fraud or deceit
dolus bonus: (leg.) permissible deceit
dolus malus: (leg.) unlawful deceit
domi [in the house]: at home
domi meae: at my house
domicilium or **domus:** a house
dominus et domina: lord and lady
domo: from home
domo carens: homeless
domo profugus: homeless
domum: homewards
Domus Procerum (D.P. or **Dom. Proc.):** the House of Lords
Dona Nobis Pacem: grant us peace (concluding section of the Latin Mass)
dono dedit (d.d.): given as a gift
donum superadditum [additional endowment]: (theo.) refers to those divine gifts humans lost at the Fall, such as knowledge, eternal happiness, and love
dorsum: the back
dramatis personae (dram. pers.): the cast of characters in a play
duces tecum [thou shalt bring with thee]: a subpoena
ductus oris: the lineaments of the face
dudum: some time ago

dulce 'Domum': sweet 'Home' or "Homeward" (English song sung at the end of the school term)
dulcis unda: fresh water
dum [while]: on the condition that
dum sola [while alone]: (leg.) while unmarried
dummodo [so long as]: provided that
duo: two
duo sextarii: a quart
duodecim: a dozen
duplex: double
duplus [twice as much]: (leg.) a double penalty
durante: during
durante absentia: (leg.) during absence
durante beneplacito [during our good pleasure]: (leg.) appointments made and unmade at the pleasure of the magistrate
durante minore aetate: (leg.) during minority
durante vita: (leg.) during life
dux: a leader or a guide
dux gregis [leader of the flock]: the leader of the pack

E

e contra: on the other hand
e contrario: on the contrary
e longinquo: from a distance
e re nata [under the present circumstances]: as matters stand
e re publica: in the interests of the state
e republica [in the public interest]: for the benefit of the state
e verbo [in word]: literally
ebriolus: mildly intoxicated (i.e., tipsy)
ebrius: drunk
Ecce Homo [behold the man!]: a representation of Christ crowned with thorns
ecce: behold!
ecce signum [behold the sign!]: here is the proof
eccere!: there you are!
ecclesia: a church
edere animam [to breathe (one's last) breath]: to die
edictum: a decree
editicius judices: jurors chosen by a plaintiff
editio cum notis variorum: an edition of a text with notes and commentary
editio princeps (pl. **editiones principes**): the first printed edition of a book
editio tribuum: (leg.) a proposal by a plaintiff for the choice of a jury

Editio Vulgata [common edition]: the Latin Vulgate version of the Bible
efferatus: stuffed full
efficiens causa: in philosophy, the efficient cause
ego: I
ego ipse: I myself
ejus modi [of this kind]: in that manner
ejusdem farinae: of the same flour
ejusdem generis: of the same kind
elapso tempore: the time having elapsed
elixir vitae: elixir of life
elogium: an epitaph on a tombstone or a codicil to a will
emeritus (fem., **emerita**) [veteran]: a title of honor denoting long and distinguished service
eminus: at or from a distance
empiricis: a physician who relies on practical rather than scientific knowledge (i.e., a quack)
emplastrum (pl. **emplastra**, pharm.): a plaster
emporium: a market or place of trade
emptor: a buyer
emunctae naris [of wiped nose]: a person of keen or mature judgment (Horace)
enim: namely
enimvero [to be sure]: certainly
enodis [without knots]: clear or plain
Ens Entium [Being of Beings]: the Supreme Being
ens (pl. **entia**): being or existence; an entity
ens rationis [a creature of reason]: a product of mental action
entia naturae: things of nature
entia rationis: things of reason
enuntiatum: a proposition
enuntio: in logic, to state a proposition
eo animo: with that intention
eo instante: at that moment
eo ipso [by that itself]: by that fact
eo loci: at that very place
eo nomine [by that name]: on this account
episcopus: a bishop
epistula: a letter
equi biiugi: two horses yoked abreast
equo admisso: at full gallop
equo incitato: at full gallop
equo vecto: mounted on horseback
equus: horse
equus bellator: a war-horse

ergo: therefore
erratum (pl. errata): an error or mistake
esse: being or existence (as opposed to **posse**)
esse in oculis: to be visible
esse in pretio: to be prized
est operae pretium: it is worth while
et: and or also
et alibi (et al.): and elsewhere
et alii (fem., aliae; et al.): and others
et cetera (etc.): and so forth
et conjunx (et conj.) [and husband or and wife]: and spouse
et hoc genus omne: and everything of this kind
et id genus omne: and everything of the kind
et nunc et semper: now and always
et sequens (et seq.): and the following
et sequentes (et seq.): and what follows
et sequentia: and what follows
et sic de ceteris: and so of the rest
et sic de similibus: and so of the like
et similia: and the like
et uxor (et ux.): and wife
etiam: yes
etiam atque etiam: again and again
eu! or **euge!** [well done!]: bravo!
Eurus: the southeast or east winds
evangelium: the Gospel
evocati: veterans called back to duty
ex abrupto [abruptly]: without preparation
ex abundante cautela: from excessive caution
ex abundantia: out of the abundance
ex acervo: out of a heap
ex adverso [from the opposite side]: in opposition
ex adyto cordis: from the bottom of the heart
ex aequo: on equal terms
ex aequo et bono: [according to what is right and good]: justly and equitably
ex animo [from the heart]: sincerely
ex animo effluere: to escape from the mind
ex auctoritate mihi commissa: by virtue of the authority vested in me
ex bona fide [in good faith]: on one's honor; sincerely
ex capite [out of the head]: from memory
ex cathedra [from the chair]: officially; with authority
ex commodo: conveniently
ex concesso [out of concession]: from what has been granted

ex consuetudine mea: according to my custom
ex contrario [on the other side]: on the contrary
ex curia: (leg.) out of court
ex delicto [from offense]: (leg.) by reason of an actionable wrong or a criminal deed
ex dono [by the gift]: as a present
ex dono Dei: by the gift of God
ex equo desilire: to dismount from a horse
ex facie [from the face]: on its face; (leg.) evidently
ex gratia [of or by favor]: (leg.) in absence of legal right
ex hypothesi: by hypothesis
ex improviso: unexpectedly
ex industria: on purpose
ex inopinato: unexpectedly
ex instituto: according to traditional usage
ex lege [arising from the law]: as a matter of law
ex libris or **e libris** [from the books of]: an inscription denoting ownership of a book (i.e., a bookplate)
ex longinquo: from a distance
ex memoria [from memory]: by heart
ex mera gratia: through mere favor
ex merito [according to one's desserts]: from merit
ex mero motu [of a mere impulse]: of one's own accord
ex morbo convalescere: to recover from a disease
ex more [according to custom]: habitually
ex necessitate rei [from the necessity of the case]: necessarily
ex officio (e.o.): by virtue of one's office
ex opere operantis [out of the work]: (theo.) refers to the efficacy of the sacrament coming from the goodness of the one dispensing it
ex opere operato [out of the operation of the work]: (theo.) refers to the efficacy of the sacrament despite the moral condition of the one dispensing it
ex parte [from one party]: in the interests of one side only; in part
ex pede Herculem [from the foot we recognize Hercules]: from a part we may divine the whole
ex post facto [after the deed is done]: after the fact
ex professo [by declaration]: avowedly or openly
ex proposito [by design]: purposely
ex propriis: from one's own resources
ex proprio judicio: from its own judgment
ex proprio motu: of his (or its) own accord
ex pueris excedere [to leave boyhood behind]: to become a man
ex quo [from which time]: since
ex quo tempore: since that time
ex quocunque capite: for whatever reason

ex re et ex tempore: according to time and circumstance
ex sanguis [without blood]: deathly pale
ex sententia: as one would wish
ex somnis: sleepless
ex tacito: tacitly
ex tempore: on the spur of the moment
ex toto: on the whole
ex usu [of use]: useful or advantageous
ex utraque parte: on either side
ex vi termini: by force of the term, limit, or restriction
ex voto: according to one's vow
ex vulnere mori: to die of wounds
exactio capitum: a poll tax
exanimis or **exanimus:** lifeless
exceptis excipiendis: (leg.) due exceptions or objections being made
excerpta [excerpts]: selections
excudit (exc.): he/she fashioned it
excursus: a digression
exempli causa: for instance
exempli gratia (e.g.) [for the sake of example]: for example
exemplum (pl. exempla): a sample or copy
exeunt (sing. exit) [they go out]: they leave the stage
exeunt omnes [all go out]: all leave the stage
exinde or **exin:** in logic, consequently or accordingly
exit (pl. exeunt): he/she leaves the stage
exlex: outside the law
expedit mihi: it is in my interest or to my advantage
experimentum crucis: a crucial test or experiment
explicit [here ends]: the end (written at the end of a book manuscript)
exploratum habeo: I am sure
expressio unius est exclusio alterius: (leg.) the express mention of the one is the exclusion of the other
expressio verbis: in express terms
exstat liber: the book is still extant
extra jocum [joking apart]: all joking aside
extra modum: beyond measure
extra muros: beyond the walls
extra ordinem: in an unusual manner; extraordinarily
extremum bonorum: the highest good
extremum malorum: the highest evil
extremus: the outermost

F

fabella: a fable or a little story
faber ferrarius: a blacksmith
faber tignarius: a carpenter
fabula: a comedy or a farce
fabulae!: nonsense!
fac sciam: let me know
fac ut sciam: tell me
facere sacramentum: to swear an oath
facies Dei revelata: (theo.) the revealed face of God
facile princeps [easily chief]: easily the first
facio ut des [I do that you may give]: (leg.) a type of commutative contract
facio ut facias [I do that you may do]: (leg.) a type of commutative contract
factum: an act or a deed
factum est: it is done
faeneus homines: men of straw
faex populi (pl. **faeses populi**) [dregs of the people]: the common rabble
fallacia consequentis [fallacy of the consequent]: in logic, a **non sequitur**
falsa lectio (pl. **falsae lectiones**): a false or erroneous reading
falsi crimen: (leg.) the crime of falsification
fama clamosa [noisy rumor]: a current scandal
fama est [it is rumored]: there is a rumor
familia: household
fanum [a temple and its grounds]: a holy place
farina: meal or flour
farrago libelli [the medley of that little book of mine]: a hodgepodge
fartum: stuffing
fas est [it is allowed]: it is lawful
fasces [bundle of sticks with protruding axe]: symbol of high office, such as a Roman Magistrate or Consul (later a symbol of fascist Italy under Benito Mussolini)
fasti [calendar of events]: annals
fasti et nefasti dies: lucky and unlucky days
faustis ominibus: with favorable omens
Favonius: the west winds
fax [a torch]: an instigator; a stimulus
febris: a fever
februum: religious purification
fecerunt (ff.) [they made it]: appended to the artists' names on a painting
fecit (fec.) [he/she made it]: appended to an artist's name on a painting
feles or **felis:** a cat
feliciter [happily]: fortunately

35

felix culpa! [O fault most fortunate!]: St. Augustine's allusion to the Fall of humanity that necessitated the coming of the Redeemer

felo-de-se (pl. **felones-de-se**): (leg.) suicide; also, an illegal act that results in the death of the felon

femina: a woman

femininum (f.): (gram.) feminine (also feminus)

femur: the thigh

fenestra [a window]: (leg.) a loophole

ferae naturae [of a wild nature]: undomesticated

ferrum (fe.): iron

ferus [a wild animal]: wild or uncivilized

fessa aetas: old age

fessus de via: travel weary

fessus viator: a weary traveler

fiat (ft.): let it be so!; (med.) let it be made

fiat haustus (ft. haust.): (med.) let a draft be made

fiat mistura (ft. mist.): (med.) let a mixture be made

fiat pulvis (ft. pulv.): (med.) let a powder be made

fictilia: pottery

fictilis (fict.) [earthen]: made of potter's clay

ficus: a fig tree; a fig

fide mea: on my word of honor

fidei defensor (F.D. or **fid. def.):** Defender of the Faith (a title of the English monarch)

fideliter: faithfully

fides publica: a promise of protection or of safe-conduct

Fiducia [trust]: an essential item in Medieval Christian faith (together with **Assensus** and **Notitia**)

fiducia sui: self-confidence

fieri facias (fi. fa.) [cause it to be done]: a writ commanding the sheriff to execute a judgment

filatim: thread by thread

filia: daughter

filioque [and from the son]: the clause later added to the Nicene creed by the Western Catholic Church that precipitated further the schism between Roman and Byzantine Christianity

filius: son

filius nullius [a son of nobody]: an illegitimate son

filius populi [a son of the people]: a bastard

filius terrae [a son of the earth]: a man of low birth or unknown origin

filiusfamilias: a son still under the power of his father

filum (pl. **fila**) [a thread]: a filament; a filar structure

finem respice [consider the end]: have regard for the outcome

finis: the end

finitum non capax infiniti [the finite cannot contain the infinite]: (theo.) a doctrine reaffirming the humanity of Christ
firmamentum: in rhetoric, the main point of an argument
fistula: a water pipe
flabellum or **flabrum:** a fan
flagrante bello [while the war is blazing]: during hostilities
flagrante delicto [while the crime is blazing]: in the very act of the crime (i.e., red-handed)
flatus vocis [a mere word]: not real (St. Anselm)
flebile ludibrium [a lamentable mockery]: a tragic farce
floreat: may it flourish
flores (fl.): flowers
floruit (fl. or **flor.):** flourished
flos: a flower or blossom
flos aetatis: the heyday
fluidum extractum (fldxt.): (med.) fluid extract
fluidus [liquid]: fluid
flumine adverso [against the stream]: upstream
flumine secundo [with the stream]: downstream
folio recto (f.r.): on the front of the page (i.e., the right-hand page)
folio verso (f.v.): on the back of the page (i.e., the left-hand page)
folium or **frons:** a leaf
fons: a fountain or fresh water spring
fons malorum: the source of evils
foramen magnum [great opening]: (anat.) the passage from the cranial cavity to the spinal canal
forceps: a pair of tongs
forfex: a pair of scissors
formica: an ant
fortitudini: for bravery
fortuna adversa: misfortune
fortuna prospera: good fortune
fortuna secunda: good fortune
forum: an open market or a public square
forum bovarium or **boarium:** the cattle market
forum holitorium: the vegetable market
forum piscarium or **piscatorium:** the fish market
fossa: a ditch
fossio: an excavation
frater (pl. **fratres**): a brother
frater germanus: one's own brother (as opposed to a step brother)
fratres: brothers and sisters
fraus est celare fraudem: (leg.) it is fraud to conceal fraud

fraus pia: a pious fraud
freno remisso: (to ride) with loose reins
frustillatim: bit by bit
frustra: in error; in vain
fuimus: we have been
fulmine ictus: struck by lightning
functus officio [having performed the office]: having resigned from office
funditus [from the bottom]: completely or entirely
fundus: the ground
fundus animae: the basis or basic essence of the soul
fungus: a mushroom
furca [two-pronged fork]: a pitch-fork
furnus: an oven
furor: madness
furor loquendi: a passion for speaking
furor poeticus: poetic inspiration
furor scribendi: a passion for writing
fusus crines: flowing free

G

Gallice [in Gaulish]: in French
gaudium certaminis: delight of battle
geminus (pl. **gemini**): twin
gemma: a gem or jewel
generalia: general principles
genesis [beginning]: the constellation that presides over one's birth
genitalis dies: birthday
genius loci (pl. **genii loci**) [the spirit of the place]: a guardian deity
gens togata [the togaed nation]: Roman citizens (Virgil); civilians generally
genus dicendi: a turn of speech or phrase
glebae ascriptus: attached to the soil
Gloria: glory
Gloria in Excelsis Deo: Glory be to God Most High (the "greater doxology")
Gloria Patri: Glory be to the Father (the "lesser doxology")
gloriae cupidus: one desirous of glory
gluten: glue
gluteus maximus: (anat.) the major muscle of the buttocks
gradarius: going step by step
gradatim [step by step]: gradually or by degrees
Gradus ad Parnassum or **Gradus** [a step to Parnassus]: an aid in writing Latin verse
grandis natu: aged

granum (gr.): (med.) a grain

gratia praeveniens [prevenient grace]: a Christian doctrine holding that God not only provides Grace but also the desire within the individual believer to receive it (St. Augustine)

gratias agere: to give thanks

gratias tibi ago: thank you

gratis dictum: a mere assertion

gratuitus: without cost

gratus animus: gratitude

gravatim: reluctantly

gravitas: serious or weighty

graviter ictus: severely wounded

gregatim [in flocks or in herds]: in droves

grege facto: (mil.) in close order

grex venalium: a venal throng

gubernaculum: a ship's rudder

gubernator [a pilot]: a governor or director

gurges: a whirlpool or eddy

guttae (gtt.): (med.) drops

guttatim: drop by drop

gyrus: a ring or a circle

H

habeas corpus ad subjiciendum or **habeas corpus (hab. corp.)** [that you have the body]: (leg) a writ requiring that officials bring a detained individual before a court to decide the legality of that individual's detention or imprisonment

habemus papa! [we have a father!]: the cheer of the people upon the election of a new Catholic pope

habet! [he has it]: he is hit (the cheer of the crowd when a gladiator is wounded, also **hoc habet!**)

hac lege [with this law]: with this proviso

hactenus: up to this point

haesitantia linguae: a speech impediment

hallex: the thumb or the big toe

haruspex: an augar who examined entrails of sacrificed animals or other natural phenomena, such as lightning, to foretell the future

haud dubie [not a doubt]: certainly

haud longis intervallis [at intervals by no means long]: at frequent intervals

haud or **haut:** by no means

haud passibus aequis [not with equal steps]: with unequal steps

haustus (haust.): (med.) a draught

Hecatean: magical

heliotropium: a sunflower
helluo librorum [a devourer of books]: a bookworm
hemina: half a pint
herba: grass
heres (pl. **heredes; her.**): (leg.) heir
heres ex asse: (leg.) a sole heir
heres ex besse: (leg.) heir to two-thirds of the property
heres ex dodrante: (leg.) heir to three-quarters of the estate
heri: yesterday
Hesperius: western
Hesperus: the Evening Star
hesterni quirites [citizens of yesterday]: slaves recently set free
hesternus: yesterday
heus: hello!
hiatus valde deflendus [a gap much to be regretted]: a person whose achievements fall short of earlier promise (also used to denote a blank space in a work)
hibernus: for the winter
hic et nunc: here and now
hic et ubique: here and everywhere
hic iacet or **hic jacet (H.I.)**: here lies
hic iacet sepultus (H.I.S.): here lies buried
hic sepultus (H.S.): here [lies] buried
hic situs est . . . : here lies . . .
hinc atque illinc: on this side and on that
hippodromos: a horse track or race course
his non obstantibus: notwithstanding these things
hoc age [this do]: mind what you are about (i.e., be attentive)
hoc anno (h.a.): in this year
hoc loco (h.l.): in this place
hoc mense (h.m.): in this month
hoc mihi placet: this pleases me
hoc monumentum posuit (H.M.P.): he/she erected this monument
hoc nocte [this night]: tonight
hoc quaere (h.q.): look for this
hoc sensu (h.s.): in this sense
hoc tempore (h.t.): at this time
hoc titulo (h.t.): under this title
hodie [this day]: today; at present
homicidium: murder
hominis iussu: with the sanction of a person
Homo Religiosus: religious man (Eliade)
Homo sapiens [wise man]: the human species of the genus **Homo**
homo (pl. **homines**): human being or man

homo ansatus: a person standing with arms akimbo
homo dissolutus: a libertine
homo doctus: a man of letters
homo ebriosus: a drunkard
homo elegans: a well-dressed person (i.e., a dandy)
homo erectus [upright man]: an early species of humans which stood upright
homo gloriosus: a braggert
homo ingeniosus: a person of talent or genius
homo liberalis: a generous or courteous person
homo ludens [playful man]: a definition of humans and human culture in terms of play (Huizinga)
homo montanus: a highlander
homo multarum literarum [a man of many letters]: a man of great learning
homo nefarius: an evil person
homo nullius coloris: a man of no party
homo plebeius: a man of the people
homo reus: (leg.) an accused or guilty person
homo Roma natus: a native of Rome
homo scelestus: a scoundrel
homo seditiosus: a rebel or insurrectionist
homo sine censu [a man without property]: the unlanded classes; the homeless
homo solitarius: a recluse
homo studiosus: a partisan
homo stultus: a fool
homo trium literarum [a man of three letters]: a thief (i.e., **fur**, a thief; Plautus)
homo viator: man the wanderer (Marcel)
homo voluptarius: a self-indulgent person
honoris causa [for the sake of honor]: with due respect; honorary
honoris gratia: honorary
hora (**H.** or **hor.**): (med.) hour
hora decubitus (**hor. decub.**): (med.) at bedtime
hora quota est?: what time is it?
horae canonicae [canonical hours]: hours for prayer
horae subsicivae: leisure hours
horno: this year
horologium: a timepiece
horribile dictu: horrible to tell
horribile visu: horrible to see
horsum: in this direction
hortus siccus [a dry garden]: an herbarium
hospes: a guest
hospes hostis: a stranger or enemy
hostia [an animal given in sacrifice]: a victim

hostis patriae: a rebel
huc et illuc: hither and thither
hui [hello!]: wow!
hujus anni: of this year
hujus mensis: of this month
Humaniora: the Humanities
humanitas: humanity
humi: on the ground
humili loco natus: of humble origin
Hydra: a many-headed water snake
hyperbole: an exaggeration
hypogeum: an underground vault

I

Iapyx or **Japyx:** the west-northwest wind
ibidem (ib. or **ibid.):** in the same place (e.g., in a book)
id aetatis: of that age
id demum: that and that alone
id est (i.e.) [that is]: that is to say
id genus omne: all that sort
id temporis: at that time
idem (id.) [the same]: the same as above
idem quod (i.q.): the same as
idem sonans [sounding alike]: having the same sound or meaning
identidem: repeatedly
iecur: the liver (thought to be the seat of the passions)
ieiunium: days of abstinence
ientaculum: breakfast
ignis: fire
ignobile vulgus [the lowborn multitude]: the great unwashed
ignorantia juris non excusat: (leg.) ignorance of the law does not excuse
ignoratio elenchi [ignorant reasoning]: in logic, the fallacy of refutation by indirection (i.e., disputing a point not raised by one's opponent)
ignotus (ign.): unknown
Ilias malorum [an Iliad of woes]: a series of calamities
ilicet [forthwith]: immediately
ilico: on the spot
illotis manibus [with unwashed hands]: unprepared
imagines majorum: portraits of ancestors
imago Dei [the image of God]: the divine aspect of the human person (Genesis 1:27)
imago mundi: a symbolic representation of the world

imitatio dei: religious rituals or other symbolic acts that replicate some divine action or sacred event (e.g., the Jewish Passover, the Christian Eucharist, the Hajj)
immedicabile vulnus: an incurable wound (Ovid)
immo: on the contrary
immodicus: excessive
immunis: exempt
immutata oratio: an allegory
imo pectore: from the bottom of the heart
impari Marte: with unequal military strength
impendio: very much
imperium singulare: absolute power
impermissus: forbidden
impietas: unbelief
implicite: by implication
impos animi [having no power over the mind]: an imbecile
impotens sui [having no power over one's self]: unrestrained; passionate
impotentia: poverty
impraesentiarum: for the present
imprimis [in the first place]: first in order
impulsu tuo: at your instigation
imum mare: the bottom of the sea
in absentia (i.a.): in absence
in absoluto: absolutely
in abstracto: in the abstract
in actu [in act or in reality]: in the very act
in adversum montem: up the mountain
in aequo: on equal terms
in aeternum [forever]: from everlasting to everlasting
in alio loco: in another place
in ambiguo [in doubt]: in a doubtful manner
in armis [in arms]: under arms
in articulo mortis: at the point or moment of death
in banco: (leg.) in full court
in banco regis: in the King's Bench
in bello: in time of war
in bonis: (leg.) in or among the goods or property
in camera [in chamber]: (leg.) at chambers (i.e., in private, not in open court); a meeting that is held in secret
in capite [in chief]: (leg.) rights bestowed by a feudal Lord
in carcerem: in prison
in cassum: in vain
in commendam [in trust for a time]: (eccles.) a benefice held by a person in absence of an incumbent

in concordia vocum: in unison
in contrarium: in an opposite direction
in contumaciam: (leg.) in contempt of court
in corpore [in body]: in substance
in cumulo: in a heap
in curia: in open court
in custodia legis: (leg.) in the custody of the law
in custodiam: in prison
in deposito [on deposit]: as a pledge
in die: on the day
in diem vivere [to live for today]: to live from hand to mouth
in dies (**in d.**): (med.) daily
in dies singulos: from day to day
in directum: in a straight line
in discrimine esse: to be at stake
in discrimine rerum [at the point of crisis]: at the turning point
in dorso: in or on the back
in dubio [in doubt]: undetermined
in dubium vocare: to call into question
in eo est [the position is such]: it depends on this
in equilibrio: in equilibrium
in esse [in being]: in actual existence (as opposed to **in posse**)
in excelsis: in the highest
in extenso: at full length (i.e., unabridged)
in extremis: at the point of death
in extremo libro: at the end of the book
in facie curiae: (leg.) in the presence of or before the court
in fieri [pending]: (leg.) in course of completion
in flagrante delicto [while the crime is blazing]: (leg.) in the very act (i.e., caught red-handed)
in folio [in leaves]: in a folio volume (i.e., in the form of a sheet folded once)
in forma pauperis [as a poor man]: (leg.) not liable to costs
in foro conscientiae: in the court or tribunal of conscience
in foro domestico: in a domestic court (as opposed to a foreign court)
in fumo: in smoke
in futuro: in the future
in futurum: for the future
in genere: in kind
in gremio legis [in the bosom of the law]: under the protection of the law
in hac parte: on this part
in horam vivere: to live for the moment
in horas: hourly

in illo tempore [in those days]: in the Golden Age (i.e., in the time when gods and goddesses walked the earth)

in incertum: for an indefinite period

in infinitum [to infinity]: forever

in intellectu: in the mind

in invidiam [in ill-will]: to excite prejudice

in invitum [against the unwilling]: compulsory

in ipso articulo temporis: in the nick of time

in ipso periculi discrimine: at the critical moment

in itinere [on the journey]: by the wayside

in jure: (leg.) according to the law

in limine (in lim.) [on the threshold]: in the beginning

in limine belli: at the outbreak of war

in litus or **in litore:** ashore

in loco [in the place]: in the proper or natural place

in loco citato (loc. cit.): in the place cited

in loco parentis: in the place of a parent

in longitudinem: length-wise

in majus: to a higher degree

in malam partem: in a bad sense

in manibus [hand to hand]: on hand

in medias res [into the midst of things]: into the heart of the matter (in literature, a story that begins in the midst of the plot)

in mediis rebus: in the midst of things

in medio: in the middle

in meditatione fugae: (leg.) in contemplation of flight

in melius mutari: to take a turn for the better

in memoriam [in memory]: in memory of

in meridiem: in the south

in mora [in delay]: (leg.) in default

in naturalibus [in a state of nature]: in the nude

in nomine: in the name of

in notis: in the notes

in nubibus [in the clouds]: befogged or confused

in nuce: in a nutshell

in obliquum [in an oblique direction]: sideways

in oculis civium [in the eyes of citizens]: in public view

in omne tempus: forever

in omnes partes: in all directions

in omnia paratus: prepared for all things

in omnibus [in all things]: in all respects

in ovo [in the egg]: undeveloped

in pace: in peace

in pari causa: in an equal cause
in pari delicto: (leg.) two equally at fault
in pari materia: in an analogous case
in partibus infidelium (i.p.i.) or **in partibus (i.p.)** [in the lands of the unbelievers]: a titular bishop whose title is that of an extinct Roman Catholic see
in pectore [in the breast]: in secret; in reserve
in periculo mortis: in danger of death
in perpetuam rei memoriam: in perpetual remembrance
in perpetuum: forever
in persona: in person
in personam [against the person]: (leg.) against a particular person as distinguished from a particular thing (**in rem**)
in plano: on a plane or level surface
in pleno: in full
in pontificalibus [in pontificals]: in episcopal robes
in posse [in possibility]: potentially (as opposed to **in esse**)
in posterum [for the next day]: for the future
in potentia [in possibility]: potentially
in praesens: for the moment
in praesens tempus: for the present time
in praesenti: at the present time
in praesentia: for the present
in primis: especially
in principio (in pr.): in the beginning
in privato: in private
in procinctu [with loins girded]: in readiness for battle
in promptu [in readiness]: at a moment's notice
in propatulo [in public]: publicly
in propria causa: (leg.) in his or her own suit
in propria persona: (leg.) in one's own person
in prospectu: in prospect
in publico [in the streets]: in public
in puris naturalibus: stark naked
in re [in the matter of]: concerning
in rebus multis [in many things]: tending to many things; busy in a matter
in rem [in or against a thing]: to one's advantage; (leg.) against a particular thing as distinguished from a particular person (**in personam**)
in rerum natura: in the nature of things
in saecula saeculorum [for ages of ages]: forever and ever
in se: in itself
in sequens: following
in singulos menses: in each month
in situ [in its place]: in proper position

in solidum or **in solido** [for the whole]: (leg.) jointly
in somnis: in a dream
in somno: asleep; in a dream
in statu pupillari: in a state of pupilage
in statu quo: in the state in which it was before
in statu quo ante bellum: in the state in which it was before the war
in tempore: at the right moment in time
in tempore ipso: at the very instant
in tempore opportuno: at the opportune time
in tempus [for a time]: temporarily
in tenebris [in darkness]: in a state of doubt
in terminis [in express terms]: definitely
in terram demergi: to sink into the earth
in terrorem: as a warning
in testimonium: in witness
in totidem verbis: in so many words
in toto [on the whole]: altogether
in toto caelo: as far as possible
in transitu (**in trans.**) [in transit]: on the way
in transversum: across
in tuto esse [to be in a position of safety]: in a safe place
in unguem [to a fingernail]: to a T (i.e., perfectly)
in universum [on the whole]: universal or universally
in unum: in or into one place
in usu: in use
in utero: in the womb
in utramque partem: pro and con
in utraque re: in both cases
in utroque fidelis: faithful in both
in utroque jure: (leg.) under both laws (i.e., civil and canon)
in utrumque paratus: prepared for either event
in vacuo: in a vacuum
in vadio: in pledge
in ventre: (leg.) in the womb
in vicem or **in vices** [in turn]: alternately; reciprocally
in vita esse: to be alive
in vitro [in glass]: in a test tube or petri dish
in vivo: (med.) in the living organism
inanis equus: riderless
Incarnatus [incarnate]: a part of the Nicene Creed referring to the incarnation of Christ
incipit: (lit.) here begins (i.e., the beginning of a literary text)
inhumatus: unburied

incoctus [uncooked]: raw

incognita causa: (leg.) without examination

incommodo tuo: to your disadvantage

incubus [nightmare]: a male spirit or demon believed to prey sexually on young women while asleep in their beds

Index Expurgatorius: a list of books from which offending passages must be purged before they may be read by Catholics

Index Librorum Prohibitorum: a list of prohibited books drawn up at the Roman Catholic Council of Trent, first published in 1557 and regularly updated

index [a sign]: the forefinger

index rerum [an index of matters]: a reference notebook

index verborum: an index of words

indicium (pl. **indicia**) [an indicating mark or sign]: a symptom

indicta causa: (leg.) without a hearing

indictum sit: be it unsaid

indidem: from the same place or matter

indolatus corpora: without funeral honors

indolentia: free from pain

inedita: unpublished compositions

inemptus: unbought

infamia: ill-fame

infaustus: unlucky

infelicitas: misfortune

infernus [below]: of the lower world

infidelis: unfaithful

infima species (pl. **infimae species**): the lowest species of a genus or class

infimo loco natus: from the lowest classes

infimus mons: at the foot of the mountain

infirmus [weak or feeble]: sickly

inflatilia: (music) wind instruments

inflatus [pompously]: on a greater scale

infra (inf.) [below]: further on (e.g., in a book)

infra dignitatem (infra dig.) [beneath one's dignity]: unbecoming

infrons: leafless

ingens aequor: the vast ocean

ingratus: thankless

ingratus animus: ingratitude

inibi: near at hand

inimicus: a public enemy

iniquus [uneven]: one-sided

initio (init.): in or at the beginning or start (usu. referring to a passage in a book)

initio anni: at the beginning of the year

inlex: lawless

inlicitus: illegal
innuba or **innupta:** unmarried
inolens: without smell
inquirendo [by inquiring]: (leg.) authority to inquire into something for the Crown
insalutato hospite [without saluting one's host]: without saying goodbye
insanabilis: incurable
insculpsit: he or she engraved it
insepultus: unburied
insomnis: sleepless
instar omnium: worth all of them
insula: an island
insuper: above; besides
integer vitae [blameless of life]: an upright person
intempesta nox: the dead of the night
inter: between or among
inter alia: among other things
inter alios: among other persons
inter cenam: during dinner
inter epulas [during the feast]: while feasting
inter nos [between ourselves]: mutually
inter pares: among equals
inter pocula [between cups]: over a glass
inter regalia: among or part of the regalia
inter se [between or among themselves]: reciprocally
inter vivos: among the living
intercus: under the skin
intercus aqua: (med.) dropsy
interdictum: a prohibition
interdius [in the daytime]: by day
interdum: now and then
interim: meanwhile
interlunium: the period of the new moon
intermundia: the space between the worlds
internus: inward; internal
interregnum: a period between two reigns
interrex: a regent or temporary chief magistrate
interrogatio: in logic, an argument (i.e., syllogism)
intertextus: interwoven
intra: inside; within
intra jactum: (mil.) within range
intra muros: within the walls [of a city]
intra parietes: within the walls [of a house]
intra vires: within the powers (of)

49

intrepidus: calm
intro: inwards; within
intuitu: in respect of
intumulatus: unburied
intus: from the inside; inwardly
inurbanus: rude
inutilis: useless
invenit (inv.): he or she designed it
inverso ordine: in inverse order
inversus: overturned; upside down
invictus: unbeaten
invidia: envy or jealousy
invitatu: by invitation
invitatus a me: at my invitation
invitatus a te: at your invitation
ipse dixit [he himself has spoken it]: a dictum
ipsissima verba: the very words
ipsissimis verbis: in the very words
ipso facto [by the fact itself]: by that very fact
ipso jure: by the law itself
ira deorum: the wrath of god; divine retribution
irrevocabile verbum: an irrevocably spoken word
ita: yes
ita res est or **ita est:** it is so
ita?: really?
Italice [in Italian]: in the Italian manner
item or **itidem:** likewise
iter impeditum: an impassable road
iter pedestre: going by foot
iter terrestre: going by land
iter unius diei: a day's journey
iterum [again]: anew; for the second time
itinera diurna nocturnaque: traveling day and night
Iudaeus: Jew
iussu: by order or by command

J

(N.B., the letter **j, J** was not known in Classical Latin but was created by Renaissance Italian humanists in order to distinguish consonated from non-consonated forms of **i, I**)

jam satis: already enough
januis clausis [with closed doors]: in secret

januae mentis [gates of the mind]: inlets of knowledge
joci causa: for the sake of the joke
judex: a judge
judex incorruptus: an impartial judge
judicia nulla [lawlessness]: anarchy
judicis: panel of jurors
judicium: a trial or legal decision
judicium Dei: the judgment of God
judicium perversum: a miscarriage of justice
jugulum (also **iugulum** or **iugulus**): the throat
jumentum: a beast of burden
junior: younger
Juppiter Tonans: Jupiter the Thunderer
jurare in verba magistri [to swear the words of the master]: a confession
jure: by right or by law
jure coronae: by right of crown
jure divino: by divine right or divine law
jure humano [by human law]: by the will of the people
jure mariti [by a husband's right]: by marital law
jure non dono: by right, not by gift
jure propinquitatis: by right of relationship
jure sanguinis: by right of blood
Juris or **Jurum Doctor [J.D.]:** doctor of law (a professional degree)
Juris Utriusque Doctor [J.U.D.]: doctor of both Canon and Civil laws
juris peritus: an expert in the law
jurisdictionis fundandae causa (or **gratia**): for the sake of establishing jurisdiction
jus (pl. **jures**) law; legal right
jus canonicum: canon law
jus civile: civil law
jus commune: common law
jus divinum: divine law
jus et norma loquendi [the law and rule of speech]: ordinary usage
jus gentium [law of nations]: international law
jus gladii [law of the sword]: supreme jurisdiction
jus in re: a real right
jus mariti: the right of a husband
jus naturae (or **naturale**): natural law
jus nullum: absence of justice
jus pignoris: right of pledge
jus possessionis [right of possession]: hypothecation
jus postliminii [law of postliminium]: restoration or repatriation of goods or persons captured during war upon coming once again under the jurisdiction of the original nation from which the goods or persons were taken

jus primae noctis: the right of the first night
jus proprietatis: right of property
jus regium: right of royalty
jus relicti: the right of the widow
jus sanguinis: the law of consanguinity (i.e., the citizenship of the parents determines the citizenship of the child)
jus soli: the law of the soil (i.e, the place of birth determines the citizenship of the child)
jusjurandum (pl. **jusjuranda**): an oath
jussu: by order or by command
justitiae tenax: tenacious of justice
justo tempore: at the right time
juxta [close by]: equally
juxta solem cadentem: in the west

K

Kyrie eleison [Lord, have mercy]: a section of the Latin Mass

L

labia or **labium:** the lip
labores solis: an eclipse of the sun
labrum: a bath tub or wash basin
lac: milk
lac concretum: curdled milk
lac recens: fresh milk
lacerta: a lizard
lacertus: the upper arm with its muscles
lacrima Christi: the tear of Christ
lacteus orbis: the Milky Way (also **orbis lacteus**)
lacuna: a gap or deficiency
laesa majestas [lese majesty]: high treason
laeva [left]: left-handed
lana caprina [goat's wool]: a nonexistent thing; a trifle
lapidarius: a stonemason
lapis (pl. **lapides**): a stone
lapis philosophorum: the philosopher's stone (an imaginary substance which alchemists believed would change base metals into gold)
lapsus [a slip]: a lapse or blunder
lapsus calami: a slip of the pen
lapsus linguae: a slip of the tongue

lapsus memoriae: a slip of the memory
lar (pl. **lares**): a tutelary deity or beneficent ancestral spirit
lar familiaris [household deity]: the spirit of the founder of the family
lares et penates [household deities]: the home
Latine [in Latin]: in the Latin manner or style
Latine dictum: spoken in Latin
Latissimus dorsi: (anat.) the back muscle
lato sensu: in a broad sense (the opposite of **stricto sensu**)
laudatio funebris: a eulogy
laudis cupidus: one desirous of praise
lectio senatus: the roll call of senators
lector benevole: gentle reader
lectori benevolo (L.B.): to the gentle reader
legalis homo [legal man]: a person of full legal rights
legatus a latere: a papal legate
legenda: things to be read
leges nullae [lawlessness]: anarchy
legis pacis: conditions of peace
Legum Baccalaureus (LL.B.): Bachelor of Laws
Legum Doctor (LL.D.): Doctor of Laws
leo: a lion
leonina societas: a leonine partnership (a legally invalid partnership in which the partner shares in the losses but not in the profits)
lepus: a hare
lex (pl. **leges**): law or statue
lex irrita est: a law is invalid
lex loci: the law of the place
lex mercatoria or **mercatorum:** mercantile law
lex non scripta [unwritten law]: common law
lex rata est: a law is valid
lex salica [law of the Salian Franks]: the ancient law denying the French monarchy to women
lex scripta [written law]: statute law
lex talionis: the law of retaliation (e.g., an eye for an eye)
lex terrae: the law of the land
libellus: a letter or petition
liber (pl. **libri; L.** or **lib.**): book
libertas: liberty or freedom
liberum arbitrium [free will]: free choice
libido (pl. **libidines**) [desire]: the sex instinct or sex drive
libra (lb.) [a pair of scales]: a Roman pound (i.e., 12 oz.)
licentia: excessive liberty or license
licentia vatum: poetic license

licet [it is permitted]: it is legal
lignator: a woodcutter
limbus [limbo]: the border regions of hell
limbus fatuorum: fool's paradise
limbus infantium [infants' paradise]: limbo for unbaptized children
limbus patrum [paradise of the Fathers]: the place for the souls of the righteous before the advent of the Christian Gospel
limbus puerorum: children's paradise
limen: a threshold
lingua [the tongue]: a language or tongue
lis pendens: (leg.) a pending lawsuit
lis sub judice: (leg.) a lawsuit before a judge yet to be decided
lite pendente: (leg.) during the trial
literati or **litterati** [persons of letters]: the learned class
literatim or **litteratim** [letter for letter]: literally
literatus or **litteratus** [well-read]: learned or educated
littera scripta manet: the written letter remains
Litterae Humaniores (Lit. Hum.): the Humanities (e.g., the ancient Classics)
litterae scriptae [written letters]: manuscripts
Litterarum Doctor (Litt.D.): Doctor of Letters
Litterarum Humaniorum Doctor (L.H.D.): Doctor of Humanties
loca deserta: the desert lands
loca inculta: uncultivated country
loca longinqua: distant places
loca plana [level country]: the plains
locatio [a letting]: (leg.) leasing
loci communes (sing. **locus communis**): public places
loco: in the place
loco citato (loc. cit. or **l.c.):** in the place cited
loco laudato (loc. laud.): in the place cited with approval
loco supra citato (l.s.c.): in the place cited before
locum tenens (pl. locum tenentes): a substitute or deputy, esp. for a physician or a cleric
locus (pl. **loci**) [a place]: a written passage
locus citatus: the quoted passage
locus classicus (pl. **loci classici**) [classical passage]: an oft-cited passage
locus communis (pl. **loci communes**) [a common place]: a public place; a place of the dead
locus criminis: the scene of the crime
locus delicti: the scene of the crime
locus in quo [place in which]: the place where a passage occurs
locus poenitentiae: a place or opportunity for repentance
locus pugnae: a battlefield
locus sigilli (L.S.): the place of the seal

locus standi [a place of standing]: recognized position; (leg.) right to appear before a court (i.e., a right to be heard by a judge)
logos: word
longitudo: length
longo intervallo: by a long interval
longus pedes sex: six feet long
loquitur (loq.): he/she speaks
lotio (lot.): (med.) a lotion
lubricus: slippery
lucescit [it grows light]: day is breaking
lucet [it is light]: it is day
lucidus ordo: a clear arrangement
lucifer [light-bringing]: the morning star
lucri causa: for the sake of gain
luctator: a wrestler
lucubratus [work done by a night lamp]: late night study
lucus a non lucendo [grove from not being light]: explanation by contraries (a play on words between *lucus* [grove] and *lucere* [to shine] which appear etymologically related but are not—hence the logical fallacy of drawing incorrect conclusions from seeming related facts)
ludus gladiatorius: a school for gladiators
ludus litterarius: an elementary school
lues: a plague
lues venerea: (med.) syphilis
lumen fidei: light of faith
lumen gratiae: light of grace
lumen naturale [light of nature]: natural intelligence
lumen naturale rationis [natural light of reason]: (theo.) knowledge of divine things without the direct assistance of God
luna: the moon
luna crescens: a crescent moon
luna decrescens: a gibbous moon
lunae lumen: moonlight
lusus naturae: a freak of nature
lux: light
lux mundi: the light of the world

M

mactatio [a sacrifice]: (theo.) refering to the sacrificial death of Christ
macte animo! [be increased in courage]: take courage!
macte virtute! [be increased in virtue]: go on and prosper!
macte!: well done! or good luck!

maculis distinctus: spotted
maculis interfusa: stained here and there
Magister Artium (M.A.): Master of Arts
magister: master or teacher
magister ceremoniarum: master of ceremonies
magister dixit: the master has spoken it (an invocation of the authority of Aristotle in Medieval scholasticism)
magister internus: inward teacher
magister ludi [master of the games]: an elementary school teacher
Magisterium: The Roman Catholic tradition, its authority, teachings, and holy offices
Magna Carta: the Great Charter of civil rights and freedoms signed by King John and the English nobility in 1215 C.E.
Magna Mater [the Great Mother]: a deity related to the ancient cult of Mithras
magna cum laude: with great praise
magna ex parte: to a great extent
magna voce: aloud
magni momenti: a great moment (i.e., a turning point)
magnificat [it magnifies]: a hymn of praise
magno cum detrimento: with great loss (of life)
magno cum fletu: with many tears
magno opere [very much]: greatly
magno pretio or **magni pretii:** at a high price (i.e., costly)
magnum bonum: a great good
magnum iter: (mil.) a forced march
magnum opus or **opus magnum** (pl. **magna opera**) [a great work]: an author's greatest work; a masterpiece
magus (pl. **magi**): a wizard or magician
Majestas Dei: (theo.) the majesty of God
major natu: older child
major pars: the majority
majusculae [uncials]: large capital letters characteristic of early Latin MSS
mala fide [in bad faith]: false or falsely; treacherously (opposite of **bona fide**)
mala in se: inherently evil
mala praxis: malpractice
male gratus: unthankful
maledictum: cursing
malevolentia: ill-will; malice
mali exempli [of bad example]: of bad precedent
malis avibus [with unfavorable birds]: under bad auspices
malleus: a hammer or mallet
malo animo: with intent to do evil
malo modo: in an evil manner

malum (pl. **mala**): an evil

malum in se [a thing evil in itself]: (leg.) a thing unlawful in itself, regardless of statute

malum prohibitum (pl. **mala prohibita**) [a prohibited evil]: (leg.) an act that is unlawful because it is forbidden by law (i.e., a legal crime though not necessarily a moral crime)

malus pudor: false modesty

mamma: the breast

mandamus [we command]: in English law, a high court writ issued to a lower court ordering performance of a legal duty or enforcement of a legal directive

mandatum: a message or commission

manes: spirits of the dead

manet [he/she remains]: he/she remains on stage

manet cicatrix: the scar remains

mania a potu [mania from drinking]: delirium tremens

manica [manicles]: handcuffs

manipulus: a handful

manu forti [with a strong hand]: by force

manu propria: with one's own hand

manumissio: emancipation from slavery

manuscriptum (**MS**; pl. **manuscripta**, **MSS**): a manuscript

mare clausum [closed sea]: a sea within the jurisdiction of a particular country

mare liberum [open sea]: a sea open to all

Mare Nostrum [our sea]: the Mediterranean Sea

margarita: a pearl

marginalia: marginal notes

marita: a wife

maritus: a husband

Marsicum bellum: the Social War between Marius and Sulla (90–88 B.C.E.)

mas or **masculus:** male or manly

masculinum (**m.**): masculine

🔴 **mater:** mother

Mater dolorosa [the sorrowing Mother]: the Holy Mother sorrowing at the Cross

materfamilias [a married woman]: the mother of the family or of the household

materia medica: (med.) notions and remedies used by physicians to heal patients

maximam partem: for the most part

maximus natu: the eldest child

me absente: in my absence

me auctore: by my advice

me duce: under my leadership or direction

me indicente: without my saying a word

me invito: against my will

me judice [I being judge]: in my opinion

57

me libente: with my pleasure or good-will
me paenitet [I regret it]: I'm sorry
me vivo: in my lifetime
mea culpa [my fault]: by my fault
mea de causa: on my account
mea gratia: for my sake
media acies: the center of the field of battle
media nox: midnight
media urbs: the city center
media via: the middle of the road; the middle way
Medicinae Doctor (M.D.): Doctor of Medicine
medicus: a physician
mediocris: middling; ordinary
meditatio fugae: (leg.) contemplation of flight
mediterraneus: inland
mel: honey
melioribus annis [in the better years]: in happier times
membratim [limb by limb]: one by one; piecemeal
membrum virile [the male member]: the penis
memento mori [remember you must die]: an object serving as a reminder of death
memorabilia: things worthy of remembrance
memoria in aeterna: in everlasting remembrance
memoria technica [artificial memory]: a system of memory (i.e., mnemonics)
memoriter [from memory]: by heart
mendicus: a beggar
mens divinior [a mind of diviner cast]: an inspired soul (Horace)
mens legis: the spirit of the law
mens rea: a guilty intent
mensa: a table or altar
mensa et toro (or **thoro**): (leg.) from bed and board
mensa secunda: dessert
mensis: month
menstruus: monthly or month long
mente captus: beside oneself
mentum: the chin
meo judicio: in my judgment
meo nomine: on my account
meo periculo [by my peril]: at my own risk
meo voto: by my wish
mercator: a merchant
mercatus: merchant business or trade
merda: excrement
meretrix: a harlot

meridies (**M.** or **m.**) [midday]: noon
messis ingrata: a poor harvest
messis opima: a good harvest
meum et tuum: (leg.) mine and thine (expressing rights of property)
meus [mine]: my friend (e.g., **Claudius meus:** my friend Claudius)
miles gloriosus: a boastful soldier
militia: warfare
mille passuum [a thousand paces]: a Roman mile
minimum: a very little
minimus: the smallest or the least
minor natu: younger
minus bene [less well]: unsatisfactorily
minusculae [small letters]: lower-case Roman letters in later Latin MSS
minutatim [bit by bit]: gradually
minutia (pl. **minutiae**) [smallness]: a trifle
mirabile dictu: wonderful to say
mirabile visu: wonderful to behold
mirabilia [wonders]: miracles
mirum in modum [in a wonderful manner]: surprisingly
misce: (med.) mix
miserabile dictu: sad to relate
miserable vulgus: a wretched mob
miserere mei: have mercy on me
misericordia [heart of mercy]: pity or compassion
Missa (pl. **Missae**): the Mass
Missa ad canones: (mus.) a Mass in canonic style
Missa ad fugal: (mus.) a Mass in fugal style
Missa bassa: Low Mass
Missa brevis: (mus.) a brief Mass
Missa cantata: Mass sung, but without deacon and sub-deacon
Missa catechumenorum: Mass of the catechumens
Missa fidelium: Mass of the faithful
Missa in Tempore Belli: Mass in Time of War (Haydn)
Missa sine nomine: (mus.) Mass without a name
Missa solemnis: High Mass
mitis sapientia: gentle wisdom
mitra [headdress]: a ceremonial hat worn by popes, bishops, and abbots
mittimus [we send]: a warrant of commitment to prison; a writ to remove records from one court to another; a dismissal or a discharge
mobile perpetuum: perpetual motion
mobile vulgus (**mob.**): the fickle masses (i.e., the mob)
modestia: sense of discipline
modo et forma: in manner and form

modo praescripto (mod. praesc.): (med.) as directed or prescribed
modus (pl. **modi**): a mode, method, or manner
modus operandi: a mode of operating
modus ponendo tollens: in logic, a mode of disjunctive syllogism that denies by affirming (e.g., either p or q; p, therefore not q; or vice versa)
modus ponens: in logic, a mode of hypothetical syllogism that affirms by affirming (e.g., if p then q; p, therefore q)
modus tollendo ponens: in logic, a mode of disjunctive syllogism that affirms by denying (e.g., either p or q; not p, therefore q)
modus tollendo tollens or **modus tollens:** in logic, a mode of hypothetical syllogism that denies by denying (e.g., if p then q; not q, therefore not p)
modus vivendi [manner of living]: (leg.) a temporary working agreement or compromise between two disputants pending a settlement of differences
moles belli: siege machines
mollia tempora: favorable occasions
momentum: movement or motion
mons: a mountain
morbo corripi: racked with disease
morbus comitialis: (med.) epilepsy
morbus ingravescit: (med.) the disease grows worse
mordicus [by biting]: with the teeth
more [after the manner of]: in the fashion of
more Anglico: in the English fashion
more dicto: in the manner directed
more Hibernico: in the Irish fashion
more meo [in my usual manner]: in my own way
more Socratico [after the manner of Socrates]: dialectically
more solito: in the usual manner
more suo [in his usual manner]: in his own way
mores (pl. **mos**) [customs, habits]: customary usages; (leg.) unwritten laws
mors immatura or **mors praematura:** an untimely death
mortis causa: by reason of impending death
mortuus: dead; defunct
morum praecepta: moral teaching
mos majorum: ancestral custom
mos pravus: a bad custom
mos pro lege [custom for law]: usage has the force of law
motu proprio [by one's own motion]: of one's own accord
mox: soon
mox nox: soon night
mulier: a woman
multa de nocte or **multa nocte:** late at night
multa paucis [much in little]: many things in few words
multi [the many]: the common crowd

multimodis [in many ways]: variously
multis cum lacrimis: with many tears
multis partibus: many times
multis rebus: in many respects
multo mane: early in the morning
multo post: much later
multorum deorum cultus: polytheism
multum in parvo: much in little
multus sermo: a long conversation
mundanus: a citizen of the world
mundi universitas: the universe
mundus: the world
mundus imaginalis: the world of images
mundus intelligibilis: the intelligible world
mundus sensibilis: the sensible world
muralis corona: the crown of honor given to the first person over the wall of a besieged city
murus: a wall
mus: a mouse
musca: a fly
muscae volitantes [flying flies]: (med.) specks before the eyes
mutanda: things to be altered
mutatis mutandis (m.m.): the necessary changes being made
mutato nomine: the name having been changed
mutuus consensus: mutual consent
mysteria: cultic mysteries or secret rites
mysterium fascinosum [a fascinating mystery]: (theo.) the feeling of awe-inspiring fascination in the presence of the Almighty God (Otto)
mysterium stupendum [an astounding mystery]: (theo.) to be dumbfounded or thunderstruck by the awareness of the presence of the Almighty God (Otto)
myterium tremendum [a tremendous mystery]: (theo) the feeling of awful dread in the presence of the Almighty God (Otto)

N

nares or **naris:** the nose
natale solum: native soil
natu: by birth
natura naturans [nature naturing]: (theo.) refers to God as the creative principle of created things (i.e., the infinite creating the finite)
natura naturata [nature natured]: (theo.) refers to created things which find their principle being in God (i.e., the finite dependent on the infinite)

naturae bona: natural advantages
naturae bonitas: innate goodness
naturalia: the sex organs
natus (n.): born
natus ad gloriam: born to glory
natus nemo [not a born soul]: not a human being; (fig.) a nobody (Plautus)
nauta: a sailor
navis: a ship
navis constrata: a decked ship
navis longa: a man-of-war
navis magister: a ship's captain
navis oneraria: a transport ship
navis praetoria: a flag ship
Ne Temere [not rashly]: a decree by the Roman Catholic Church invalidating all marriages not consecrated before a priest and the proper witnesses
ne admittas: do not admit
ne exeat regno or **ne exeat** [let him not go out of the realm]: a writ of restraint
ne multa: in brief
ne nimium [not too much]: do nothing in excess
ne obliviscaris [lest ye forget]: do not forget
ne plus ultra [not more beyond]: the highest point attainable or attained
nebula: a fog; a vapor
nebulo: a fog-headed person (i.e., good-for-nothing)
nec caput nec pedes [neither head nor foot]: in confusion
nec cede malis: yield not to misfortunes
nec cupias nec metuas: neither desire nor fear
nec more nec requies [neither delay nor rest]: without intermission (Virgil)
nedum: not to say
nefasti dies: unlucky days (in ancient Rome, assemblies did not convene and legal pronouncements were not made on these days)
negotia publica: public affairs
nemine contradicente: no one contradicting
nemine dissentiente: no one dissenting
nemo alius: no one else
nemo doctus: no man of learning
nemo est heres viventis: (leg.) no one is heir of a living man
nemo non: everyone
nepos: nephew or grandson
neptis: a granddaughter
nervus probandi [the sinew of proof]: the chief argument
nervus rerum [the sinew of things]: the strength of things
nescio quid: I know not what
neuter [neither]: of neither sex; in neither direction

neutrum (n.): neuter
nexus [a tying together]: connectedness
niger cycnus [black swan]: a prodigy (v.i., **rara avis**)
nigro notanda lapillo [to be marked with a black pebble]: a bad day
nihil: nothing
nihil ad rem [nothing to the point]: beside the point (i.e., irrelevant)
nihil attinet: it is pointless
nihil debet [he/she owes nothing]: (leg.) a plea denying a debt
nihil dicit or **nil dicit** [he says nothing]: (leg.) a common-law judgment when the defendant declines to enter a plea or to answer a charge
nihil non: everything
nihil obstat: there is no objection
nihil obstat quominus imprimatur [nothing hinders the work from being published]: the phrase that indicates acceptability to the Censor of the Roman Catholic Church printed on the title page of a published work
nihil omnino: not in the least
nil ultra [nothing beyond]: the farthest point or utmost limit
nimbus: a cloud; a rain cloud
nimis: more than enough; too much
ningit: it is snowing
nisi [if not]: unless
nisi prius [unless before]: (leg.) a trial held for civil cases before a judge and a jury
nisus: effort; striving
nisus formativus [creative effort]: the vital principle
nitrum: soda
nix: snow
nobilis [of noble birth]: known or celebrated
nobilis genere natus: of noble birth
nocte (n.): at night
nocte intempesta: at dead of night
noctiluca [light of the night]: the moon
noctu or **nocturnus:** by night
nolens volens [whether willing or not]: perforce (i.e., willy-nilly)
nolle prosequi (nol. pros.) [to be unwilling to prosecute]: an entry into court records indicating a stay or discontinuance of proceedings, either wholly or in part
nolo contendere [I do not wish to contest]: (leg.) a plea of "no contest" to criminal charges by the defendant without admitting guilt
nolo espiscopari [I do not wish to be made a bishop]: official refusal of a royal offer of a bishopric
nomen (pl. **nomina**): name
nomen atque omen: a name and also an omen (Plautus)
nomen genericum: a generic name
nomen nudum (pl. **nomina nuda**) [naked name]: in biology, a mere name without a proper description

nomen Romanum: the Roman Power
nomen specificum: a specific name
nomenclator: a servant or slave who reminded his master of names
nomine meo [in my name]: on my behalf
non: no
non adfici: to remain unaffected
non assumpsit [he/she did not undertake]: (leg.) a general denial in an action of *assumpsit*
non bis in idem [not twice for the same thing]: the legal principle of double jeopardy
non causa pro causa [not a cause for a cause]: in logic, the fallacy of false cause
non compos mentis: (leg.) not of sound mind
non constat [it does not appear]: (leg.) the evidence is not before the court
non dolet: it does not hurt
non ens [nonexistent]: a nonentity
non erat his locus: that was not the appropriate place for them
non esse [nonbeing]: nonexistence
non est: he/she/it is not
non est inventus [he/she has not been found]: (leg.) a statement by a sheriff on return of a writ of arrest when the defendant is not to be found
non est mens actus: (leg.) it is not my act
non est tanti: it is not worthwhile
non ita: not particularly
non laccessitus: unprovoked
non legitimus: unconstitutional
non libet: it is not pleasing
non licet (n.l.): it is not permitted
non liquet (n.l.) [it is not clear]: (leg.) the case is not proven
non nihil: something
non obstante (non obs.): notwithstanding
non obstante veredicto [notwithstanding the verdict]: (leg.) a verdict for the plaintiff setting aside a verdict for the defendant
non placet [it does not please]: a negative vote
non possumus [we cannot]: a statement expressing inability to act in a matter
non prosequitur (non pros.) [he/she does not prosecute]: a judgment where the plaintiff does not appear
non sequitur (non seq.): it does not follow
non sine causa [not without cause]: with good reason
nondum: not yet
nondum editus: unpublished
nondum natus: unborn
norma: a rule; a standard
nostri: our people
nostro periculo: at our own risk

nota bene (**N.B.** or **n.b.**) [note well]: take notice
nota per experientiam: in logic, a proposition that is evident by experience as derived by the principle of induction
notandum (pl. **notanda**): a memorandum
notatu dignum: worthy of note
Notitia [understanding]: an essential item in Medieval Christian faith (together with **Assensus** and **Fiducia**)
notitia illata: acquired knowledge
notitia innata: innate knowledge
notitia intuitiva: intuitive knowledge
nova luna: a new moon
novae res: a political revolution
novae tabulae [new ledgers]: a cancellation of debts
novalis: fallow ground; also a cultivated field
novena (pl. **novenae**): a nine-day period of religious observance or devotion
novissima verba: a person's last words
novus homo [a new man]: an upstart; a parvenu
novus rex, nova lex: new king, new law
nox (pl. **noctis**): night
nox luna inlustris: a moonlit night
nucleus: a pit or stone
nuda veritas: the naked truth (Horace)
nudatum corpus: the naked body
nudis verbis: in plain words
nudius tertius: the day before yesterday
nudum pactum [a nude pact]: (leg.) an informal contract or agreement without consideration or cause and therefore invalid unless under seal
nugae [trifles]: trivial works
nugae canorae [melodious trifles]: nonsense
nulla bona [no goods]: (leg.) no effects
nulli secundus: second to none
nullius filius [nobody's son]: an illegitimate son
nullo modo: by no means
nullo negotio: without any trouble
nullo pacto: by no means
numen: a spirit or deity
numen divinum: the will of heaven
numen loci [spirit places]: sacred places
numen praesens: (theo.) the feeling of some spiritual presence
numerus clasus [closed number]: a quota
nummi adulterini: bad money
nummi boni: a genuine coin
nunc: now

nunc aut nunquam: now or never

nunc pro tunc [now for then]: in law, designating a delayed action which takes effect as if it were done at the proper time

nupta: married

nuptiae [nuptials]: marriage

nutus et pondus: gravity

nux: a nut

O

ob rem: with advantage

obesus: fat or swollen

obiit (ob.): he/she died

obiit sine prole (ob.s.p.): he/she died without issue

obiter (ob.) [by the way]: incidentally; in passing

obiter dictum (pl. **obiter dicta**) [an incidental remark]: an unofficial expression of opinion

obiter scriptum (pl. **obiter scripta**): an incidental composition

oblique: sideways

obscuro loco natus: of unknown origin

observandum (pl. **observanda**): a thing to be observed

obsignator: (leg.) a witness to a will

obsoletus [worn out]: out of date

obviam: in or on the way

occidens [setting]: the setting sun (i.e., the West)

occultus: hidden; concealed

occupatus: busy; engaged

Oceanus: in ancient time, the ocean believed to encompass the earth

octarius (o.): (med.) a pint

octipes: having eight legs

oculatus [having eyes]: conspicuous; catching the eye

oculis et auribus captus: blind and deaf

oculis opertis: a blindfold

oculus: the eye

oculus dexter (o.d.): the right eye

oculus sinister (o.s.): the left eye

odium: hatred; bitter dislike

odium aestheticum [the hatred of artistic rivals]: the bitterness of aesthetical controversy

odium medicum [the hatred of rival physicians]: the bitterness of medical controversy

odium musicum [the hatred of rival musicians]: the bitterness of musical controversy

odium theologicum [the hatred of rival theologians]: the bitterness of theological controversy
odor lucri [the smell of profit]: the expectation of gain
officina [workshop]: a laboratory
officina gentium: the laboratory of the nations
officium: sense of duty; a dutiful act
oleo tranquillior: smoother than oil
oleum (ol.): oil (also olive oil)
oleum perdisti [you have lost oil]: you have wasted your time
olim [at that time]: formerly; for a long time now
olivum: olive oil
omen faustum: a favorable omen
omen infaustum: an evil omen
omen sinistrum: an evil omen
omne scibile: everything knowable
omnes ad unum [all to a person]: unanimous
omni ex parte: from every point of view
omni hora (o.h.): every hour
omni nocte (o.n.): every night
omni quadranta hora (o.q.h.) [every quarter hour]: every fifteen minutes
omni mane vel nocte: every morning or night
omnibus idem: the same to everyone
omnibus rebus: in every respect
omnigenus: of all kinds
omnimodis: in every manner or way
omnino [altogether]: in general; in all
omniparens: all-producing
omnipotens: all-powerful
omnipotentia Dei: almighty God
omnituens: all-seeing
onus probandi: (leg.) the burden of proof
ope et consilio [with aid and counsel]: (leg.) an accessory to the crime
opera mea: thanks to me
operae pretium: worth while
opere citato (op. cit. or **o.c.):** in the work cited
opere in medio: in the midst of the work
operis exactor: a task-master
opinio dei: belief in god
opinio vana: an illusion
oportet [it is proper]: one should; one ought
opposuit natura [nature has opposed]: it is contrary to nature
opprobrium medicorum [the reproach of physicians]: (med.) an incurable disease
optato: according to one's wish

optimas [one of the best]: aristocratic
optimates [the aristocrisy of ancient Rome]: the noble class
optime [most excellent]: very good
optimo jure: with full right
opus (pl. **opera**; **op.**) [a work]: a musical composition
opus est [there is work]: there is need
opus magnum or **magnum opus** [a great work]: a masterpiece
opus operatum (pl. **opera operata**) [a work wrought]: in Christian theology, the inherent efficacy of the sacrament
oraculum: an oracle
orate fratres: pray, brothers
orate pro anima: pray for the soul of. . . .
oratio composita: an elaborate speech
oratio gravis: a weighty address
oratio meditata: a prepared speech
oratio obliqua [a second-hand report]: hearsay
oratio subita: an extemporaneous speech
orationem concludere: to end a speech
Orbis Factor: Maker of the World
Orbis Pictus: the World in Pictures (Comenius)
orbis finiens: the horizon
orbis lacteus: the Milky Way (also **lacteus orbis**)
orbis medius: the temperate zone
orbis scientiarum: the circle of the sciences
orbis signifer: the Zodiac
orbis terrae or **orbis terrarum:** the world (i.e., all those countries comprising the Roman Empire)
ordinandi lex: procedural law
ordinatum est [it is ordered]: so ordered
ordine [in turn]: in due order
ordines majores [major orders]: the higher offices of the Catholic Church
ordines minores [minor orders]: the lower offices of the Catholic Church
ordo albus [white order]: the Augustinian Order
ordo griseus [grey order]: the Cistercian Order
ordo niger [black order]: the Benedictine Order
ordo salutis [orders of salvation]: (theo.) the Holy Orders of the Catholic Church
ore rotundo [with a round mouth]: a nicely given speech (Horace)
ore tenus [merely from the mouth]: by word of mouth
oriens [rising]: the rising sun (i.e., the East)
origo mali: (theo.) the origin of evil
os (pl. **ora**) [mouth]: an opening
os (pl. **ossa**): a bone
oscillatio: swinging to and fro

osculum pacis: kiss of peace
ossa: a skeleton
ossium compages: the skeletal system
ostiatim: from door to door
ostrinus: purple
otiosus: at leisure
otium [leisure]: free time
ovis: a sheep
ovum: an egg
Oxoniensis (Oxon.): of Oxford

P

pabulum animi [food of the soul]: learning
pace [by leave of]: with all deference to
pace tua [by your leave]: with your approval
pacta conventa [the conditions agreed upon]: a diplomatic agreement
pactum (pl. **pacta**) [pact]: a contract or agreement
pactum illicitum: an unlawful or illegal contract or agreement
pactum vestitum: an enforceable contract or agreement
paganus: rustic; rural
pagina: a page of a book or letter
pallida mors: pale Death (Horace)
pallidus irae: pale with rage
pallium: a ceremonial mantle worn over the shoulders by a priest
panacea [a plant believed to heal all ailments]: a cure-all
panis: bread
panis cibarius: common or ordinary bread
pannis obsitus: in rags
papae!: wonderful!
papilio: a butterfly
par [equal]: a match
par est: it is appropriate
par oneri: equal to the task
par pari refero [I return like for like]: tit for tat
parabola: an application; a comparison
paralysis agitans: (med.) Parkinson's disease
parens: a parent or ancestor
parentalia: a festival honoring dead ancestors
pares cum paribus: equals with equals
pari passu [with equal pace]: equally and simultaneously; without partiality
pari ratione [for a like reason]: neither is acceptable; an impasse

pars adversa: the opposite party
pars pro toto: a part for the whole
partes aequales (p.ae.): equal parts
partes primae: the leading part in a story or play
particeps criminis: (leg.) an accomplice in the crime
participium (ptc.): a participle
partim (p.): in part
parum: too little; not enough
passim (pass.) [here and there]: throughout (as in references found throughout the pages of a book)
Passionale: a book containing the Acts of the Christian Martyrs
passis crinibus: with tossled hair
passus [a measure equal to five Roman feet]: in literature, a portion or division of a poem or story
pater: father
pater patriae: [father of his country]: a national hero
paterfamilias [father of a family]: head of a household
Paternoster or **Pater Noster** [Our Father]: the Lord's Prayer
patres: forefathers
patres conscripti (PP.C.) [conscript fathers]: a title of the Roman Senators
patria potestas [parental authority]: in ancient Rome, the power of a father over the members of his family
patriis virtutibus: by ancestral virtues
patrimonium: (leg.) inherited property
patris est filius [his father's son]: like father, like son
pauca dixit: he said little
paucis verbis: in or with few words
Pax [peace]: peace established by law
Pax Britannica: British peace
Pax Dei: Peace of God (i.e., the Church's protection of non-combatants during war)
Pax Ecclesiae: Peace of the Church (i.e., the Church's protection of non-combatants during war)
Pax Romana: Roman peace (referring to the period from the emperors Augustus to Commodus, ca. 27 B.C.E. to 192 C.E.)
pax in bello: peace in war
pax orbis terrarum [the peace of the world]: universal peace
pax regis: king's peace
peccavi (pl. peccavimus) [I have sinned]: a confession of guilt
pecunia mutua: a loan
pedalis: a foot long or wide
pedes: going on foot
pedes muscarum [flies' feet]: (mus.) a system of musical notation
pedibus [on foot]: by land
pedibus nudis: barefoot

pedilavium: ritual foot-washing (cf., St. John 13:2–17)
pedis digitus: a toe
peior or **pejor:** worse
penates: Roman household gods
pendente lite: (leg.) pending the suit
pendere filo: to hang by a thread
penes se esse: to be in one's senses
penetralia mentis [the inner chambers of the mind]: a person's innermost thoughts
penis: a tail
penna: a feather or a wing
per [by or through]: by means of; throughout
per accidens [by accident]: by chance
per acria belli: through the bitterness of war
per ambages [by circuitous ways]: indirectly
per annum (p.a.) [by the year]: annually
per capita [by heads]: for each individual
per centum (per cent. or **p.c.** or **pct.**): by the hundred
per contra: on the contrary
per curiam: (leg.) by the court *in toto*
per diem [by the day]: daily
per dolum: by craft
per essentiam [by essential means]: essentially
per eundem [by the judge]: (leg.) by the same judge
per extensum: at length
per fas et nefas [through right and wrong]: by fair means or foul
per gradus: step by step
per hominen stare: (leg.) occurring through the fault of someone
per impossibile: as is impossible
per incuriam: through carelessness
per infortunium: by accident
per interim: in the meantime
per jocum: in jest
per Jovem: by Jove
per ludibrium: in sport or in fun
per mare per terram: by sea and by land
per mensem [by the month]: monthly; for each month
per mese: by the month
per mille: by the thousand
per minas: by threats
per os: by mouth
per pares: (leg.) by one's peers
per procurationem (p.p. or **per. pro.)** [by proxy]: by the action of
per quod [through which]: by which

per recto et recto: forward and backward
per saltum [by a leap]: in a single bound
per saturam: indiscriminately
per se [by or in itself]: intrinsically
per se esse: to exist by its own being
per se nota: in logic, a proposition, derived by the principle of deduction, that is evident by the meaning of its own terms
per se subsistere: to subsist by itself
per somnum [asleep]: in a dream
per stirpes: (leg.) by families; by representation
per studium: partially
per totam curiam [by the entire court]: unanimously
per viam: by way of
per viam dolorosam: by the way of sorrows
per vias rectas [by the straight road]: directly
per vices [by retaliation]: reciprocally
per vivam vocem: by the living voice
perdiu: for a very long time
perdudum: a long time ago
peregrinatio [travelling abroad]: a foreign journey
peregrinatio sacra: a pilgrimage
perennis: lasting throughout the year
perfervidum ingenium: an ardent temperment
perfidia Punica: Punic treachery
perfidus: treacherous; faithless
perfugium [a shelter for fugitives]: a place of refuge
permissu: by permission
pernox [throughout the night]: lasting all night
perpetuum mobile: perpetual motion
perserverando: by perservering
persona [a mask worn by stage players]: a person or personality
persona ficta: a fictitious person
persona grata (p.g.): an acceptable person
persona gratissima: a most acceptable person
persona muta: a silent actor
persona non grata (p.n.g.) [an unacceptable person]: a diplomatic representative who is not welcome by the government to which he or she is assigned
persona prima: the hero or heroine in a play
pervagatus: widespread; well-known
pes or pedis: the foot
pessimi exempli: of a very bad example
pessimus: worst
pestis: plague or pestilence

petasus: a broad-brimmed hat
petitio principii: (rhet.) begging the question
phalanx: soldiers in close formation
pharmaceutria: a sorceress
pharmacopola: a druggist; also, a quack
phiala prius agitata: the bottle being first shaken
philologia [lover of learning]: philology
philosophia [lover of wisom]: philosophy
philosophia moralis [moral philosophy]: ethics
philosophia mundi: philosopher of the world
Philosophiae Baccalaureus (Ph.B.): Bachelor of Philosophy
Philosophiae Doctor (Ph.D.): Doctor of Philosophy
philtrum: a love potion
phrenesis: madness or frenzy
physica or **physiologia:** physics or natural science
pia fraus: a pious fraud (Ovid)
pictor: a painter
pictor ignotus: an unknown painter
pictura textilis: embroidery
pietas: piety or devotion
pietatis causa: for the sake of piety
pila: a ball
pilarius: a juggler
pilosus: hairy
pilula (pl. **pilulae**; **pil.**): (med.) a pill
pinxit (pinx. or **pxt.):** he or she painted it
pirum: a pear
pirus: a peartree
piscator: a fisherman or fishmonger
piscis: a fish
pistor: a baker
pistris: a sea-monster
pius: godly or devoted
placebo [I shall please]: (med.) a prescription given to please a patient; (Eccles.) the first antiphonal in the vespers for the dead
placet [it seems good]: it is agreed
placitum (pl. **placita**) [a decree]: (leg.) a decision
plaudite, cives [citizens, applaud]: a curtain call at the end of a performance
plebeius [of the people]: common
plebiscitum: a decree of the people of Rome
plebs: the common people
plectrum: a stick used to play a stringed instrument
plenilunium: a full moon

pleno jure: with full right or authority
pleno modio [in full measure]: abundantly
plenus: full or complete
plexus: braided or plaited
plumbum (pb.): lead
plumbum album [white lead]: tin
pluralis (pl.): plural
plus solito: more than usual
pluvia: rain
pocula ex auro: gold cups
poena damni [pain of the damned]: (theo.) refers to the anguish the damned experience in hell as a result of their separation from God
poena sensus [pain of judgment]: (theo.) refers to the means by which humans will be tortured in hell (e.g., Dante's *Inferno*)
poeta epicus: an epic poet
pollex: the thumb or big toe
pollice verso [with thumb turned]: the "thumb's down" signal by which spectators indicated the judgment of death to a beaten gladiator
polus glacialis: the North Pole
pomarius: a fruit vendor
pompa: a solemn procession
pompa funebris: a funeral procession
pondere non numero: by weight not by number
pons (pl. **pontes**) [a bridge]: (anat.) a part connecting two parts
pons asinorum [ass's bridge]: a term applied to the fifth proposition of the first book of Euclid, concepts difficult for the unlearned to grasp
pons Varolii: (zool.) in higher species of veterbrates, a band of traverse fibers on the ventral surface of the brain
Pontifex Maximus [the high priest of the Roman cultus]: a papal appellation
pontifex: a priest
pontificalia [pontificals]: the vestments and insignia of a bishop
porca [pig]: a sow
porcus [pig]: a hog
portorium circumvectionis: port customs or transit duties
portus: a port or harbor
posse [to be able]: potential or possibility (as opposed to **esse**)
posse comitatus [the power of the county]: a sheriff's posse
posse videor [seem to be able]: I think I can
post bellum auxilium [aid after the war]: assistance offered too late
post Christum natum (P.Ch.N.): after Christ's birth
post cibum (p.c.): (med.) after meals
post diem: (leg.) after the appointed day
post hoc ergo propter hoc [after this, therefore, on account of this]: in logic, a fallacy of cause and effect

post litem motam: (leg.) after litigation began
post meridiem (p.m.): after noon
post mortem (P.M.): after death
post obitum: after death
post partum: after birth
post postscriptum (PPS): an additional postscript
post terminum: after the conclusion
postpartor: an heir
postremo: at last
postremum: for the last time
postridie [the day after]: on the next day
postscriptum (PS): a postscript
postulata [postulates]: fundamental assumptions
postulatus: a legal complaint or suit
potestas est: it is possible
prae: in front of; before
prae quam: in comparison with
praecognitum (pl. **praecognita**) [something foreknown]: a branch of knowledge necessary to the understanding of something else
praecox: premature
praedium [land]: landed property; an estate
praefectus urbis: governor of the city of Rome
praenomen: first name
praesentia animi: presence of mind
praestat [it is better]: it is preferable
praeter: past, beyond, or beside
praeteriti anni: bygone years
praeterito anno: in the past year
praetexta: a toga with purple borders worn by magistrates
praetorius cohors: the bodyguard or military detail protecting a general
prandium: lunch or brunch
precibus infirmis: with ineffective prayers (Livy)
pretium: worth, value, price, or reward
pretium affectionis [the price of affection]: (leg.) the sentimental value of a thing distinct from its market value
pretium periculi: an insurance premium
pretium puellae [the price of a maiden]: the marriage price demanded by a young woman's guardian
prex: a prayer
pridie: on the day before
prima facie [at first appearance]: a judgment based on the first impression
prima inter pares: first among equals
prima luce [at first light]: early in the morning

prima lux [first light]: the break of day
primas partes: to play the leading part
primitus: for the first time
primo [in the first place]: first
primo intuitu: at the first glance
primo vere: in the beginning of spring
primordium: origin or first beginnings
primoribus labris: superficially
primum cognitum: the first thing known
primum mobile [the first moving thing]: in Ptolemaic astronomy, the prime source of the motion of the universe
principia rerum: the principle elements
priore anno: last year
privatim [privately]: in private life
pro: before
pro bono publico [for the public good]: without charge (also known as **pro bono**)
pro certo [for sure]: you bet!
pro certo habeo: I feel sure
pro confesso [for the confession]: (leg.) as if confessed
pro consule (or **proconsul**) [an officer in place of a consul]: the governor of a province
pro eo quantum [in proportion as]: proportionally
pro et contra: for and against
pro forma [for the sake of form]: as a matter of form
pro hac vice: for this occasion only
pro mea parte [for my part]: to the best of my ability
pro memoria [for memory]: for a memorial
pro meritis: deservedly
pro merito: according to merit
pro nunc: for now
pro rata [according to rate]: in proportion; proportionally
pro re: according to circumstance
pro re nata (p.r.n.): (med.) whenever necessary
pro sua parte: to the best of one's ability
pro tanto [for so much]: so far; to that extent
pro tempore (p.t. or **pro tem.)** [temporarily]: for the time being
pro verbo [according to the word]: literally
pro viribus [to the best of one's ability]: as well as can be done
pro virili parte [for a man's part]: to the best of one's ability
probatum est: it has been proven
procul dubio: without doubt
procurator: a viceroy
proelium justum: a pitched battle

profanum vulgus [the profane rabble]: the ungodly multitude
profanus: not sacred
progenitor: an ancestor
proletarius: a citizen of the lowest class
promotor fidei: promoter of the faith (opposite of **advocatus diaboli** in an ecclesiastical argument in favor of the beatification of a person)
propediem [at an early date]: very soon
propositi tenax: firm of purpose
propositio [a purpose]: in logic, the major premise of a syllogism
propria natura: individuality
propria quae maribus [things appropriate to males]: the rudiments of Latin
propria vis: the literal sense; proper meaning
proprio jure: of his own right
proprio motu [by its own motion]: spontaneously
proprio vigore [of its own strength]: independently; by its own power
propter: on account of; because of
propter hoc: on this account
prosit [may it do you good]: to your health!
prosit tibi: may it be well with thee!
prospectus: an outlook or view
provisio [foresight]: a provision
provocatio: (leg.) an appeal to a higher court
proxime accessit (pl. **accesserunt**; **prox. acc.**) [he/she came very near (to winning)]: the runner-up in a contest
proximo (prox.): in the following month
proximo mense (prox. m.): in the following month
proximum genus: the nearest kind
prudens futuri: thoughtful of the future
pruina: hoarfrost
publice: publicly
publicum juris: of the public right
pudet me: I am ashamed
puella: a female youth
puer: a male youth
pugil: a fighter
pugna navalis: a naval battle
pulex: a flea
pullus: a chick or chicken
pulmo (pl. **pulmones**): a lung
pulvis (pulv.): dust; powder
punctatim: point for point
puncto temporis: in an instant
punctum (pl. **puncta**): a point; a spot

punctum caecum: (anat.) the blind spot of the eye
punctum contra punctum [note against note]: counterpoint
punctum saliens: a salient point
punctum temporis: a point of time
punctum vegetationis: (bot.) the growing point of a plant
pupa: a little girl; a doll
purpuratus [clothed in purple]: a person of high rank
puto or **ut puto:** I suppose (said parenthetically)
pyorrhea alveolaris: (med.) Rigg's disease

Q

qua: as
quadra or **quadrum:** a square
quadragesima [fortieth]: the forty day period of fast preceding Easter that begins on Ash Wednesday
quadriennium: a period of four years
quadrimus: four years old
Quadrivium [a crossroads]: the four principle subjects of advanced study in medieval universities (i.e., arithmetic, astronomy, geometry, and music), following the **Trivium**
quadrupes: four-footed
quadruplex: quadruple
quae cum ita sint: in these circumstances
quae est eadem: which is the same
quae summa est?: what does it amount to?
quae vide (qq.v.): (pl.) which see
quaere (qu.): a question or query
quaeritur [it is sought]: the question arises
quaesitum [that which is sought]: the solution to a problem
quaestio vexata (pl. **quaestiones vexatae**): a vexed or vexing question
quaestiones perpetuae: (leg.) standing courts of justice
qualibet: wherever you like; in any way you please
qualis: of what kind?
qualis ab incepto: such as from the beginning (Horace)
quam celerrime: as fast as possible
quam libet or **quamlibet:** as much as you please
quam maxime: as much as possible
quam primum or **quamprimum:** as soon as possible
quam proxime: as nearly as possible
quamvis [as much as you please]: ever so much
quantum (pl. **quanta**): a concrete quantity or specified amount

quantum [as much as]: how much
quantum in me est: as far as in me lies
quantum libet (**q.l.** or **q.lib.**) [as much as you please]: liberally
quantum meruit: as much as he or she deserved
quantum placet (**q.pl.** or **q.p.**): as much as you please
quantum satis: as much as is sufficient
quantum scio: as far as I know
quantum sufficit (**q.s.** or **quant. suff.**) [as much as suffices]: a sufficient quantity
quantum valeat: as much as it may be worth
quantum valebat: as much as it is worth
quantum vis (**q.v.**): as much as you will
quaque hora (**Q.H.**): (med.) every hour
quaque mane (**Q.M.**): (med.) every morning
quare impedit [why does he hinder?]: (leg.) a writ issued against the objector to a disputed right or claim
quarta pars: one quarter
quarto die (**q.i.d.**): on the fourth day
quartus: the fourth; the fourth hour
quasi [as it were; about]: a sort of
quasi dicat (**q.d.**): as if one should say
quasi dictum (**q.d.**): as if said
quasi dixisset: as if he had said
quater [four times]: again and again
quater in die (**q.i.d.**) (also **quater die**): four times a day
quaterni: four each
querela (pl. **querelae**) [bill of complaint]: (leg.) a court action
qui tam [who as well]: (leg.) action to recover (brought by an informer in conjunction with the State)
quia timet: because he fears
quid agis?: how do you do?
quid est rei?: what is the matter?
quid est veritas?: what is truth? (Pontius Pilate in St. John 18:38)
quid faciendum?: what is to be done?
quid hoc sibi vult?: what does this mean?
quid ni?: why not?
quid novi? [what news?]: what's new?
quid nunc?: what now?
quid pro quo [this for that]: something given in return for a favor
quid rides?: why do you laugh?
quid times [what do you fear?]: what are you afraid of?
quidam: a person known though unnamed (i.e., an unknown person)
quidditas [whatness]: the essence of a thing

Quinque Viae [The Five Ways]: the five arguments of St. Thomas Aquinas for the existence of God
quinquennis: five years old
quinquennium: a five year period
quo animo?: with what spirit or intention?
quo in genere: from this standpoint; from this point of view
quo jure?: by what right?
quo modo? or **quomodo?:** by what means?; in what way?
quo tendis?: where are you going?
quo vadis?: whither goest thou?
quoad [as to]: as regards; so far as
quoad hoc [as to this]: as regards this particular matter; as far as this goes
quoad minus: as to the lesser matter
quoad ultra: as regards the past
quocunque modo [in whatsoever manner]: in whatever way
quocunque nomine: under whatever name
quod abominor!: God forbid!
quod absurdum est: it is absurd
quod ad hoc [as far as this]: to this extent
quod ad me attinet: as far as I am concerned
quod bene notandum [which is to be well marked]: take especial notice
quod erat demonstrandum (Q.E.D.): which was to be demonstrated or shown
quod erat faciendum (Q.E.F.): which was to be done
quod est (q.e.): which is
quod hoc sibi vult?: what does this mean?
quod sciam: as far as I know
quod vide (q.v.): which see
quodlibet [what you please]: a subtle or debatable point
quomodo vales? [how do you fare]: hello
quondam [former]: formerly; at times
quot annis or **quotannis:** every year
quota pars?: how large a part?
quotidianus or **quotidie:** daily
quousque tandem?: to what lengths? (Cicero)
quovis modo: in whatever manner

R

radicitus: by the roots
radix: a root or foundation
rana: a frog
raptor: a robber or plunderer

rara avis (pl. **rarae aves**) [a rare bird]: a prodigy
raro: seldom; rarely
rata [rate]: an individual share
ratio [a reckoning or reasoning out]: a calculation; a transaction
ratione domicilii: (leg.) by reason of domicile
ratione soli: (leg.) by reason of soil
re: regarding or concerning
re infecta: the business being unfinished
re vera or **revera** [in truth]: in fact
rebus sic stantibus: things being the way they are
recessim: backwards
recitatio: a reading; a recitation
recta linea: a straight line
recta via: straight ahead
recte est: all is well
recto or **recto folio:** the right-hand page of a book (opposite of **verso**)
rector: a ruler; a director
rectus (pl. **recti**): straight or upright
rectus abdominis: (anat.) the abdominal muscles
rectus femoris: (anat.) the major thigh muscle surrounding the femur bone
rectus in curia [upright in court]: blameless
rectus musculus or **rectus:** (anat.) any of various straight muscles
redivivus [restored to life]: resuscitated; renewed
reductio ad absurdum [reduction to the absurd]: in logic, to prove the falsity of a proposition or conclusion by reducing it to the point of absurdity
reductio ad impossibile [reduction to the impossible]: in logic, an impossible conclusion
redux: a bringing back; a restoring
Regina Caeli [Queen of Heaven]: the Virgin Mary
regina (**R.**): a queen
regio meridiana: the south
regium donum: a royal gift or grant
rei publicae causa: for political reasons
religio illicita: in the Roman Empire, an unlawful or illegal religion
religio laici: a layperson's religion
religio licita: in the Roman Empire, a lawful or legal religion
religio loci: the sanctity of a place (Virgil)
reliquiae [the remains]: relics
remedium efficacissum: a sovereign remedy (i.e., an effective cure)
remisso animo [the mind relaxed]: listlessly
renes: the kidneys
renovato nomine: by a revived name
repertorium (pl. **repertoria**): a catalogue

repetatur (**rep.** or **repet.**): (med.) let it be repeated
requiem [rest]: a mass for the dead
requiescat in pace (pl. **requiescant; R.I.P.**): may he/she rest in peace
requiescit in pace (**R.I.P.**): he/she rests in peace
rerum natura [realm of nature]: the natural world; the universe
rerum primordia: the first beginnings of things
rerum progressio: evolution
Res Tota Simul [the whole thing at the same time]: a medieval Christian definition of eternity (also **Totum Simul**)
res (pl. **res**): a thing, matter, or circumstance; a cause or action
res adjudicata [a matter already settled]: (leg.) a decided case
res adversae: misfortune
res alienae [things belonging to others]: debt
res bene gesta: a successful military campaign or exploit
res cogitans [a thinking thing]: the natural state of the mind without reference to space or time (Descartes)
res confecta est: the question is settled
res corporales [corporeal things]: tangible things
res discrepat: non agreement
res divina [divine things]: sacrificial service to the gods
res expedit: it is useful, expedient, or advantageous
res extensa [an extended thing]: the body in motion (i.e., the natural state of the body with reference to space and time is motion; Descartes)
res fessae: distress
res gesta: a deed
res gestae [things done]: deeds, transactions; (leg) the attendant circumstances; exploits in war
res hereditaria: an heirloom
res incorporales [things incorporeal]: nontangible things
res inter alios: a matter between others
res judicata [a matter already settled]: (leg.) a decided case
res judicata pro veritate accipitur: (leg.) a case decided is accepted as just
res militaris: (mil.) military strategy
res mobiles: movable things
res nihili [a none thing]: a nonentity
res nullius [a none thing]: a nonentity
res publica: the state
res repetundae: extortion
res rustica: a rural affair
res secundae: prosperity; success
respublica: commonwealth; republic
respublica forum: public life
resurgam: I shall rise again

rete (pl. **retia**) [a net]: (anat.) plexus of nerves; vascular network
retro: backwards
retro Satana!: Satan, behind!
reus: (leg.) an accused person
rex (R.): a king
rex regum: king of kings
rhombus: a magician's circle
rhythmus [measured motion]: rhythm
ridicula imitatio: a parody
rigor mortis [rigor of death]: the stiffening of the body after death
risus [a laugh]: laughter
rite: in proper form
rituale: a ritual manual for priests
rivus: a stream
Romae natus: a native of Rome
ros marinus: rosemary
rosa: a rose; a garland of roses
rosarium: a rose garden
rota: a wheel
rotula: a yo-yo
rotundus: circular or round
rubrica [red earth]: a law with its title written or printed in red ink
rudera [rubbish]: debris
rudis indigestaque moles: a rude and disorderly mass
ruri or **rure:** in the country
rus in urbe: the country in a city (Martial)

S

sacer or **sacra:** holy; consecrated
sacerdos: a priest
Sacrae Theologiae Baccalaureus (S.T.B.): Bachelor of Sacred Theology
Sacrum Romanum Imperium (S.P.I.): the Holy Roman Empire
saeculum [a century]: a generation or age
saga: a prophetess; a fortune-teller
sagitta: an arrow
sagittarius: an archer
sal: salt
sal amarus [bitter salt]: a cathartic (e.g., Epsom salt)
sal Atticum [Attic salt]: a keen wit (also **sal Atticus**)
sal catharticus: a cathartic (e.g., Epsom salt)
sal culinarius [cooking salt]: table salt

sal gemmae: rock salt
saltem [at least]: at all events
saltus ad funem: to play jump-rope
salus: health or welfare; safety or salvation
salus mundi: the salvation or welfare of the world
Salutem dicit! (**Sal.** or **S.**): Greetings!
salve! [may you be safe]: God's speed!
salvo jure: without prejudice; (leg) without infraction of law
salvo ordine: with due regard to one's rank
salvo pudore: without offense to modesty
salvo sensu: without violation of sense
sanae mentis esse: to be in one's right mind
sanctio: (leg.) a clause in a law defining a penalty for breach
sanctum sanctorum [holy of holies]: a private room; a place of retreat
sanctus: holy or consecrated
sane quam: exceedingly
sanguine suffusus: bloodshot
sanguis: blood
sapientia: wisdom; discernment
sarcophagus: a coffin; a grave
satis: enough
Saturnalia: the winter festival
Saturnia regna [the reign of Saturn]: the Golden Age (Virgil)
saxum: a rock or stone
saxum quadratum: hewn stone
scala: a ladder
scalae: a staircase
scandalum magnatum (pl. **scandala magnatum**; **scan. mag.**) [scandal of magnates]: the defamation of notables or of high ranking persons
scarabaeus: a beetle
scienter [knowingly]: willfully
scientia [knowledge]: science
scilicet (**sc.**) [that is to say]: namely
scintilla: a spark
scire facias (**sci. fa.**) [cause it to be known]: (leg.) a writ to enforce, annul, or vacate a judgment, patent, charter or other matter of record
scorpio: a scorpion
scribere scientes: skilled in writing
scripsit: he/she wrote (it)
scriptura: a composition or a piece of writing
sculpsit (**sc.** or **sculpt.**): he/she sculptured (it)
se defendendo: in defending him/herself
secunda mensa: dessert

secundo: secondly
secundo flumine: downstream
secundum (sec.): according to
secundum artem (sec. art.) [according to art]: scientifically; artificially
secundum formam statuti: (leg.) according to the form of the statute
secundum genera: according to classes
secundum legem (sec. leg.): according to law
secundum naturam (sec. nat.) [according to nature]: naturally
secundum ordinem [according to order]: in an orderly manner
secundum quid [according to some one thing]: with limitations
secundum regulam (sec. reg.): according to rule
secundum usum: according to usage
secundum veritatem [according to truth]: universally true
sedes: a seat or chair
selibra: half a pound
selpuchra: a cemetery
semel: once; one time only
semel pro semper: once for all
semen: seed
semihora: half an hour
seminex: half-dead
semis (ss): (med.) half or one half
semper: always
semper florens: perennials
sempiterna gloria [everlasting glory]: immortality
semuncia: half an ounce
Senatus Populusque Romanus (S.P.Q.R.): the Senate and People of Rome (motto of the Roman Republic)
senatus consultum: a decree of the Roman Senate
senior: older
seniores priores: elders' first
sensu bono: in a good sense
sensu malo: in a bad sense
sententia legis: the spirit of the law
sententiae judicum: (leg.) the finding of the jury
separatio a mensa et toro (or **thoro**) [separation from room and board]: legal separation
separatio a vinculo matrimonii [separation from the bond of marriage]: divorce
septemtriones or **septentrio:** the north or northwind
Septemviri epulones: a college of priests in charge of sacrificial feasts (previously **Tresviri epulones**)
septimana: a week
sepultus (S.): buried

sequens (seq.): the following
sequentia (seqq.): the following things
sequitur (seq.) [it follows]: a logical inference
seriatim [in a series]: point by point; also, one volume in a series of publications
serra: a saw
servare modum: to keep within the bounds
Servus Servorum Dei [Servant of the Servants of God]: a papal appellation
servus ad manum or **servus a manu:** a secretary; an amanuensis
sescenaris: a year and a half old
sescenti [six hundred]: countless
sesqui [one half more]: half as much again
sesquialter: one and a half
sesquihora: an hour and a half
sesquipedalia verba [words a foot and a half in length]: very long words
sexangulus: hexagonal
sexennis: six years old
sexennium: a period of six years
sextarius: a pint
sexus: sex (i.e., gender)
sexus muliebris: the female sex
sexus virilis: the male sex
si modo: if only
si opus sit (s.o.s.): (med.) if necessary
si placet [if it pleases]: please
si quis: if anyone
sic [thus]: usually found in brackets following a doubtful word in a quotation to indicate that the original passage is being followed *verbatim*
sic in originali: thus in the originals
sic jubeo: thus I command
sic passim [thus throughout]: here and there
sic totidem verbis: thus in as many words
sicarius: an assassin
sicut ante: as before
signa (S. or **Sig.)** [write]: (med.) that which is to be written on the label of a prescription
signum: a signet or seal
sigillum: a seal
silentio noctis: in the silence of night
silentium altum: deep silence
silex [a hard rock]: a flint stone
silva: a wood or forest
similiter: in like manner
similitudo Dei: the likeness of God
simpliciter [absolutely]: without reservation or reserve

simul [at once]: at the same time
simulare morbum: to feign illness
sincerus: genuine; pure
sine: without
sine anno (s.a.): without date
sine auxilio: unaided
sine controversia: indisputably
sine cortice natare [to swim without corks]: to need no assistance
sine cura [without care]: all the benefits of office without all the responsibilities
sine die (s.d.) [without a day]: without fixing a day for future action or meeting (e.g, indefinitely adjourned)
sine dolore: painless
sine dubio: without doubt
sine fraude [without deceit or offense]: honorably; without harm
sine fuco [without pretense]: frankly
sine ictu: without a blow
sine ira: without anger
sine invidia: without envy
sine joco [without jesting]: seriously
sine legitima prole (s.l.p.): without legitimate issue
sine loco (s.l.): without place
sine loco et anno (s.l.a.): without place and year
sine loco, anno, vel nomine (s.l.a.n.): without place, year, or name
sine maculis [without stain]: spotless
sine mascula prole (s.m.p.): without male issue
sine mora: without delay
sine nervis [without strength]: weak
sine nomine (s.n.) [without name]: anonymous
sine odio: without hatred
sine omni periculo: without any danger
sine ope: without help
sine praejudicio: without prejudice
sine proba causa: without approved cause
sine prole (s.p.): without issue
sine prole supersite (s.p.s.): without surviving issue
sine qua non [without which not]: something essential; an indispensible condition
sine sapore: tasteless
sine ulla dubitatione: without any hesitation
singillatim or **singulatim:** one by one
singularis (sg. or **sing.):** singular
singulis annis [year by year]: every year
singulis diebus [day by day]: every day
sinister: left

sinistra manu: with the left hand
sinus urbis: the heart of the city
Sirius: the Dog-Star
Sitio: I thirst (one of the Seven Last Words of Christ; St. John 19:29)
sobrius: sober or sober-minded
societas: a partnership or association
socius criminis: (leg.) an associate in crime
sodalis [a companion]: a member of a secret society
sodes [if you please]: with your leave
Sol Invictus [the Invincible Sun]: the Sun God of ancient Mithraism whose festival was celebrated on December 25th of each year
sol: the sun
sol occidens: setting sun
sol oriens: rising sun
sola fide: faith alone (a doctrine of Martin Luther)
sola gratia: grace alone (a doctrine of the Protestant Reformers)
sola scriptura: scripture alone (a doctrine of the Protestant Reformers)
solarium: a sundial; an open terrace
solea (pl. **soleae**): a sandal
solis defectio: a solar eclipse
solis occasus: sunset
solis ortus: sunrise
solstitium: the summer solstice
solus: by oneself
solutio (sol.): (med.) a solution
solvendo non esse: to be insolvent
somnium: a dream
somnus: sleep
sonus: sound
sonus dulcis: a sweet or pleasant sound (i.e., euphony)
sophia: wisdom
sorbilo [by sipping]: drop by drop
soror: a sister
sortes Biblicae [casting a fortune with the Book]: divination by the selection of random passages from the Christian Bible
sortes Homericae [casting a fortune with Homer]: divination by the selection of random passages from Homer
sortes Vergilianae (or **sortes Virgilianae**) [casting a fortune with Virgil]: divination by the selection of random passages from Virgil
soter: a savior
speciali gratia: by special favor
specimen: a model or an example
spectaculum: a spectacle or a show

spectator (fem. **spectatrix**): a spectator; an observer
speculum: a mirror
speculum aeterni Patris: mirror of the eternal Father (a reference to the Crucifixion as an image of the eternal love of God)
speravi: I have hoped
spes: hope
spina: a thorn
spinosus: thorny or prickly
spiritus: spirit
spiritus asper: in Greek grammar, rough breathing (i.e., asperated)
spiritus lenis: in Greek grammar, smooth breathing (i.e., nonasperated)
spolia opima [the richest spoils]: a supreme achievement (originally, the spoils taken from a vanquished general by a victorious general in a single contest)
spolia sua [from one's own spoils]: out of one's excess
sponte sua or **sua sponte** [of one's own accord]: unsolicited
sportula (pl. **sportulae**) [small basket]: a present, gratuity, or largess
Stabat Mater [the Mother was standing]: Latin hymn inspired by the suffering of the Holy Virgin Mother at the Crucifixion
stadium [a measure of distance]: a race course
stannum (**sn.**): tin
stans pede in uno [standing on one foot]: a certain posture taken by orators during a speech (Horace)
statim (**stat.**) [immediately]: on the spot; at once
statu quo: as things were before
statua: a statue
status in quo [the state in which]: an existing condition or unchanged position
status quo [the state which]: an existing condition or unchanged position
status quo ante bellum: the state existing before the war
stella: a star
stella comans: a comet
stella crinita [long-haired star]: a comet
sterilis: barren; fruitless
stet [let it stand]: to leave as is (i.e., not to be changed or deleted)
stomachus: the stomach
stomachus bonus [good digestion]: good humor
stratum super stratum: layer upon layer
strena [a new year's gift]: a favorable omen
stricto sensu: in a strict sense (the opposite of **lato sensu**)
strictum jus [strict law]: the strict letter of the law
stultus: silly or foolish
sua sponte or **sponte sua** [of one's own accord]: unsolicited
sub: under or underneath
sub audi or **subaudi** (**sub.**) [to supply the missing word or words by subaudition]: to read between the lines

sub colore juris: under color of law
sub dio or **sub divo** [under the open sky]: in the open air
sub ferula: under the rod
sub finem: toward the end
sub initio: at the beginning
sub Jove [under Jupiter]: in the open air
sub Jove frigido [under cold Jupiter]: under the cold sky
sub judice [before the judge]: under judicial consideration
sub modo: in a qualified sense
sub noctem: at nightfall
sub poena: under penalty
sub quocunque titulo: under whatever title
sub rosa [under the rose]: confidentially
sub sigillo [under seal]: in the strictest confidence
sub silentio [in silence]: privately
sub spe rati: in the hope of a decision
sub specie: under the appearance of
sub verbo (s.v., pl. **s.vv.):** look under the word
sub vino: under the influence of wine
sub voce (s.v., pl. **s.vv.):** look under the word
subito: suddenly
subscriptio [a writing beneath]: a signature
subter or **subtus:** beneath or below
subterraneus: underground
suburbanus: near the city
succubus: a female spirit or demon believed to prey sexually on young men while they sleep
sufficit (pl. **sufficiunt**): it is enough
suffragium [a voting tablet]: the right to vote
suggestio falsi [suggestion of a falsehood]: an indirect lie or misrepresentation
sui generis [of its own kind]: unique; one of a kind; something in a class by itself
sui impotens: beside oneself
sui juris [in one's own right]: of full legal capacity
sulfur (s.): sulfur
Summa or **Summae:** a compendium of philosophical thoughts or theological conclusions, the most famous being the *Summa Theologica* of St. Thomas Aquinas
summa aestas: midsummer
summa aqua: the surface of the water
summa cum laude: with highest honors
summa gloria: the height of glory
summa pax: a great peace
summa res publica: the welfare of the state
summa summarum [the sum of sums]: the sum of all things

summa urbs: the highest point of the city
summa vitae: life span (also **vitae summa**)
summo loco natus: of noble origin
summum bonum: the highest or chief good
summum genus (pl. **summa genera**): in logic, the highest genus
summum jus: the highest law
summus collis: the brow of a hill or ridge
summus mons: the mountain summit
sumptibus publicis or **sumptu publico:** at the public expense
sumptio: in logic, the premise of a syllogism
suo jure: in one's own right
suo loco: in its proper place
suo Marte: by one's own prowess
suo motu: by its own motion
suo periculo: at one's own peril
suo tempore: at its own time
super: over or above
superas ad auras: to the light of day
supercilium [an eyebrow]: (fig.) arrogance
superiore anno: last year
supinus: lying face-up
supinus manus: lying on one's back with palms facing upwards
suppositio terminorum [substitution of terms]: in logic, the claim that an affirmative proposition is true only when the subject and predicate terms stand for the same thing
suppressio veri [a suppression of the truth]: concealment of facts
supra (sup.): over, above, or on the top
supra vires: beyond one's powers
supremo vitae die: on one's last day
supremum vale: a last farewell
sursum deorsum [up and down]: backwards and forwards
sursum versus: upwards
suspensio per collum (sus. per col.) [suspension by the collar]: execution by hanging
suspenso gradu: on tiptoe
suum cuique: to each his/her own

T

tabella (tab.): (med.) a tablet
tabellarius: a letter carrier
tabernaculum: a tent

tabernarius: a shopkeeper
tabula: a map, record book, or register
tabula rasa (pl. **tabulae rasae**) [a blank writing tablet]: the mind at birth (Locke)
tabulae publicae: a public archives
tace!: be silent!
tacet [it is silent]: in music, a direction indicating that a certain instrument (or instruments) is not played during a particular section or movement of a piece
tacitus: silent; unmentioned
taedium: boredom
taedium vitae: weariness of life
talis qualis: such as it is
tamquam alter idem or **tanquam alter idem** [as if a second self]: a completely trustworthy person
tandem: at length
tandem denique: in the end
tangere ulcus: to touch a sore
Tantum Ergo [so great, therefore]: a Eucharistic hymn
tantum quantum: just as much as is required
taurus: a bull
Te Deum, Laudamus: We praise Thee, O God (an ancient Christian hymn)
Te Igitur [Thee, therefore]: part of the Eucharistic liturgy of the Latin mass
te judice [you being the judge]: in your judgment
tempestas: bad weather; a violent storm
templum: consecrated ground
tempora matutina: the morning hours
tempore (**temp.** or **t.**): in the time of
temporis causa: on the spur of the moment
temporis puncto: in the twinkling of an eye
tempus: time
tempus in ultimum: to the last extremity
tempus ludendi: the time for play
tenax propositi: tenacious of purpose
tendo calcaneus: (anat.) the Achilles tendon
tenebrae aeternae: (theo.) eternal darkness
tepidus: warm or lukewarm
ter [thrice]: three times
ter in die (**t.i.d.**): (med.) three times a day
tere bene: (med.) rub well
terminus a quo [the end from which]: the starting point
terminus ad quem [the end to which]: the finishing point; the destination
terra: the earth
terra firma [solid earth]: dry land; firm footing

terra incognita (pl. **terrae incognitae**) [an unknown land]: an unknown region or subject

terrae filius (pl. **terrae filii**) [son of the earth]: a person of lowly birth

terrae motus: an earthquake

terrestris: terrestrial

Tersanctus [thrice holy]: the Trisagion

tertia hora est: it is the third hour (i.e., 9 a.m.)

tertium: for the third time

tertium quid [a third something]: something in between two fixed points or positions; a third alternative or choice beyond two fixed choices

tertius: third

teste [by the evidence of]: a witness

testimonium internum (or **testimonium Spiritus Sanctus internum**) [internal testimony]: (theo.) the internal witness of the Holy Spirit that inspires faith within those who seek the truth of the Gospel

testis gravis: (leg.) an important witness

testis unus, testis nullus: (leg.) one witness is no witness

textor: a tailor or weaver

textus receptus (**text. rec.**): the received text (i.e., the scripture tradition that has been handed down from generation to generation)

theologia crucis [theology of the cross]: the emphasis of Protestant reformers on the sacrificial death of Christ on the Cross (as opposed to **theologia gloriae**)

theologia gloriae [theology of glory]: Martin Luther's pejorative label for Church doctrines that did not lay proper stress on the sacrificial death of Christ on the Cross (as opposed to **theologia crucis**)

thermae: warm springs or baths

thesaurus: a store-house or treasury

thorax: a breastplate

thyrsus: a stalk of a plant, such as corn, symbolizing fertility

tibia: the shin-bone

tigris: a tiger

tintinnabulum: a bell

titulus: a label or inscription

toga candida [the white robe]: the white robe worn by Roman candidates for office

toga praetexta: a white robe bordered with purple and worn by Roman magistrates and freeborn children

toga virilis [the manly robe]: the toga worn by Roman freemen from ages fourteen and older

togata: a freed woman (sometimes, a prostitute)

totidem verbis [in so many words]: in these very words

toties quoties [as often as]: repeatedly or on each occasion

totis viribus: with all one's might

toto caelo [by the whole heaven]: by a great distance; diametrically opposite

Totum Simul [the whole at the same time]: a medieval Christian definition of eternity (also **Res Tota Simul**)

totum: the whole

toxicum: poison (usu. for arrows)

tractim [in managed bits]: by degrees

trans: across, over, or beyond

transfugium [going across]: desertion

transmarinus [from beyond the sea]: foreign

tremulus: trembling

Tresviri epulones: a college of priests who had charge of sacrificial feasts (later **Septemviri epulones**)

Treuga Dei (or **Treva Dei**) [Truce of God]: during the Middle Ages, the suspension of hostilities and private warfare during certain religious holidays, on pain of excommunication

triangulus [triangular]: three-cornered

tribuni plebis: tribunes or magistrates of the people

tributum: tax or taxation

triceps: having three heads or three points of origin

tricuspis: having three points

tridens: having three teeth or three prongs

triduum: a period of three days

triennia: a festival celebrated every three years

triennium (pl. **triennia**): a period of three years

trilibris: three pounds in weight

trinitas [trinity]: (theo.) the doctrine of the Christian Trinity (i.e., Father, Son, and the Holy Ghost)

trimus: three years old

tripartito: having three parts

tripedalis: three feet in length or width

tripes: having three feet

triplex munus [triple service]: (theo.) refering to Christ as fulfilling the triple roles of prophet, priest, and king

triplex or **triplus** [threefold]: triple

Trisagion: thrice holy

tristes kalendae (or **calendae**) [the unhappy calends]: the day interest on borrowed money was due to the lender

trium literarum homo [a man of three letters]: a thief (properly, **homo trium literarum**)

triumvir (pl. **triumviri**): a ruling board of three members (referring specifically to the first and second Roman triumvirs: Julius Caesar, Pompeius, and Crassus; and Octavian, Marcus Antonius, and Lepidus)

Trivium: the three principle subjects of basic study in medieval universities (i.e., dialectic, grammar, and rhetoric), followed by the **Quadrivium**

trivium: a junction where three roads meet

tu quoque [you as well]: (leg.) a statement accusing the accuser of the same charge

tuba: a straight war trumpet

tuebor: I will defend
tumor [a swelling]: a protuberance
tumulus: a burial mound
tunica: a sleeved garment
turris: a tower
tutamen (pl. **tutamina**) [protection]: a protective pact
tutor et ultor: protector and avenger
tuum [yours]: your property
tuum est: it is yours
tuum est?: is it yours?
tyrannis: an absolute ruler

U

uberrima fides [superabounding faith]: implicit trust
ubi gentium?: where in the world?
ubi supra (**u.s.**) [where above]: in the place mentioned above
ubique: everywhere
ultima forsan: perhaps the last [moment] (an inscription on clocks)
ultima ratio: the final argument (i.e., force)
ultima ratio regum [the last argument of kings]: a resorting to arms
ultima Thule [farthest Thule]: the utmost limit; an unknown region (Virgil)
ultimo (**ult.**): last month
ultimum: for the last time
ultimum vale: a last farewell
ultimus haeres [the last of the heirs]: the final heir
ultimus regum: the last of the kings
ultimus Romanorum: the last of the Romans
ultra: beyond
ultra licitum: beyond the legal limit
ultra valorem: beyond the value
ultra vires [beyond one's power]: transcending legal authority
ultro: to the far side
ultro citroque: to and fro
ultro et citro [up and down]: hither and thither
umbilicus: the navel
umbra: shade or shadow
umerus: the shoulder
una sancta [one holy]: a reference to the divine nature of the Christian Church
una voce [with one voice]: unanimously
unanimus: of one mind or spirit
uncia: one twelfth (i.e., one ounce)

unciatim: little by little
unicus: sole or unique
unigena [of the same race]: (theo.) only-begotten
unio mystica [mystical union]: (theo.) referring to the mystical union of the human consciousness with the divine consciousness
Unitas Fratrum [unity of brethren]: official name of the Moravian Church
unius diei: ephemeral
uno animo [with one spirit]: unanimously
uno consensu: unanimously
uno ictu: at one blow
uno ore [one mouth]: unanimously
uno saltu [in one leap]: in a single bound
uno tempore: at the same time
uno verbo: in a word
unus et alter: one or two
urbanus [of a city]: elegant; refined
urbs: a walled city
urbi et orbi [to the city and to the world]: words traditionally occurring in a special Papal benediction
urceus [an earthen jug]: urn
Ursa Major [Great Bear]: the Big Dipper
Ursa Minor [Little Bear]: the Little Dipper
usque a Romulo [ever since Romulus]: since the beginning of time
usque ad aras [even to the altars]: to the last extremity
usque ad nauseum [even to nausea]: to the point of disgust
usque Romam: as far as Rome
usu venit [it comes]: it happens
usus et fructus or **ususfructus:** (leg.) the use of the property of another
usus loquendi: usage in speaking
ut adsolet: as is usual
ut dictum (ut dict.): (med.) as directed
ut fata trahunt [as the fates pull]: at the mercy of fate
ut infra (ut i. or **ut inf.)** [as below]: as stated or cited below
ut pignus amicitiae: as a token of friendship
ut prosim [that I may be of service]: that I may do good
ut puto or **puto:** I suppose (said parenthetically)
ut solet: as usual
ut supra (ut sup. or **u.s.):** as above
ut videtur: apparently
uterlibet: whichever of the two you please
uterus: a womb
uti possidetis [as you possess]: (leg.) with the possessions held at the present time
utilis: useful

uva: a bunch of grapes
uxor (ux.): a wife

V

vacatio: freedom; immunity
vacca: a cow
vacuo: in a vacuum
vacuum: an empty place
vade mecum [go with me]: a companion; a reference volume
vadium mortuum [a dead pledge]: a mortgage
vagina: a sheath
vagitus: (med.) the first cry of a newborn child
vale or **valete:** farewell
valgus: a bow-legged person
varia lectio (pl. **variae lectiones**): a variant reading
varicus: straddling
variorum notae: notes of various commentators
vas (pl. **vasa**) [utensil]: a vessel or duct
vas deferens (pl. **vasa deferentia**): (anat.) the sperm duct
vasculum: a small vessel
velociter: quickly
vena (pl. **venae**): a vein
vena cava (pl. **venae cavae**): one of the large veins flowing into the heart
venire facias [to make to come]: (leg.) a writ from a judge ordering the sheriff to summon a jury
Venite [O, Come]: a musical setting of Psalm 95 which begins *Venite, exultemus Domino*
ventriculus: the belly or stomach
ventus adversus [winds fore]: an unfavorable wind
ventus Africus or **Africus:** the southwest wind
ventus secundus [winds aft]: a favorable wind
venus: love; a loved one
ver: spring
ver sacrum: an offering of the first fruits
vera causa: a true cause
verbatim et literatim [word for word and letter for letter]: exactly
verbatim et literatim et punctatim [word for word and letter for letter and point for point]: with the utmost accuracy
Verbi Dei Minister (V.D.M.): minister of the Word of God
verbi causa: for instance
verbo: in name only
verbosus: wordy

veri similis: probable
veritas: truth
veritas entis [truth of being]: metaphysical truth
veritas signi: the truth of a symbol
vermis: a worm or grub
verso or **verso folio** (**v.** or **vo.**) [reverse side]: the left-hand page of a book (opposite of **recto**)
versus (**v.** or **vs.**): towards; against
verte [turn]: turn the page over
veritas victrix: truth the conqueror
vertigo [whirling round]: dizziness or light-headedness
vesania: (med.) insanity
vesica piscis [a fish bladder]: the aura surrounding the heads of sacred figures in medieval and renaissance Christian art (also, **cum nimbus**)
vesper [evening]: the Evening Star
vesperi: in the evening
vestigia (pl. of **vestigium**) [vestiges]: footprints; traces
vestigia nulla retrorsum: no footsteps backward (i.e., no retreat)
vestigium Dei [vestige of God]: doctrine teaching that, despite the Fall, creation still reflects traces of its divine origins
veteranus: an old soldier
veterator: an experienced or skilled person (i.e., an old hand)
vexata quaestio: a vexed or disputed question (also **quaestio vexata**)
Via Dolorosa [the way of sorrows]: the route taken by Jesus on his way to crucifixion
via (pl. **viae**): a street or way
via affirmativa [the affirmative way]: (theo.) the way to knowledge of or union with God that is gained through affirmation of the positive aspects of the world (also known as **via positiva**)
via amicabili: in a friendly way
via compendiaria: a short cut
via eminentiae [the way of eminence]: (theo.) the positive way to knowledge of or union with God that is gained by affirming those perfections in the world that point to the eminence to God (St. Thomas Aquinas)
via illuminativa [the way of enlightenment]: (theo.) the way to God through illumination, whether mystical, inspirational, or relevatory
via Lactea: the Milky Way
via Matris: the Seven Sorrows of Mary, the Mother of God, en route to the crucifixion of Christ
via media: the middle way
via militaris: a military road
via negativa or **via negationes** [the negative way]: (theo.) the way to knowledge of or union with God that is gained through negation of the world (Maimonides)
via positiva [the positive way]: (theo.) the way to knowledge of or union with God that is gained through affirmation of the positive aspects of the world (also known as **via affirmativa**)

via purgativa [the way of purgation]: (theo.) the way to knowledge of or union with God that is gained through purification by ascetic practices
via strata: a street
via trita: a well-traveled road
via unitiva [the way of union]: (theo.) the way to knowledge of or union with God that is gained by perfection of the self
viator: a wayfarer
vice versa (**V.V.**) [with the meaning or order reversed]: conversely
victus cotidianus: daily bread
victus tenuis: a meager diet
vide (**v.**): see
vide ante: see before
vide infra (**v.i.**): see below
vide post: see after this
vide supra (**v.s.**): see above
vide ut supra [see as above]: see the above comment
videlicet (**viz.**): namely
videtur [it appears]: it seems
vigilantibus: to be watchful
villa: a country estate
vinarius: a vintner
vinculum matrimonii: the bond of marriage
vindex injuriae: an avenger of wrong
vinitor: a vinedresser
vir: a man
vir bonus dicendi peritus: a good man skilled in rhetoric
vir doctus: a scholar
vir et uxor: husband and wife
vir insignis: a celebrity
vir literatus or **vir litteratus** [a man of letters]: a scholar
vir privatus: a private person
viribus totis: with all one's strength
viribus unitis: with united strength
virago [a female warrior]: a heroine
vires corporis: bodily strength
virginibus puerisque: for young women and men
Virgo: the Virgin
Virgo Sapientissima: The Virgin Wisest of All
Virgo Sponsa Dei: the Virgin Bride of God
virgo: a maiden girl or virgin
virgo vestalis: a vestal virgin
viritim [man by man]: individually
virtus [manly excellence]: virtue or valor

vis (pl. **vires**): force, power, or strength
vis a fronte: a propelling force from in front
vis a tergo: a propelling force from behind
vis comica: comic genius
vis conservatrix: the preservative power
vis inertiae [power of inertia]: the power of passive resistance
vis insita [the innate force of matter]: an aspect of Newton's first law of motion
vis major [superior force]: (leg.) an inevitable accident
vis medicatrix: healing power
vis medicatrix naturae: the healing power of nature
vis mortua [dead force]: force that does not work
vis poetica: poetic genius
vis vitae: vital force
vis viva [living force]: kinetic energy
viscus (pl. **viscera**): internal organs (i.e., the guts)
vita: life
vita beata [the blessed life]: happiness
vita honesta: a virtuous life
vita occidens: the evening of life
vita privata: private life
vita turpis: an immoral life
vitae curriculum [course of life]: a résumé (also **curriculum vitae**)
vitae societas: social life
vitae summa: life span (also **summa vitae**)
vitellus: an egg yolk
vitium: a fault or crime
vitrum: a glass
viva voce [by a living voice]: orally (i.e., by oral examination)
vivarium [a fish pond]: an animal preserve
vivendi causa [cause of living]: the source of life
vivere parvo: to live on little
vivida vis animi: the living force of the mind
vixit ... annos (**v.a.**): he lived ... years
vocis imago: an echo
volenti non fit injuria: (leg.) no injury is done to consenting parties
voluntas: freewill
voluntas legis: the spirit of the law
voluptates corporis [the pleasures of the body]: sensual pleasures
vortex or **vertex:** a whirlpool
vox (pl. **voces**): voice
vox angelica: an organ stop producing a stringlike sound
vox barbara [strange or barbaric voice]: (gram.) an incorrectly formed word (e.g., a hybrid)

vox clandestina: a whisper
vox humana: an organ stop producing a sound like a human voice
vox populi (pl. **voces populi**): the voice of the people
vox stellarum [voice of the stars]: music of the spheres
vulgi opinio: public opinion
vulgo: commonly or generally
vulgus [the common people]: a mob
vulneribus confectus: weakened by battle wounds
vulnus: an injury or wound
vulpes: a fox

Z

zelotypus: jealousy
zephyrus: a warm westwind
zonam solvere [to untie the girdle]: to marry a maiden (during the Roman wedding ceremony, the woman's apron is untied and laid aside as a rite symbolizing her change of marital status)

DICTA
Common Phrases and Familiar Sayings

A

a cruce salus: salvation comes from the Cross

a Deo et rege: from God and the king

a Deo lux nostra: our light comes from God

a fronte praecipitium a tergo lupi [a precipice before (me), wolves behind (me)]: between a rock and a hard place

a verbis legis non est recedendum: (leg.) from the words of the law there is no departure

ab abusu ad usum non valet consequentia: the usefulness of something is not invalidated by the consequences of its abuse

ab actu ad posse valet illatio: it is possible to infer the future from the past

ab hoc et ab hac et ab illa [from this and from this and from that]: from here, there, and everywhere (i.e., confusedly)

ab Jove principium: from Jove is the beginning (of all things; Virgil)

ab ovo usque ad mala [from the egg to the apples]: from appetizer to the dessert (i.e., from beginning to end)

ab uno disce omnes [from one learn all]: from one sample we judge the rest

abeunt studia in mores: pursuits become habits (Ovid)

abi in malam crucem: (fig.) to the devil with you!

absens haeres non erit [the absent one will not be the heir]: out of sight, out of mind

abundans cautela non nocet: abundant caution does no harm

Acheruntis pabulum [food for Acheron]: marked for death (Plautus; referring to corrupt and depraved persons)

acta est fabula: the play is over (the dying words of Caesar Augustus)

actio personalis moritur cum persona: (leg.) a personal right dies with the person

actori incumbit onus probandi: (leg.) the burden of proof falls to the plaintiff

actum est de me [it is all over with me!]: all is lost!

actum est de nobis [it is all over with us!]: all is lost!

actum est de republica: [it is all over with the Republic!]: the Republic is lost!

actum ne agas [do not do what is done]: leave well enough alone (Terence)

actus Dei nemini facit injuriam: (leg.) acts of God do injury to no one

actus Dei nemini nocet: (leg.) acts of God bring harm to no one

ad astra per aspera: to the stars through adversities (motto of Kansas)

ad augusta per angusta: to honors through difficulties

ad instar omnium: in the likeness of all

ad kalendas (or **calendas**) **Graecas** [at the Greek calends]: never (the Greeks did not have a calends, only the Romans had)

ad majorem Dei gloriam (A.M.D.G.): to the greater glory of God (motto of the Society of Jesus, the Jesuits)

ad meliora vertamur: let us turn to better things

ad perpetuam rei memoriam: for the perpetual remembrance of the matter

ad praesens ova cras pullis sunt meliora [eggs today are better than chickens tomorrow]: a bird in the hand is worth two in the bush

adjuvante Deo labor proficit: with God's help, work prospers

adulescentia deferbuit: the fires of youth have cooled

adversus solem ne loquitor [neither speak against the sun]: do not dispute with what is obvious

aedificatum solo, solo cedit: (leg.) the thing built on the land goes with the land

aegrescit medendo [he grows worse with the treatment]: the remedy is worse than the disease (adapted from Virgil)

aequitas sequitur legem: equity follows the law

aeternum servans sub pectore vulnus: tending an eternal wound within the heart

age quod agis [do what you are doing]: attend to the work you have at hand

alea jacta est: the die is cast

alia tendanda via est: another way must be tried

alis volat propriis: she flies with her own wings (motto of Oregon)

alitur vitium vivitque tegendo [the taint is nourished and lives by being concealed]: vice lives and thrives by secrecy

alter ego est amicus: a friend is another self

alter ipse amicus: a friend is a second self

alteri sic tibi: do to another as to thyself

alterum alterius auxilio eget: one thing needs the help of another

altiora peto: I seek higher things

amantes amentes or **amantes sunt amentes:** lovers are lunatics (Terence)

amicus usque ad aras [a friend as far as the altar]: a friend in everything save religion

amo ut invenio: I love as I find

amor gignit amorem: love begets love

amor vincit omnia: love conquers all things

anguillam cauda tenes [you hold an eel by the tail]: you have caught a lion by the tail.

anima in amicis una: one mind among friends

animal bipes implume [a two-legged animal without feathers]: man (Plato's definition of man)

animis opibusque parati: prepared in minds and resources (a motto of South Carolina)

animo et fide: by courage and faith

animo non astutia: by courage, not by craft

animis opibusque parati [prepared in spirit and resources]: ready for anything

animus et prudentia: courage and discretion

animus hominis est anima scripti: (leg.) the intention of the person is the intention of the written instrument

animus non deficit aequus [a well-balanced mind is not wanting]: equanimity does not fail us

annona cara est [corn is dear]: the cost of living is high (also **annonae caritas**)

annuit coeptis: He (God) has favored our undertaking (a motto of the United States of America)

ante tubam trepidat [he trembles before the trumpet sounds]: he cries before he is hurt (Virgil)

apage Satanus!: away with you, Satan!

apage!: be off!

aperto vivere voto [to live with unconcealed desire]: to live life as an open book (Persius)

appetitus rationi pareat: let your desires be governed by reason (Cicero)

aqua profunda est quieta: still water runs deep

aquila non capit muscas: an eagle does not catch flies

arbitrium est judicium: (leg.) an award is a judgment

arma pacis fulcra: arms are the props of peace

arma tuentur pacem: arms maintain peace

arma virumque cano: sing of arms and of a man (the opening lines of Virgil's epic poem *The Aeneid*)

armat spinat rosas: the thorn arms the rose

ars est celare artem: true art is to conceal art

ars est longa, vita brevis: art is long, life is short

ars gratia artis: art for art's sake (motto of Metro-Goldwyn-Mayer)

arte magistra: by the aid of art (Virgil)

arte perire sua [to perish by one's own trickery]: to be caught in one's own trap

artes honorabit: he will adorn the arts

artes, scientia, veritas: arts, science, truth (motto of the University of Michigan)

asinus ad lyram [an ass at the lyre]: to be all thumbs

asinus asino, et sus sui pulcher: as an ass is beautiful to an ass so a is pig to a pig

asinus asinum fricat [the ass rubs the ass]: one fool rubs another fool's back (i.e., mutual praise)

astra castra, numen lumen: the stars my camp, the divine Spirit my light

at spes non fracta: but hope is not broken

Athanasius contra mundum [Athanasius against the world]: referring to the stand made by St. Athanasius against heresy in the early fourth century C.E.

auctor pretiosa facit: the giver makes the gifts precious (adapted from Ovid)

audaciter at sincere: boldly and frankly

audax et celer: bold and swift

aude sapere: dare to be wise

audemus jura nostra defendere: we dare to defend our rights (motto of Alabama)

audentes (or **audaces**) **fortuna juvet:** fortune favors the bold

audi alteram partem: (leg.) hear the other side (the right of the defendant to answer a charge or to speak in his or her own defense)

audita et altera pars: let the other side be heard as well

aureo hamo piscari [to fish with a golden hook]: gold is the surest of lures

auri sacra fames: accursed craving for gold

auribus teneo lupum [I have a wolf by the ears]: I am in desparate trouble

auro quaeque janua panditur: a golden key opens any door

aurora musis amica est: Dawn is the friend of the muses

auspicium melioris aevi [an omen of a better age]: a pledge of better times (motto of the Order of St. Michael and St. George)

Austriae est imperare orbi universo (A.E.I.O.U.): all the world is to be ruled by Austria (motto of Frederick III)

aut bibat aut abeat: either drink or go away

aut Caesar aut nihil [either Caesar or nothing]: either first or not at all

aut disce aut discede: either learn or depart

aut inveniam viam aut faciam: I will either find a way or make one

aut mors aut victoria: either death or victory

aut non tentaris, aut perfice: either do not try it or go through with it

aut vincere aut mori: either to conquer or to die

auxilium ab alto: help from on high

ave atque vale: hale and farewell

ave, Caesar, morituri te salutamus!: Hail, Caesar, we who are about to die salute you (salutation of the gladiators to the Roman emperors)

avi memorantur avorum [my ancestors recall their ancestors]: my ancestral line is long

avito viret honore [he flourishes upon ancestral honors]: his honor is not of his own doing

B

barbae tenus sapientes [men are wise as far as their beards]: referring to those who pretend to have knowledge they do not in fact possess

basis virtutum constantia: constancy is the foundation of virtue

beati pacifici: blessed are the peacemakers

beati pauperes spiritu: blessed are the poor in spirit

bella, detesta matribus: war, the horror of mothers

bella, horrida bella: wars, horrid wars

bene est tentare: it is as well to try

bene orasse est bene studuisse: to have prayed well is to have striven well

bene qui latuit bene vixit [well has he lived who has lived a retired life]: he who has lived in obscurity has lived in security (Ovid)

beneficium accipere libertatem est vendere: to accept a favor is to sell one's liberty

bibere venenum in auro: to drink poison from a golden cup

bis dat qui cito dat: he gives twice who gives quickly
bis peccare in bello non licet: it is not permitted to err twice in war
bis pueri senes: old men are twice children
bis repetita placent: that which pleases is twice repeated
bis vincit qui se vincit in victoria: he conquers twice who conquers himself in victory (Publius Syrus)
bis vivit qui bene vivit: he lives twice who lives well
blandae mendacia linguae: the lies of a flattering tongue
bona fide polliceor: I promise in good faith
boni judicis est lites dirimere: (leg.) a good judge is one who prevents litigation
bonis nocet quisquis pepercerit malis: whoever spares the bad injures the good (Publius Syrus)
bonis quod bene fit haud perit: whatever is done for good men is never done in vain (Plautus)
bonum vinum laetificat cor hominis: good wine makes men's hearts rejoice
brevis esse haboro, obscurus fio: in trying to be concise, I become obscure (Horace)

C

caeca invidia est: envy is blind
caeli enarrant gloriam Dei: the heavens are telling the glory of God
caelitus mihi vires: my strength is from heaven
candide et constanter: frankly and firmly
candor dat viribus alas: sincerity gives wings to strength
cane pejus et angue: worse than a dog or a snake
cantabit vacuus coram latrone viator: the penniless man has nothing to lose (Juvenal)
cantilenam eandem canis: he sings the same old song (Terence)
capiat qui capere possit [let him take who can]: catch as catch can
captantes capti sumus [we catchers have been caught]: the biter is bitten
captus nidore culinae: caught by the odor of the kitchen
caput inter nubia condo: I hide my head among the clouds (i.e., fame; Virgil)
caret initio et fine: it lacks beginning and end
carpe diem [seize the day]: enjoy today; make the most of the present
carpe diem, quam minimum credula postero: seize the day, trusting little in tomorrow (Horace)
carpent tua poma nepotes: your descendants will pick your fruit
carpere et colligere: to pick and gather
cassis tutissima virtus [virtue is the safest helmet]: an honest person need not fear a thing
castigat ridendo mores: it corrects manners by laughing at them (i.e., comedy)
causa latet, vis et notissima: the cause is hidden but its strength is well noted (Ovid)

cave canem: beware of the dog
cave ignoscas: take care not to overlook (or forgive)
cave ne cadas [take heed you do not fall]: beware of falling from your high position
cave quid dicis, quando et cui: beware what you say, when and to whom
caveat actor: let the doer beware
caveat emptor: let the buyer beware
caveat venditor: let the seller beware
caveat viator: let the traveler beware
cavendo tutus: safe by taking heed
cedant arma togae [let arms yield to the toga]: let the military yield power to civil authority (Motto of Wyoming)
cede Deo: submit to God
celeritas et veritas: swiftness and truth
certum est quia impossibile est: it is true because it is impossible (Tertullian)
certum scio: I know for certain
certum voto pete finem: set a definite limit to your desire (Horace)
cessante causa, cessat effectus: when the cause ceases, the effect ceases
Christi crux est mea lux: the cross of Christ is my light
Christo et Ecclesiae: for Christ and for the Church
cineri gloria sera est: glory paid to ashes comes too late (Martial)
cito maturum, cito putridum: soon ripe, soon rotten
civilitas successit barbarum: civilization succeeds barbarism (territorial motto of Minnesota)
civis Romanus sum: I am a citizen of Rome
clarior ex obscuro: (I shine) more brightly from out of obscurity
clarior ex tenebris: (I shine) more brightly from out of the darkness
clarum et venerabile nomen: an illustrious and venerable name
classicum canit: the trumpet sounds attack
coelitus mihi vires: my strength is from heaven
coetus dulces valete [happy meetings]: fare you well (Catullus)
cogito ergo sum: I think, therefore I am (Descartes)
colubrem in sinu fovere: to hold a snake in one's bosom
comes jucundus in via pro vehiculo est: a pleasant companion on the road is as good as a vehicle (Publius Syrus)
commune periculum concordiam parit: a common danger begets unity
communis error facit jus: (leg.) sometimes common error makes law
compendia dispendia: short cuts are round-abouts
compesce mentem: control your temper
confido et conquiesco: I trust and I am at rest
conscia mens recti: a mind conscious of integrity (Ovid)
conscientia mille testes: conscience is as a thousand witnesses
consensus facit legem: consent makes law
consensus tollit errorem: (leg.) consent takes away error

consequitur quodcunque petit: he attains whatever he attempts
consilia et facta: by thoughts and deeds
consilio et animis: by wisdom and courage (also **consilio et animo**)
consilio et prudentia: by wisdom and prudence
consilio manuque: by work and wisdom
consilio, non impetu: by wisdom, not impulse
constantia et virtute: by constancy and courage
consuetudo quasi altera natura: habit is as second nature (Cicero)
consule Planco [when Plancus was consul]: in my younger days (Horace)
consummatum est: it is finished (one of the Seven Last Words of Christ on the Cross: St. John 19:30)
cor unum, via una: one heart, one way
corda serata fero: I carry a heart locked up
corpora lente augescunt cito extinguuntur: bodies are slow in growth, rapid in decay (Horace)
corruptio optimi pessima: the corruption of the best is the worst
corruptissima re publica plurimae leges: in the most corrupt state exist the most laws (Terence)
crambe repetita [warmed-over cabbage]: the same old thing (Juvenal)
cras credemus, hodie nihil: tomorrow we will believe, not today
credat Judaeus Apella [let Apella the Jew believe it]: only the credulous believe it (Horace)
crede quod habes, et habes: believe that you have it, and you have it
credite posteri: believe it, posterity (Horace)
credo quia absurdum (est): I believe it because it is absurd
credo quia impossibile (est): I believe it because it is impossible
credo ut intelligam [I believe so that I might understand]: belief precedes knowledge (St. Augustine)
credula res amor est: a credulous thing is love (Ovid)
crescere ex aliquo: raising oneself through the fall of another
crescit eundo: it grows as it goes (motto of New Mexico)
crescit sub pondere virtus: virtue grows under oppression
crescite et multiplicamini: increase and multiply (motto of Maryland)
cribro aquam haurire: to draw water with a sieve
cruce, dum spiro, fido: while I have breath, I trust in the Cross
crux mihi ancora: the Cross is my anchor
cucullus non facit monachum: the cowl does not make the monk
cui Fortuna ipsa cedit: to whom Fortune herself yields (Cicero)
cuilibet in arte sua perito credendum est: every skilled man is to be trusted in his own art
cujus regio, ejus religio [whose region, his religion]: the faith of the people is determined by their king
culpam poena premit comes: punishment presses hard upon the heels of crime (Horace)

cum tacent, clamant [when they are silent they cry loudest]: silence speaks louder than words
cuneus cuneum trudit: wedge drives wedge
cura facit canos: care brings grey hairs
curae leves loquuntur, ingentes stupent: light griefs find utterance, great ones hold silent (Seneca)
curiosa felicitas: nice felicity of expression (Petronius)
currus bovem trahit [the cart draws the ox]: to put the cart before the horse
curta supellex [scanty supply of furniture]: meager stock of knowledge

D

da fidei quae fidei sunt: give to faith that which belongs to faith
da locum melioribus: give place to your betters (Terence)
dabit Deus his quoque fine: God will put an end to these troubles as well (Virgil)
dabit qui dedit: he will give who gave
damna minus consulta movent: losses to which one grows accustomed affect one much less (Juvenal)
damnant quod non intelligunt: they condemn what they do not understand
damnum sentit dominus: (leg.) the master suffers the loss
damnum sine injuria esse potest: (leg.) loss without injury is deemed possible
dare cervices [give the neck]: submit to the executioner
dare pondus idonea fumo [fit only to give weight to smoke]: utterly worthless (Persius)
data fata secutus: following what is decreed by faith (Virgil)
date obolum Belisario: give alms to Belisarius (a Roman general who, according to legend, was reduced to poverty)
date, et dabitur vobis: give and it shall be given to you (St. Luke 6:38)
Davus sum, non Oedipus [I am Davus, not Oedipus]: I am a simple man, not a genius
de asini umbra disceptare [to argue about the shadow of an ass]: to argue over trifling matters
de duobus malis, minus est semper eligendum: of two evils, always choose the lesser (Thomas à Kempis)
de fumo in flammam [out of the smoke into the flame]: out of the frying pan and into the fire
de gustibus non est disputandum (or **de gustibus non disputandum**): there is no disputing about tastes
de minimis non curat lex: the law does not concern itself with trifles
de minimis non curat praetor: a magistrate does not concern himself with trifles
de mortuis nil nisi bonum: of the dead say nothing but good
de nihilo nihil: from nothing nothing can come (Persius)
de omni re scibili et quibusdam aliis [of all things knowable and certain others]: a "know it all"

de omnibus rebus et quibusdam aliis [of all things and of certain others]: a book that rambles on and on

de similibus idem est judicium: (leg.) in similar cases, the judgment is the same

de te fabula narratur: the story relates to you (Horace)

debellare superbos: to overthrow the proud (Virgil)

debile fundamentum fallit opus: a weak foundation destroys the work upon which it is built

decies repetita placebit: though repeated ten times, it is still pleasing (Horace)

decipimur specie recti: we are deceived by the semblance of what is right (Horace)

decipit frons prima multos: the first appearance deceives many

decori decus addit avito: he adds honor to his ancestral honor

decus et tutamen: honor and defense

deficit omne quod nascitur: everything which is born passes away (Quintilian)

degeneres animos timor arguit: fear betrays ignoble souls (Virgil)

Dei gratia: by the grace of God

Dei gratias: thanks be to God

Dei irati: the wrath of God

Dei memor, gratus amicus: mindful of God, grateful to friends

delectando pariterque monendo: by giving pleasure and at the same time instructing (Horace)

delegatus non potest delegare: a delegate cannot delegate

delenda est Carthago [Carthage must be destroyed]: the war must be carried on to the bitter end

deliciae humani generis: the delight of mankind (a reference to the Emperor Titus)

delphinum natare doces: you are teaching a dolphin to swim

delphinum silvis appingit, fluctibus aprum [he portrays a dolphin in the woods and a boar in the waves]: he introduces objects unsuited to the scene (Horace)

deme supercilio nubem [remove the clouds from your brow]: come down from your cloud

denique caelum: heaven at last (Crusaders' battle cry)

dente superbo: with a disdainful tooth (Horace)

Deo adjuvante non timendum: with God's help, nothing need be feared

Deo date: give unto God

Deo duce, ferro comitante: with God as my leader and a sword as my friend

Deo et regi fidelis: loyal to God and king

Deo favente [with God's favor]: by the grace of God

Deo gratias: thanks be to God

Deo juvante: with God's help (motto of Monaco)

Deo monente [with God's warning]: a warning from God

Deo volente (D.V. or **d.v.):** God willing

deo dignus vindice nodus [a knot worthy of a god to unloose]: a great dilemma

Deo, non fortuna: from God, not chance

Deo, Optimo, Maximo (D.O.M.): to God, the Best, the Greatest (motto of the Benedictine order)

Deo, patriae, amicus: for God, homeland, and friends
deorum cibus est: it is food for the gods
deos fortioribus adesse: the gods are said to aid the stronger (Tacitus)
deprendi miserum est: it is wretched to be found out
desipere in loco [to act foolishly at the proper time]: to unwind occasionally (Horace)
detur digniori: let it be given to those more worthy
detur pulchriori: let it be given to those more beautiful
Deum cole, regem serva: worship God, serve the king
Deum esse credimus: we believe in the existence of God
Deus avertat!: God forbid!
Deus det!: God grant!
Deus est regit qui omnia: there is a God who rules all things
Deus est summum bonum: God is the greatest good
Deus est suum esse: God is his own being
Deus gubernat navem: God pilots the ship
Deus misereatur: God be merciful
Deus nobis haec otia fecit: a god has given us this place of rest (Virgil)
Deus nobiscum, quis contra?: God with us, who can be against us?
Deus providebit: God will provide
Deus sive natura: God or nature (Spinoza)
Deus vobiscum: God be with you
Deus vult: God wills it (the rallying cry of the First Crusade)
di meliora: god forbid!
di or **dii pia facta vident:** the gods see virtuous deeds (Ovid)
dicamus bona verba: let us speak words of good omen (Terence)
dictis facta suppetant: let deeds suffice for words
dictum ac factum [said and done]: no sooner said than done
dictum sapienti sat est: a word to the wise is sufficient
diem perdidi [I have lost a day]: I have done nothing of worth (attributed to Titus)
difficilia quae pulchra: things that are beautiful are difficult to attain
dimidium facti qui coepit habet: a work that is begun well is already half done (Horace)
dirige nos Domine: direct us, O Lord
dirigo: I direct (motto of Maine)
dis aliter visum: it seemed otherwise to the gods
dis bene juvantibus: with the help of the gods
dis ducibus: under the direction of the gods
disce pati: learn to endure
discere docendo: to learn through teaching
disjecti membra poetae: limbs of a dismembered poet (Horace)
ditat Deus: God enriches (motto of Arizona)
divide et impera: divide and rule

divinitus accidit: it happened miraculously
divitiae virum faciunt: riches make the man
dixit Dominus: the Lord has spoken it
doce ut discas: teach that you may learn
docendo discimus: we learn by teaching
docta ignorantia: learned ignorance (Nicolas of Cusa)
dolium volvitur: an empty cask is easily rolled
domi militiaeque: at war and at peace
Domine illuminatio mea: O Lord, my light!
Domine, dirige nos: O Lord, direct us (motto of the city of London)
Domino, Optimo, Maximo (D.O.M.): the Lord, the Best, the Greatest (an alternate rendering of the motto of the Benedictine Order)
Dominus illuminatio mea: the Lord is my light (motto of Oxford University)
Dominus providebit: the Lord will provide
Dominus vobiscum: the Lord be with you
domus et placens uxor: home and a pleasing wife (Horace)
donec eris felix multos numerabis amicos: as long as you are prosperous you will have many friends (Ovid)
dormitat Homerus [even Homer nods off]: sometimes even the best of us are caught napping (Horace)
duabus sellis sedere: to sit in two saddles
ducit amor patriae: love of country leads me
dulce bellum inexpertis: war is sweet to those not acquainted with it
dulce est desipere in loco: it is sweet to unwind upon occasion (Horace)
dulce et decorum est pro patria mori: sweet and seemly it is to die for one's country
dulce quod utile: what is useful is sweet
dulce sodalicium [sweet society]: what a sweet thing is companionship
dulces moriens reminiscitur Argos: as he died he remembered Argos (the home of his youth) (Virgil)
dulcis amor patriae: sweet is the love of one's homeland
dum fortuna fuit: while fortune lasted
dum loquor, hora fugit: time is flying while I speak (Ovid)
dum spiro, spero: while I breathe, I hope (a motto of South Carolina)
dum tacent clamant [though they are silent, they cry aloud]: their silence speaks loudly
dum vita est, spes est: while there is life, there is hope
dum vitant stulti vitia in contraria current: in shunning one kind of vice, fools run to the opposite extreme (Horace)
dum vivimus, vivamus: while we live, let us live
duplici spe uti: to have a double hope
dura lex, sed lex: the law is hard, but it is the law
durate et vosmet rebus servate secundis: carry on and preserve yourselves for better times (Virgil)
dux femina facti: the leader of the action was a woman (Virgil)

E

e flamma petere cibum [to snatch food out of the flame]: to live by desperate means (Terence)

e pluribus unum: out of many one (motto of the United States of America)

Ecce Agnus Dei: Behold the Lamb of God!

ecce iterum Crispinus [here's that Crispin again]: here's that bore again

Ecclesia non moritur: the Church does not die

ego et rex meus [my king and I]: I and my king (as rendered by Cardinal Wolsey)

ego spem pretio non emo [I do not purchase hope for a price]: I do not buy a pig in a poke (Terence)

egomet mihi ignosco: I myself pardon myself (Horace)

eheu! fugaces labuntur anni: alas! the fleeting years slip by (Horace)

elephantem ex musca facis: you are making an elephant out of a fly (i.e., making a mountain out of molehill)

empta dolore docet experientia: experience bought with pain teaches effectually

ense et aratro: with sword and plow

ense petit placidam sub libertate quietem: by the sword she seeks peaceful quiet under liberty (motto of Massachusetts)

Epicuri de grege porcus [a hog from the drove of Epicurus]: a glutton (Horace)

epulis accumbere divum: to recline at the feast of the gods (Virgil)

equis virisque [with horse and foot]: with all one's might

errare humanum est: to err is human

errores Ulixis: the wanderings of Ulysses

erubuit; salva res est: he blushed; the affair is safe (Terence)

esse est percipi: to be is to be perceived (Berkeley)

esse quam videri: to be rather than to seem (motto of North Carolina)

est ars etiam male dicendi: there is even an art of maligning

est deus in nobis: there is a god within us (Ovid)

est mihi honori: it reflects well on me

est modus in rebus: there is a method in all things (Horace)

est quaedam flere voluptas: there is a certain pleasure in weeping (Ovid)

esto perpetua [be thou eternal]: may she be everlasting (motto of Idaho)

esto perpetuum: let it be everlasting

esto quod esse videris: be what you seem to be

et campos ubi Troja fuit: and the fields where once was Troy (Virgil)

et cum spiritu tuo: and with thy spirit (liturgical response to **Dominus vobiscum**, the Lord be with you)

et decus et pretium recti: both the ornament and the rewards of virtue

et ego in Arcadia [I too have been to Arcadia]: I know all about it

et genus et formam regina pecunia donat: like a queen, money bestows both rank and beauty (Horace)

et nos quoque tela sparsimus [we too have hurled javelins]: we are also veterans

et sceleratis sol oritur: the sun shines even on the wicked (Seneca)

et tu, Brute [and you too, Brutus!]: last words of Caesar indicating betrayal by a trusted ally (Shakesphere's *Julius Caesar*)

etiam periere ruinae [even the ruins have perished]: there is nothing left (Lucan)

etiam quod esse videris: be what you seem to be

eventus stultorum magister: experience is the teacher of fools

ex Africa semper aliquid novi: out of Africa there is always something new

ex desuetudine amittuntur privilegia: it is out of disuse that rights are lost

ex facto jus oritur: the law goes into effect after the fact

ex fide fortis: strong through faith

ex granis fit acervus: many grains make a heap

ex malis moribus bonae leges natae sunt: from bad usages, good laws have sprung (Coke)

ex nihilo nihil fit [from nothing, nothing is made]: nothing produces nothing

ex ore parvulorum veritas: out of the mouth of little children comes truth

ex ungue leonem [from a claw, the lion]: the lion is known by its claws (i.e., from a part one can determine the whole)

ex uno disce omnes [from one learn all]: from one we judge the rest

excelsior: ever higher (motto of New York State)

exceptio probat regulam: the exception establishes the rule (i.e., gives greater definition)

excitari, non hebescere: to be spirited, not sluggish

exegi monumentum aere perennius: I have raised a monument more lasting than bronze (Horace)

exempla sunt odiosa: examples are odious

exercitatio optimus est magister: practice is the best teacher

exitus acta probat [the ending proves the deeds]: all's well that ends well

expende Hannibalem: weigh the dust of Hannibal (Juvenal)

experientia docet: experience teaches

experientia docet stultos: experience teaches fools

experto crede or **experto credite:** believe one who has had experience

expertus dico: I speak from experience

expertus loquitur: he speaks from experience

expertus metuit [having had experience, he is afraid]: once burnt, twice shy (Horace)

explorant adversa viros: misfortune tries men

extinctus amabitur idem: (though hated in life), the same man will be loved after he is dead (Horace)

F

faber est quisque fortunae suae: everyone is the architect of his or her own fortune (Sallust)

fabes indulcet fames [hunger sweetens beans]: hunger makes everything taste good

facere non possum quin: I cannot but

DICTA

facile est inventis addere: it is easy to add to things already invented
facile largiri de alieno: it is easy to be generous with what is another's
facilis descensus Averno: the descent to hell is easy (Virgil)
facit indignatio versum [indignation produces verse]: righteous anger flames into verse (Juvenal)
facta non verba: deeds not words
faenum habet in cornu, longe fuge: flee far from the danger; beware, he is vicious (Horace)
fallentis semita vitae: the narrow path of an unnoticed life (Horace)
falsus in uno, falsus in omnibus: false in one thing, false in everything
fama fert [the story goes]: rumor runs away
fama malum quo non aliud velocius ullum: there is no evil swifter than a rumor (Virgil)
fama nihil est celerius: nothing is swifter than rumor
fama semper vivat!: may his/her fame live forever!
fama volat: the report or rumor flies (Virgil)
famam extendere factis: to spread abroad his fame by deeds (Virgil)
fames optimum condimentum: hunger is the best of seasonings
fare fac: speak and act
fari quae sentiat: to say what one feels (Horace)
fas est ab hoste doceri: it is allowable to learn even from an enemy (Ovid)
Fata obstant: the Fates oppose (Virgil)
Fata viam invenient: the Fates will find a way (Virgil)
Fata volentem ducunt, nolentem trahunt: the Fates lead the willing and drag the reluctant
fatetur facinus qui judicium fugit: to flee the law is to confess one's guilt
favete linguis [favor with your tongues]: be silent (Horace)
fax mentis incendium gloriae: the passion for glory is the torch of the mind
felicitas multos habet amicos: happiness (or prosperity) has many friends
felix qui nihil debet: happy is the one who owes nothing
felix qui potuit rerum cognoscere causas: happy is the one who understands the causes of all things (Virgil)
ferrum ferro acuitur: iron is sharpened by iron
fervens difficili bile tumet jecur: my hot passion swells with savage wrath (Horace)
fervet olla, vivit amicitia: while the pot boils, friendship lives (or endures)
fervet opus: the work boils (Virgil)
festina lente: make haste slowly
fiat Dei voluntas: God's will be done
fiat experimentum in corpore vili: let the experiment be done upon a worthless body (or object)
fiat justitia, ruat caelum: let justice be done, though the heavens fall
fiat lux: let there be light (Genesis 1:3)
fiat voluntas tua: Thy will be done (Matthew 6:10)
fictio cedit veritati: fiction yields to truth

fide et amore: by faith and love
fide et fiducia: by faith and confidence
fide et fortitudine: by faith and fortitude
fide, non armis: by faith, not by arms
fide, sed cui vide: trust, but be careful whom
fidei coticula crux: the cross is the touchstone of faith
fideli certa merces: to the faithful one, reward is certain
fidelis ad urnam [faithful to the urn]: true till death
fides ante intellectum: faith before understanding
fides et justitia: faith and justice
fides facit fidem [faith creates faith]: confidence begats confidence
fides non timet: faith does not fear
fides probata coronat: faith approved confers a crown
fides Punica [Punic faith]: treachery
fides quaerens intellectum or **fidens quaerens intellectum** [faith seeking understanding]: belief before understanding (St. Augustine)
fides servanda est: faith must be protected
fidus Achates [faithful Achates]: a trustworthy friend
fidus et audax: faithful and courageous
finem respice [look to the end]: consider the outcome
finis coronat opus: the end crowns the work
finis finem litibus imponit: (leg.) the end put an end to litigation
finis unius diei est principium alterius: the end of one day is the beginning of another
fit via vi: a way is made by force
flamma fumo est proxima [flame is close to smoke]: where there is smoke, there is fire
flectere si nequeo superos, Acheronta movebo: if I cannot bend heaven then I'll stir hell (Virgil)
flecti, non frangi: to be bent, not broken
floreat Etona: may Eton flourish (motto of Eton College)
flores curat Deus: God takes care of the flowers
flosculi sententiarum: flowerets of thought
fluctuat nec mergitur: she is tossed by the waves but she does not sink (motto of Paris, which has a ship as its emblem)
fons et origo: the source and origin
forensis strepitus: the clamor of the forum
forma bonum fragile est: beauty is a transitory blessing (Ovid)
forma flos, fama flatus: beauty is a flower, fame is a breath
forte scutum, salus ducum: a strong shield is the safety of leaders
fortem posce animum: pray for a strong will (Juvenal)
fortem te praebe: be brave!
fortes fortuna [ad]juvat: fortune favors the strong
forti et fideli nihil difficile: to the brave and faithful, nothing is difficult

fortis cadere, cedere non potest: the brave may fall, but they cannot yield
fortis et fidelis: brave and faithful
fortiter et recte: bravely and uprightly
fortiter geret crucem: he will bravely bear the cross
fortiter in re, suaviter in modo [strongly in deed, gently in manner]: resolute in deed, but gentle in manner
fortiter, fideliter, feliciter: fearlessly, faithfully, felicitously
fortitudine et prudentia: by courage and prudence
fortuna caeca est: fortune is blind
fortuna favet fatuis: fortune favors fools
fortuna favet fortibus: fortune favors the brave
fortuna mea in bello campo: the fortune is mine in a fair fight
fortuna meliores sequitur: fortune follows the better man (Sallust)
fortuna multis dat nimium, nulli satis: to many fortune gives too much, to none does it give enough (Publius Syrus)
fortuna sequatur: let fortune follow
fortunae cetera mando: I commit the rest to fortune
fortunae filius: a child of fortune (Horace)
fortunae objectum esse: abandoned to fate
fortunae vicissitudines: the vicissitudes of fortune
fossoribus orti [sprung from ditch diggers]: from humble origins
frangas, non flectes: you may break, you will not bend (me)
frons est animi janua: the forehead is the door of the mind (Cicero)
fronti nulla fides: there is no trusting appearances (Juvenal)
fructu non foliis arborem aestima: judge a tree by its fruit, not by its leaves (Phaedrus)
fruges consumere nati: born merely to consume the fruits of the earth (Horace)
frustra laborat qui omnibus placere studet: he labors in vain who tries to please everybody
fugaces labuntur anni: the fleeting years glide by
fugit hora: the hour flies (Ovid)
fugit irreparabile tempus: irretrievable time flies (Virgil)
fuimus Troes [we were once Trojans]: our day is over (Virgil)
fuit Ilium [Troy once was]: its day is over (Virgil)
fulmen brutum [a harmless thunderbolt]: an empty threat
fumum et opes strepitumque Romae: the smoke, the wealth, the din of Rome (Juvenal)
fundamentum justitiae est fides: the fountain of justice is good faith (Cicero)
furiosi absentis loco est: a madman is like a man who is absent
furiosi solo furore punitur: (leg.) a madman is to be punished by his madness alone
furor arma ministrat: rage supplies arms (Virgil)

G

gaudeamus igitur (juvenes dum sumus): let us be joyful (while we are young)
gaudet tentamine virtus: virtue rejoices in trial
genus est mortis male vivere: to live an evil life is a type of death (Ovid)
genus irritabile vatum: the irritable race of poets (Horace)
Gloria Tibi, Domine: Glory be to Thee, O Lord
gloria virtutis umbra: glory is the shadow of virtue
gradatim vincimus: we conquer by degrees
gradu diverso, una via [with different pace, but on the same road]: the same way by different steps
Graeculus esuriens [hungry young Greek]: a parasite (Juvenal)
grammatici certant, et adhuc sub judice lis est: the grammarians quibble and still the question is unresolved (Horace)
grata testudo: the pleasing lyre
gratia Dei: by the grace of God
gratia gratiam parit: kindness produces kindness
gratia placendi: the grace of pleasing
Gratias agimus tibi: we give Thee thanks
graviora manent [more grievous perils remain]: the worst is yet to come
graviora quaedam sunt remedia periculis: some remedies are worse than the disease (Publius Syrus)
gravis ira regum est semper: the wrath of kings is always heavy (Seneca)
gravissimum est imperium consuetudinis: the power of custom is most weighty (Publius Syrus)
gutta cavat lapidem, non vi, sed saepe cadendo: the drop hollows the stone, not by force but by constant dripping

H

habemus confitentem reum: (leg.) we have an accused person who pleads guilty
habent sua fata libelli: books have their own destiny (attributed to Horace)
habere et dispertire: to have and to distribute
habere, non haberi: to hold, not to be held
habet et musca splenem: even a fly gets angry
hac mercede placet: I accept the terms
hac urgent lupus hac canis: on one side a wolf menaces, on the other, a dog (Horace)
hae nugae in seria ducent mala: these trifles will lead to serious evils (Horace)
haec generi incrementa fides: this faith will bring increase to our race
haec olim meminisse juvabit: it will be a pleasure to remember these things hereafter (Virgil)
haec tibi dona fero: these gifts I bear to thee (motto of Newfoundland)

haerent infixi pectore vultus: his face is graven on her heart (Virgil)
Hannibal ad portas [Hannibal is at the gate]: the enemy is close at hand (adapted from Cicero)
haud ignota loquor [I speak of things by no means unknown]: I speak of well-known events
heroum filii: sons of heroes (motto of Wellington College)
heu pietas! heu prisca fides: alas for piety! alas for the ancient faith! (Virgil)
hic domus, haec patria est [here is our home]: this is our country (Virgil)
hic est enim sanguis meus novi testamenti: this is the new covenant in my blood (St. Matthew 26:28)
hic et ubique terrarum: here and everywhere throughout the world (motto of the University of Paris)
hic finis fandi [here was an end of the speaking]: here the speech ended (Virgil)
hic funis nihil attraxit [this line has taken no fish]: this scheme has failed
hic jacet lepus [here lies the hare]: here lies the difficulty
hiems subest: winter is at hand
hinc illae lacrimae: hence these tears (Terence)
hinc lucem et pocula sacra: from hence we receive light and sacred drafts (motto of Cambridge University)
hoc certum est: this much is certain
hoc erat in more majorum: this was in the manner of our ancestors
hoc erat in votis [this was among my wishes]: this was one of my desires (Horace)
hoc est corpus meum: this is my body (St. Matthew 26:26)
hoc genus omne: all of this class (Horace)
hoc habet! [he has it!]: he is hit! (the cry of the spectators at gladiatorial contests)
hoc indictum volo [I wish this unsaid]: I withdraw the statement
hoc opus, hic labor est [this is the task, this is the toil]: there's the rub (Virgil)
hoc opus, hoc studium: this work, this pursuit (Horace)
hoc sustinete, majus ne veniat malum: endure this evil, lest a greater come upon you (Phaedrus)
hoc tibi est honori: this reflects well on you
hoc volo, sic jubeo, sit pro ratione voluntas: this I write, thus I command, let my will stand for reason
hodie mecum eris in paradiso: Today, you shall be with me in Paradise (one of the Seven Last Words of Christ; St. Luke 23:43)
hodie mihi, cras tibi [today for me, tomorrow for thee]: my turn today, your turn tomorrow
hodie, non cras: today, not tomorrow
hominem quaero: I am looking for a man (Phaedrus)
hominis est errare: to err is human
homo antiqua virtute ac fide: a man of the old-fashioned virtue and loyalty
homo doctus in se semper divitias habet: a learned person always has wealth within
homo homini aut deus aut lupus: to man, man is either a god or a wolf (Erasmus)

homo homini lupus: man is a wolf to man

homo mensura [man is the measure]: man is the measure of all things (Protagoras)

homo sum; humani nihil a me alienum puto: I am a man; nothing that relates to man do I deem alien to me (Terence)

homo unius libri: a man of one book (Thomas Aquinas's definition of a learned man)

homo vitae commodatus non donatus: a man is lent, not given, to life (Publius Syrus)

homunculi quanti sunt: what insignificant creatures we men are (Plautus)

honesta mors turpi vita potior: an honorable death is better than a base life (Tacitus)

honesta quam splendida [honorable things rather than brilliant ones]: reputable rather than showy

Honor est a Nilo: honor is from the Nile (anagram for Admiral **H**oratio **N**elson, who won the Battle of the Nile)

honor virtutis praemium: honor is the reward of virtue

honores mutant mores: honors alter mannners

honos alit artes: honor nourishes the arts (Cicero)

honos habet onus [honor has its burdens]: honor carries responsibilty

hora fugit: the hour flies

horas non numero nisi serenas: I number none but shining hours (an inscription on a sun dial)

horresco referens: I shudder to relate it

horror ubique: terror everywhere (motto of the Scots Guards)

hos ego versiculos feci, tulit alter honores: I wrote these lines, another has taken the credit (Virgil)

hostis honori invidia: envy is the foe of honor

hostis humani generis: an enemy of the human race

humani nihil alienum: nothing that relates to man is alien to me (Terence)

humanum est errare: to err is human

hunc tu, Romane, caveto: of him, Romans, do thou beware (Horace)

hypotheses non fingo [I frame no hypothesis]: I deal entirely with the facts (Sir Isaac Newton)

I

idem velle atque idem nolle: to like and dislike the same things (Sallust)

idoneus homo [a fit man]: a man of proved ability

Iesus Nazarenus, Rex Iudaeorum (I.N.R.I.) [Jesus of Nazareth, King of the Jews]: the title placard appended to the Cross of Christ by Pontius Pilate at the Crucifixion (St. John 19:20)

ignavis semper feriae sunt: to the indolent it is always a holiday

ignis fatuus (pl. **ignes fatui**): a delusive hope

ignorantia legis neminem excusat: ignorance of the law excuses no one

ignorantia judicis est calamitas innocentis: the ignorance of a judge is calamitous to an accused person

ignoscito saepe alteri nunquam tibi: forgive others often, yourself never
ignoti nulla cupido [no desire is felt for what is unknown]: ignorance is bliss
ignotum per ignotius: the unknown explained by the unknown
Ilias malorum: an Iliad of woes
illaeso lumine solum: an undazzled eye to the sun
imitatores, servum pecus: ye imitators, servile herd (Horace)
impavidum ferient ruinae [ruins strike him without dismay]: nothing can shatter the steadfastness of an upright man (Horace)
imperat aut servit collecta pecunia cuique: money is either our master or our slave (Horace)
imperium et libertas: empire and liberty
imperium in imperio: an empire within an empire (motto of Ohio)
imponere Pelion Olympo: to pile Pelion on Olympus
impunitas semper ad deteriora invitat: impunity is always an invitation to a greater crime
in aqua scribis [you are writing in water]: it is without effect
in arena aedificas [you are building on sand]: it will not last (i.e., it is in vain)
in beato omnia beata: with the blessed, all things are blessed (Horace)
in caelo quies: in heaven is rest
in caelo salus: in heaven is salvation
in cauda venenum [in the tail is poison]: beware of danger
in Christi nomine: in Christ's name
in cruce spero: I hope in the Cross
in Deo speravi: in God have I trusted
in ferrum pro libertate ruebant: for freedom they rushed upon the sword
in generalibus latet error: in generalities lies error
in hoc salus: there is safety in this
in hoc signo spes mea: in this sign is my hope (a reference to the Cross of Christ)
in hoc signo vinces: by this sign you will conquer (Emperor Constantine's vision before the Battle of the Milvian Bridge, 312 C.E., which, according to Eusebius, inspired the Chi-Rho [XP] monogram the laborum)
in lumine tuo videbimus lumen: in your light we shall see the light (motto of Columbia University)
in manus tuas commendo spiritum meum: into Thy hands I commend my sprit (one of the Seven Last Words of Christ; Luke 23:46)
in maxima potentia, minima licentia: in the greatest power exists the least liberty
in medio tutissimus ibis: safety is in going the middle course
in necessariis unitas, in dubiis libertas, in omnibus caritas: in things essential unity, in things doubtful liberty, in all things love (a motto of the Christian Church, Disciples of Christ)
in nocte consilium [in the night is counsel]: sleep on it
in nomine Domini: in the name of the Lord
in nomine Patris et Filii et Spiritus Sancti: in the name of the Father, the Son, and the Holy Spirit

in omnibus caritas: in all things love
in perpetuam rei memoriam: in everlasting remembrance of the event
in silvam ligna ferre: to carry wood to the forest
in solo Deo salus: in God alone is salvation
in te omnia sunt: everything depends on you
in te, Domine, speravi: in thee, O Lord, have I put my trust
in vino veritas [in wine is truth]: under wine's influence, the truth is told
incessu patuit dea: by her gait the goddess was revealed (Virgil)
incredulus odi: being skeptical, I detest it (Horace)
incudi reddere [to return to the anvil]: to revise or retouch (Horace)
inde irae et lacrimae: hence this anger and these tears (Juvenal)
index animi sermo est: speech is an indicator of thought
indignante invidia florebit justus: the just man will flourish in spite of envy
indocilis pauperiem pati: one that cannot learn to endure poverty (Horace)
industriae nil impossibile: to industry, nothing is impossible
inest clementia forti: clemency belongs to the brave
inest sua gratia parvis: even little things have a charm of their own
infandum renovare dolorem: to renew an unspeakable grief (adapted from Horace)
infecta pace: without effecting a peace (Terence)
infixum est mihi [I have firmly resolved]: I am determined
ingens telum necessitatis: necessity is an enormous weapon
injuria non excusat injuriam: one wrong does not justify another
inopem me copia fecit: abundance made me poor (Ovid)
inopiae desunt multa, avaritiae omnia: poverty is the lack of many things, but avarice is the lack of all things
insanus omnis furere credit ceteros: every madman thinks all others insane (Publius Syrus)
integer vitae scelerisque purus: blameless of life and free from crime (Horace)
integra mens augustissima possessio: a sound and vigorous mind is the highest possession
integros haurire fontes: to drink from pure fountains
integrum est mihi: I am at liberty
intelligenti pauca: to the understanding, few words suffice
intentio caeca mala: a hidden intention is an evil one
inter arma leges silent: in time of war, the laws are silent (Circero)
inter canem et lupum [between dog and wolf]: twilight
inter malleum et incudem: between the hammer and the anvil
inter spem et metum: between hope and fear
interdum vulgus rectum videt: sometimes the common folk see correctly
intra verba peccare: to offend in words only
invictus maneo: I remain unconquered
invita Minerva [Minerva being unwilling]: lacking inspiration
invitum sequitur honor: honors follow him unsolicited

io Triumphe! [Hail, god of Triumph]: the shout of the Roman soldiers and populace on the occasion of a procession of a victorious general
ipsa quidem pretium virtus sibi: virtue is its own reward
ipse dixit Dominus: the Lord himself has spoken it
ira furor brevis est: anger is a brief madness (Horace)
irritabis crabones: you will stir up the hornets
ita lex scripta est [thus the law is written]: such is the law
ite missa est: go, the mass is over

J

jacta est alea or **jacta alea est:** the die is cast (words attributed to Julius Caesar upon crossing the Rubicon)
jam redit et Virgo: now returns the Virgin (the return of Astraea, goddess of Justice, was thought by Romans to be a signal for the return of the Golden Age)
jejunus raro stomachus vulgaria temnit: a hungry stomach rarely despises common things (Horace)
Joannes est nomen ejus: his name is John (St. Luke 1:63; the Motto of Puerto Rico)
Jubilate Deo: rejoice in God
jucundi acti labores: [the memory of] past labors are pleasant (Cicero)
judex damnatur cum nocens absolvitur: the judge is condemned when the guilty is acquitted (Publius Syrus)
judex est lex loquens: a judge is the law speaking
judicium parium aut leges terrae: judgment of one's peers or else the laws of the land (Magna Carta)
juncta juvant: union is strength
juniores ad labores: the younger men for labors
jus est ars boni et aequi: law is the art of the good and the just
jus summum saepe summa malitia est: extreme law is often extreme wrong (Terence)
justitia omnibus: justice for all (motto of the District of Columbia)
justitiae soror fides: faith is the sister of justice
justum et tenacem propositi virum: one who is upright and firm of purpose (Horace)
juvante Deo: God helping

L

labor ipse voluptas [work itself is a pleasure]: labor is its own reward
labor omnia vincit: labor conquers all things (motto of Oklahoma)
laborare est orare: to work is to pray
labore et honore: by labor and honor
laborum dulce lenimen: the sweet solace of my labors (Horace)

labuntur et imputantur: the moments slip away and are entered into our account (a popular saying for a sundial)

lacrimae rerum: the tears of things

lacrimae simulatae [simulated tears]: crocodile tears

lacrimus oculos suffusa nitentis: her glittering eyes filled with tears (Virgil)

lateat scintillula forsan: perchance a little spark of life may lie hidden (motto of the Royal Humane Society, founded in 1774 for the rescue of drowning persons)

latet anguis in herba: a snake lies hid in the grass

laudari a laudato viro: to be praised by a man of praise (Cicero)

laudator temporis acti [a praiser of times past]: one who prefers the good old days (Horace)

laudem virtutis necessitati damus: we give to necessity the praise of virtue

laudumque immensa cupido [and a immense desire for praise]: passion for praise (Virgil)

laus Deo: praise be to God

laus propria sordet: self-praise is base

lege, quaeso: I beg you read (a note appended to the top of student papers inviting tutors to read their work)

leges mori serviunt: laws are subservient to custom

legimus, ne legantur: we read that others may not read (Lactantius, referring to censors and reviewers)

leone fortior fides: faith is stronger than a lion

leve fit quod bene fertur onus: light is the load that is cheerly borne (Ovid)

liberavi animam meam: I have freed my soul

libertas et natale solum: liberty and native land

libertas in legibus: liberty under the laws

libertas sub rege pio: liberty under an upright king

libido dominatur: the passions have gained control

ligonem ligonem vocat [he calls a hoe a hoe]: to call a spade a spade

limae labor et mora [the toil and delay of polishing]: the tedious revising of a literary work before publication (Horace)

linguae verbera: lashings of the tongue

lis litem generat: strife begats strife

litem lite resolvere [to settle strife by strife]: to clarify one's obscurity by another

litem quod lite resolvit: resolving one controversy by creating another (Horace)

longe aberrat scopo [he wanders far from the goal]: to be wide of the mark

longe absit [far be it from me]: God fobid

longe lateque: far and wide

longinquae nationes: distant tribes or nations

longo sed proximo intervallo: the next, but after a long interval (Virgil)

luce lucet aliena: it shines with a borrowed light (e.g., the moon)

lucernam olet: it smells of a lamp

ludere cum sacris: to trifle with sacred things

ludibrium fortunae: the plaything of Fortune

lumenque juventae purpureum [the light of purple youth]: the radiant bloom of youth (Virgil)

lupum auribus tenere [to hold a wolf by its ears]: to catch a Tartar (i.e., to oppose someone stronger than oneself)

lupus est homo homini: man is a wolf to his fellow man

lupus in fabula [the wolf in the fable]: speak of the devil

lupus pilum mutat, non mentem: the wolf changes its coat, not its disposition

lux: light (motto of the University of Northern Iowa)

lux et veritas: light and truth (motto of Yale University)

lux in tenebris: light in darkness

lux venit ab alto: light comes from above

M

magis mutus quam piscis: quieter than a fish

magistratus indicat virum: the office shows the man

magna civitas, magna solitudo: great city, great solitude

magna est veritas et praevalebit: truth is mighty and will prevail

magna est vis consuetudinis: great is the force of habit (Cicero)

magna servitus est magna fortuna: a great fortune is a great slavery (Seneca)

magnae multae pecuniae: large sums of money

magnae spes altera Romae [another hope of mighty Rome]: a youth of promise

magnas inter opes inops: poor amid great riches (Horace)

magni nominis umbra: the shadow of a great name

magnificat anima mea Dominum [my soul magnifies the Lord]: the Hymn of the Virgin at the Annunciation (St. Luke 1:46)

magno conatu magnas nugas [a great effort for great trifles]: so much for so little

magnum in parvo: a great amount in a small space

magnum vectigal est parsimonia: economy is a great revenue (Cicero)

magnus ab integro saeculorum nascitur ordo: the mighty cycle of the ages begins its turn anew (Virgil)

major e longinquo reverentia [greater reverence from afar]: no one is a hero in his or her own city

majores pennas nido [wings greater than the nest]: to rise above the position in which one is born (Horace)

male parta male dilabuntur [things ill-gotten are ill lost]: ill-gotten, ill-spent; easy come, easy go (Cicero)

malesuada fames: hunger that impels the crime (Virgil)

mali principii malus finis: the bad end of a bad beginning

malignum spernere vulgus: to scorn the wicked rabble

malo mori quam foedari: I had rather die than be dishonored

manet alta mente repostum: it remains stored deep in the mind (Virgil)

manibus pedibusque [with hands and feet]: with might and main

manu e nubibus [a hand from the clouds]: help from above
manus haec inimica tyrannis: this hand is an enemy to tyrants
margaritas ante porcos: pearls before swine
Mars gravior sub pace latet: a more grievous war lies beneath peace
mater artium necessitas [necessity is the mother of the arts]: necessity is the mother of invention
materiam superabat opus: the workmanship surpassed the material (Ovid)
matre pulchra filia pulchrior: a daughter more beautiful than her beautiful mother
maturato opus est: there is need of haste (Livy)
maxima debetur puero reverentia: the greatest respect is due to a child (Juvenal)
maximus in minimis [greatest in the least]: very great in little things
me, me adsum qui feci: it is I, here before you, who did the deed (Virgil)
mea nihil interest: it is all the same to me
mea virtute me involvo: I wrap myself up in my virtue (Horace)
medice, cura te ipsum: physician, heal thyself (St. Luke 4:23)
medio tutissimus ibis: a middle course will be safest (Ovid)
mediocria firma [the middle course is most secure]: moderation is safer than extremes
medium tenuere beati: blessed are they who have kept a middle course
medius fidius!: so help me God!
meliores priores [the better, the first]: the better ones first
memor et fidelis: mindful and faithful
mendacem memorem esse oportet: a liar should have a good memory
mens aequa in arduis: [a mind undisturbed in adversities]: equanimity in difficulties
mens agitat molem [mind moves the mass]: mind moves matter (Virgil)
mens conscia recti: a mind conscience of uprightness
mens invicta manet: the mind remains unconquered
mens sana in corpore sano: a sound mind in a healthy body
mens sibi conscia recti [a mind conscious of its own uprightness]: a good conscience
mentis gratissimus error: a most delightful hallucination (Horace)
meret qui laborat: he is deserving who is industrious
merum sal [pure salt]: genuine Attic wit
metus autem non est, ubi nullus irascitur: there is no fear where none is angry (Lactantius)
mihi cura futuri: my care is for the future
mihi non constat: I have not made up my mind
mihi persuasum est [I am persuaded]: I firmly believe
militat omnis amans: every lover serves as a soldier (Ovid)
militiae species amor est: love is a kind of military service (Ovid)
minima de malis [the least of evils]: choose the lesser of two evils
minor jurare non potest: (leg.) a minor cannot swear (i.e., serve on a jury)
misce stultitiam consiliis brevem: mix a little foolishness with your wisdom (Horace)
miscebis sacra profanis: you will mix sacred things with profane (Horace)

miseris succurrere disco: I am learning to help the distressed (Virgil)
moderata durant: things used in moderation endure
mole ruit sua [it falls down of its own bulk]: it is crushed under its own weight (Horace)
mollia tempora fandi: favorable occasions for speaking (a misquotation of Virgil)
mollissima fandi tempora: the most favorable occasions for speaking (Virgil)
Montani semper liberi: mountaineers are always free (motto of West Virginia)
monumentum aere perennius: a monument more lasting than brass (Horace)
morituri morituros salutant: those about to die salute those about to die
morituri te salutamus: we who are about to die salute thee
mors janua vitae: death is the gate of life
mors omnia solvit: death dissolves all things
mors omnibus communis: death is common to all persons
mors tua, vita mea [your death, my life]: you die that I might live
mors ultima linea rerum est: death is the final goal of things (Horace)
mortui non mordant [the dead do not bite]: dead men tell no tales
mortuo leoni et lepores insultant: even hares insult a dead lion
mox nox in rem: night is approaching, let's get on with the matter
multa acervatim frequentans: crowding together a number of thoughts
multa docet fames: hunger teaches us many things
multa fidem promissa levant: many promises weaken faith (Ovid)
multa gemens: with many a groan (Virgil)
multa petentibus desunt multa: to those who seek many things, many things are lacking (Horace)
multa tulit fecitque: much has he suffered and done
multi sunt vocati, pauci vero electi: many are called but few are chosen (St. Matthew 22:14)
multum demissus homo: a very modest or unassuming man (Horace)
multum, non multa: much, not many (Pliny)
munditiis capimur: we are captivated by neatness (Ovid)
mundus vult decipi: the world wishes to be deceived
munus Apolline dignum: a gift worthy of Apollo (Horace)
murus aeneus conscientia sana: a sound conscience is a wall of brass
mutare vel timere sperno: I scorn to change or to fear
mutato nomine, de te fabula narratur [the name being changed, the story is told of you]: with only the change of a name, the story applies to you (Horace)
mutum est pictura poema: a picture is a silent poem

N

nam et ipsa scientia potesta est: for knowledge is itself power (Francis Bacon)
nam tua res agitur, paries cum proximus ardet: (fig.) you too are in danger when your neighbor's house is on fire

nascentes morimur: from birth we begin to die
natio comoeda est: it is a nation of comics (Juvenal, referring to the Greeks)
natura abhorret a vacuo: nature abhors a vacuum
natura appetit perfectum: nature desires perfection
natura non facit saltum [nature makes no leaps]: there are no gaps in nature
naturae vis maxima: the greatest force is that of nature
Ne Aesopum quidem trivit [neither has he encountered Aesop]: he knows nothing
ne cede malis: neither yield to evils
ne fronti crede: trust not to appearances
ne Juppiter quidem omnibus placet: not even Jupiter can please everyone
ne puero gladium: do not entrust a sword to a boy
ne quid detrimenti respublica capiat: (fig.) take care to protect the republic from harm
ne quid nimis [not anything too much]: avoid excess
ne tentes, aut perfice [attempt not, or accomplish]: do not attempt what you do not intend to accomplish
ne teruncius quidem: not a penny!
ne vile fano: bring no vile thing to the temple
ne vile velis: incline to nothing base
nec amor nec tussis celatur: neither love nor a cough can be hidden
nec aspera terrent: not even hardships deter us
nec habeo, nec careo, nec curo: I have not, I want not, I care not
nec male notus eques [a knight of no stigma]: a knight of good repute
nec placida contentus quiete est: nor is he content with calm repose
nec pluribus impar [not equal to many]: a match for the whole world (motto of Louis XIV of France)
nec prece nec pretio: neither by entreaty nor by bribery
nec quaerere nec spernere honorem: neither to seek nor to shun honors
nec scire fas est omnia: nor is it permitted to know all things (Horace)
nec tecum possum vivere, nec sine te: neither can I live with you nor without you
nec temere nec timide: neither rashly nor timidly
nec timeo nec sperno: I neither fear nor despise
necessitas non habet legem [necessity has no law]: necessity knows no law
nemo bis punitur pro eodem delicto: no one is punished twice for the same crime
nemo dat quod non habet: no one can give what he does not have
nemo malus felix: no bad person is happy
nemo me impune lacessit: no one attacks me with impunity
nemo mortalium omnibus horis sapit: no mortal is wise all the time
nemo repente fuit turpissimus [no one ever was suddenly base]: no one ever became a villain all at once (Juvenal)
nemo solus satis sapit [no one is sufficiently wise alone]: two heads are better than one (Plautus)
nemo tenetur se ipsum accusare: no one is bound to accuse himself
nervi belli pecunia infinita: war's strength lies in an unlimited supply of money

nescit vox missa reverti: the word once spoken can never be recalled
nihil amori injuriam est: there is no wrong that love will not forgive
nihil dat qui non habet: a person gives nothing who has nothing
nihil est ab omni parte beatum [nothing is blessed in all its parts]: there is no perfect happiness
nihil ex nihilo: nothing comes from nothing
nihil quod tetigit non ornavit: he touched nothing which he did not adorn
nihil sub sole novum: there is nothing new under the sun
nil admirari: to wonder at nothing (Horace)
nil consuetudine majus: nothing is greater than custom (Ovid)
nil desperandum [nothing must be despaired of]: never despair
nil magnum nisi bonum: nothing is great unless it is good
nil mortalibus arduum est: nothing is too difficult for mortals
nil nisi bonum [nothing unless good]: say nothing but good about the dead
nil nisi Cruce: nothing except by the Cross
nil novi sub sole: there is nothing new under the sun
nil sine Deo: nothing without God
nil sine magno vita labore debit mortalibus: life has given nothing great to mortals without labor
nil sine numine: nothing without divine will (motto of Colorado)
nimium ne crede colori [trust not too much in a beautiful complexion]: trust not too much in appearances
nisi Dominus frustra: except the Lord [build it, those who build it build] in vain (motto of Edinburgh after Psalm 127)
nitor in adversum: I strive against opposition (Ovid)
nobilitas sola est atque unica virtus: only nobility is the one virtue above all (Juvenal)
nobilitatis virtus non stemma character: virtue, not pedigree, is the mark of the most noble
nocet empta dolore voluptas: pleasure bought by pain is injurious
noli irritare leones: do not provoke the lions
noli me tangere: touch me not (St. John 20:17)
nomina stultorum parietibus haerent [fool's names stick to the walls]: fools' names and fools' faces are always found in public places
nominis umbra: the shadow of a name
non Angli sed angeli: not Angles but angels (Pope Gregory the Great, upon seeing English youths for sale in the slave market at Rome)
non cuivis homini contingit adire Corinthum [not all men are fortunate enough to go to Corinth]: not everyone is blessed with an easy and luxurious life
non datur tertium [no third is given]: there is no third choice
non decipitur qui scit se decipi: the one who knows he/she has been deceived is not deceived
non deficiente crumena [the purse not failing]: while the money holds out (Horace)
non est vivere, sed valere, vita: life is not mere living but the enjoyment of health

non generant aquilae columbas: eagles do not beget doves

non ignara mali, miseris succerrere disco: not unacquainted with misfortune, I learn to give aid to those in misery (Virgil)

non inferiora secutus: having followed nothing inferior (Virgil)

non licet omnibus adire Corinthum [not everyone is permitted to go to Corinth]: we cannot all be wealthy

non mihi, non tibi, sed nobis: not for you, not for me, but for us

non mihi sed Deo et regi: not for myself but for God and the king

non multa, sed multum: not many things, but much

non nobis solum nati sumus: not for ourselves alone are we born (Cicero)

non nobis, Domine: not to us, Lord (Psalm 115:1)

non nova sed nove: not new but a new way

non olet: it has not a bad smell (i.e., money, no matter its source)

non omne licitum honestum: not every lawful thing is honorable

non omnia possumus omnes: we cannot all do all things (Virgil)

non omnis moriar: not all of me shall die (Horace, referring to his works)

non passibus aequis: not with equal steps (Virgil)

non possidentem multa vocaveris recte beatum: you cannot correctly call happy the one who possesses many things (Horace)

non pugnat sed dormit: instead of fighting, he sleeps

non quis sed quid: not who but what

non quo sed quomodo: not by whom but how

non revertar inultus: I shall not return unavenged

non semper erit aestas: it will not always be summer (Hesiod)

non semper erunt Saturnalia [it will not always be Saturnalia]: the carnival will not last forever

non sibi sed omnibus: not for himself but for all

non sibi sed patriae: not for himself but for his country

non sine numine: not without divine aid

non subito delenda: not to be hastily destroyed

non sum qualis eram: I am not what I once was (Horace)

non tali auxilio: not for such aid as this (Virgil)

non vobis solum: not for you alone

nonum(que) prematur in annum: let it be kept back from publication until the ninth year (Horace)

nos duo turba sumus: we two are a multitude (Ovid)

nosce te ipsum or **nosce teipsum:** know thyself

noscitur a sociis: he is known by his companions

novus ordo seclorum: a new order for the ages (a motto of the United States)

nox senatum dirimit [night breaks upon the session]: the meeting is called on account of darkness

nugis addere pondus: to add weight to trifles (Horace)

nugis armatus: armed with trifles

nulla dies sine linea [no day without a line]: no day without something done

nulli desperandum, quamdiu spirat: (fig.) while there is life there is hope
nullo meo merito: I had not deserved it
nullum quod tetigit non ornavit: he touched nothing which he did not adorn
numini et patriae asto: I stand on the side of God and my country
Nunc Dimittis (servum tuum, Domine): Lord, now let thy servant depart (Simeon's holy prayer of rejoicing at the sight of the Christ child; St. Luke 2:29)
nunc est bibendum: now is the time for drinking
nunquam dormio [I never sleep]: I am always on guard
nunquam minus solus quam cum solus: never less alone than when alone (Cicero)
nunquam non paratus [never unprepared]: always ready
nusquam tuta fides: nowhere is there true honor (Virgil)

O

O dea certe!: O Thou, who are a goddess surely! (Virgil)
O fama ingens, ingentior armis!: great in fame, greater still in deeds
O imitatores, servum pecus [O servile herd of imitators!]: miserable apes! (Horace)
O laborum dulce lenimen: O sweet solace of labors (Horace, in reference to Apollo's lyre)
O mihi praeteritos referat si Juppiter annos: O that Jupiter would give me back the years!
O Salutaris Hostia: O saving Victim (first words of the hymn used at the beginning of the Benediction of the Blessed Sacrament)
O sancta simplicitas!: O sacred simplicity
O si sic omnis [O, if all things were thus!]: O that he had always done or spoken thus!
O tempora! O mores!: O times! O customs!
O ubi campi! [O, where are those fields]: O for life in the country! (Virgil)
obscuris vera involvens: shrouding truth in darkness (Virgil)
obscurum per obscurius: explaining an obscure thing by something more obscure
obsta principiis: resist the beginning (more properly, **principiis obsta**)
occasio furem facit: opportunity makes the thief
occasionem cognosce: know your opportunity
occupet extremum scabies: Plague, take the hindmost (Horace)
occurrent nubes: clouds will intervene
oderint dum metuant: let them hate, so long as they fear (Cicero)
odi et amo: I hate and I love (Catullus)
odi profanum vulgus et arceo: I detest the ungodly rabble and keep them at a distance
odora canum vis: the strong scent of the hounds
ohe! jam satis est: hey there!, that is enough (Horace)
olet lucernam [it smells of the lamp]: it bears the mark of nightly toil
oleum addere camino [to pour oil onto the fire]: add fuel to the flame (i.e., to make things worse)

omne bonum desuper: all good is from above

omne ignotum pro magnifico (est): all things unknown are thought to be magnificat (Tacitus)

omne solum forti patria: to a brave man, all soil is his homeland

omne trinum perfectum: every perfect thing is threefold

omne vivum ex ovo: everything living thing comes from an egg

omnem movere lapidem: to leave no stone unturned

omnia ad Dei gloriam: all things for the glory of God

omnia bona bonis: to the good all things are good

omnia desuper or **omnia de super:** all things are from above

omnia mea mecum porto: everything that is mine I carry with me

omnia mors aequat: death levels all things

omnia munda mundis: to the pure all things are pure

omnia mutantur, nos et mutamur in illis: all things change and we change with them

omnia praeclara rara: all excellent things are rare (Cicero)

omnia suspendens naso: turning up his nose at everything

omnia tuta timens: fearing all things, even those that are safe (Virgil)

omnia vanitas: all is vanity

omnia vincit amor: love conquers all things

omnia vincit labor: labor overcomes all things

omnibus hoc vitium est: all have this vice (Horace)

omnibus invideas, livide, nemo tibi: you may envy everyone, envious one, but no one envies you

omnis amans amens: every lover is demented

omnium rerum principia parva sunt: the beginnings of all things are small (Cicero)

onus segni impone asello: lay the burden on the lazy ass

ope et consilio: with help and counsel

opera illius mea sunt: his works are mine

operae pretium est [there is a reward for work]: it is worth doing (Terence)

operose nihil agunt: they are busy about nothing (Seneca)

opinione asperius est: it is harder than I thought

optima mors Parca quae venit apta die: the best death is that which comes on the day that Fate determines (Propertius)

optimi consiliarii mortui: the best counselors are the dead

optimum obsonium labor [work is the best of relishes]: work is the best means to eating

opum furiata cupido: frenzied lust for wealth (Ovid)

opus artificem probat [the work proves the craftsman]: the worker is known by his work

ora et labora: pray and work

ora pro nobis: pray for us

orando laborando: by prayer and by toil (motto of Rugby School, England)

orator fit, poeta nascitur: the orator is made, the poet is born
osculo Filium hominis tradis?: you betray the Son of Humanity with a kiss? (St. Luke 22:48)
otia dant vitia: leisure begats vices
otiosa sedulitas: leisurely zeal
otium cum dignitate [leisure with dignity]: dignified leisure (Cicero)
otium sine dignitate: leisure without dignity
otium sine litteris mors est: leisure without literature is death

P

pabulum Acheruntis [food for Acheron]: one deserving of death (Plautus)
pace tanti viri [by leave of so great a man]: if so great a man will pardon me (said ironically)
palmam qui meruit ferat: let him bear the palm who has deserved it (motto of Lord Nelson and of the University of Southern California
panem et circenses [bread and the games of the circus]: food and amusement (according to Juvenal, the sole interests of the ancient Roman plebeian class)
par in parem imperium non habet: an equal has no authority over an equal
par negotiis, neque supra: equal to his business and not above it (Tacitus)
par nobile fratrum [a noble pair of brothers]: two people just alike (Horace)
parce, parce, precor: spare me, spare me, I pray
parcere subjectis, et debellare superbos: to spare the vanquished and subdue the proud (Virgil)
parem non fert: he endures no equal
parendo vinces: you will conquer by obedience
paritur pax bello: peace is produced by war
Parthis mendacior: more mendacious than the Parthians
parva componere magnis: to compare small things with great
parva leves capiunt animas: little minds are caught up with little things (Ovid)
parvum parva decent: small things benefit the small (Horace)
Pater, in manus tuas commendo spiritum meum: Father, into Your hands I commend my spirit (one of the Seven Last Words of Christ; St. Luke 23:46)
patria cara, carior libertas: the nation is dear, but liberty is dearer
patriae infelici fidelis [faithful to my misfortunate homeland]: (fig.) It is my country, wrong or right
pauca sed bona [few things, but good]: quality, not quantity
paulo majora canamus: let us sing of somewhat greater things (Virgil)
paupertas omnium artium repertrix: poverty is the inventor of all the arts
pax huic domui: peace be to this house
pax paritur bello: peace is produced by war
pax potior bello: peace is more powerful than war
pax quaeritur bello: peace is sought by war (motto of the Cromwell family)

pax vobiscum: peace be with you
pectus est quod disertos facit: it is the heart that makes one eloquent (Quintillan)
pecunia non olet: money does not smell
pecunia obediunt omnia: all things are obedient to money
Pelio imponere Ossam: to pile Ossa on Pelion
Pelion imposuisse Olympo: to have piled Pelion on Olympus (Horace)
per angusta ad augusta: through adversity to honor
per ardua ad astra: through difficulties to the stars (motto of the R.A.F.)
per aspera ad astra: a variation of **ad astra per aspera** (motto of Kansas)
per deos immortales!: for heaven's sake!
per tot discrimina rerum: through all manner of calamitous events (Virgil)
per viam dolorosam: by the way of sorrows
pereunt et imputantur: the hours pass away are reckoned against us (a saying used for a sundial)
periculum fortitudine evasi: by courage I have escaped danger
periculum in mora: there is danger in delay
perjuria ridet amantum Juppiter: Jupiter laughs at lovers' deceits
permitte divis caetera: leave the rest to the gods
persta atque obdura: be steadfast and endure
pessimum genus inimicorum laudantes: flatters are the worst type of enemies
Pia Desideria: the desire after things religious (motto of the Pietistic movement)
piscem natare docere: to teach a fish how to swim
plures crapula quam gladius: drunkenness kills more than the sword
plus aloes quam mellis habet [he has more aloes than honey]: the bitter outweighs the sweet (Juvenal)
plus salis quam sumptus [more of good taste than expense]: more tasteful than costly (Nepos)
poesis est vinum daemonum: poetry is the wine of demons
poeta nascitur, non fit: a poet is born, not made
populus me sibilat, at mihi plaudo: the people boo me, but I applaud myself (Horace)
populus vult decipi, ergo decipiatur: the people wish to be deceived, therefore let them be deceived
porro unum est necessarium: there is still one necessary thing
possunt quia posse videntur: they can because they think they can
post cineres gloria sera venit [glory comes after one is reduced to ashes]: fame comes too late for one to enjoy it
post equitem sedet atra cura [behind the horseman sits dark cares]: even the nobleman cannot escape his worries
post factum nullum consilium: counsel is of no effect after the fact
post festum venisti: you have come after the feast
post nubila, Phoebus: after the clouds, the sun
post proelia praemia: after battles come rewards
post tenebras lux: after darkness, light

137

post tot naufragia portum: after so many shipwrecks, then the harbor
potestas vitae necisque: power over life and death
potius mori quam foedari: rather to die than to be dishonored
praefervidum ingenium Scotorum: the fervently serious disposition of the Scots
praemonitus, praemunitus: forewarned, forearmed
praestat sero quam nunquam: better late than never
praesto et persto: I stand in front and I stand firm
presto maturo, presto marcio: soon ripe, soon rotten
pretiosum quod utile: what is useful is valuable
pretium laborum non vile: no cheap reward for the labors (motto of the Order of Golden Fleece)
primus inter pares: first among his equals
principia, non homines: principles, not men
principibus placuisse viris non ultima laus est: to have won the approval of important people is not the lowest of praise (Horace)
principiis obsta [resist the beginnings]: nip the evil at the bud (Ovid)
prior tempore, prior jure [first by time, first by right]: first come, first served
pristinae virtutis memores: mindful of the courage of earlier times
pro aris et focis [for our altars and our hearths]: for civil and religious liberty
pro Deo et Ecclesia: for God and the Church
pro Ecclesia et Pontifice: for Church and Pope
pro libertate patriae: for the liberty of my country
pro mundi beneficio: for the benefit of the world (motto of Panama)
pro patria [for the country]: for one's country
pro patria et rege: for country and king
pro pelle cutem: the hide for the sake of the fir (motto of the Hudson Bay Company)
pro rege et patria: for king and country
pro rege, lege, et grege [for king, law, and the people]: for ruler, rule, and ruled
pro salute animae: for the welfare of the soul
probitas laudatur et alget: honesty is praised and is left to freeze to death
probitas verus honor: honesty is true honor
probum non poenitet: the honest man does not repent
prodesse quam conspici [to be of service instead of being stared at]: Get busy!
proh pudor!: for shame! (properly **pro pudor**)
proprie communia dicere: to speak commonplace things as if they were original
proximus ardet Ucalegon: Ucalegon's house, the one next door, is on fire (Virgil)
prudens quaestio dimidium scientiae: half of science is putting forth the right questions (Bacon)
pugnis et calcibus [with fists and heels]: with all one's might
pulvis et umbra sumus: we are but dust and shadow (Horace)
Punica fides [Punic faith]: treachery

Q

quae amissa salva: things lost are safe
quae fuerunt vitia mores sunt: what were once vices are now customary
quae nocent docent: that which hurts teaches
quae sursum volo videre: I desire to see the things that are above
quaere verum: seek after truth
qualis artifex pereo: what an artist dies in me (Nero, shortly before his death)
qualis pater, talis filius: like father, like son
qualis rex, talis grex: like king, like people
qualis vita, finis ita: as is the life, so is the end
quam parva sapientia mundus regitur!: with how little wisdom the world is governed!
quam te Deus esse jussit: what God commanded you to be
quamdiu se bene gesserit: so long as he conducts himself well
quandoque bonus dormitat Homerus: sometimes even good Homer nods off (Horace)
quanti est sapere!: what a great thing it is to be wise! (Terence)
quanti fama?: at what price fame?
quantum mutatus ab illo!: how changed from what he once was (Virgil)
quem di diligunt adolescens moritur: the one whom the gods esteem dies young
quem Juppiter vult perdere, prius dementat: the one whom Jupiter desires to destroy is first driven insane
qui bene amat bene castigat: the one who loves well chastises well
qui capit ille facit [if the hat fits, put it on]**:** if the shoe fits, wear it
qui desiderat pacem, praeparet bellum: the one wishing peace must prepare for war
qui docet discit: he who teaches learns
qui facit per alium facit per se: a man is responsible for the deeds he does through another
qui invidet minor est: he who envies is the lesser of the two
qui laborat orat: he who labors prays
qui nimium probat nihil probat: he who proves too much proves nothing
qui non improbat, approbat: the one who does not disapprove, approves
qui non proficit deficit: he who does not make progress loses ground
qui scribit bis legit: the one who writes reads twice
qui stat, caveat ne cadat: let the one who stands be careful lest he or she fall (1 Corinthians 10:12)
qui tacet consentit: he who is silent consents
qui timide rogat docet negare: he who asks timidly courts denial
qui transtulit sustinet: he who transplanted sustains (motto of Connecticut)
qui uti scit ei bona: one should profit who knows how to use it
quicunque vult servari: whoever will be saved (the beginning of the Creed of Athanasius, or the Quicunque Vult)

DICTA

quid leges sine moribus vanae proficiunt?: what good are laws when there are no morals?
quid opus est verbis: what need is there for words?
quid sit futurum cras, fuge quaerere: avoid asking what the future will bring (Horace)
quid verum atque decens: what is true and becoming
quidquid agas prudenter agas: whatever you do, do so with caution
quieta non movere [not to move quiet things]: (fig.) let sleeping dogs lie
quis custodiet ipsos custodes?: who shall guard the guards? (Juvenal)
quis fallere possit amantem: who can deceive a lover? (Virgil)
quis separabit?: who shall separate? (motto of the Order of St. Patrick; referring to Britain and Ireland)
quisque sibi proximus: everyone is nearest to himself
quisque suos patimur manes: everyone suffers from the spirits of his or her own past
Quo Vadis, Domine?: whither goest Thou, Lord?
quo celerius eo melius: the faster the better
quo fas et gloria ducunt: where duty and glory lead
quo Fata vocant: whither the Fates call
quo pax et gloria ducunt: where peace and glory lead
quo spinosior fragrantior: the more thorns, the greater the fragrance
quod avertat Deus! [which may God avert!]: God forbid!
quod Deus bene vertat!: may God grant success!
quod dixi dixi: what I have said I have said
quod non legitur non creditur: what is not read is not believed
quod scripsi scripsi: what I have written I have written (Pontius Pilate)
quorum pars magna fui: of which things I was an important part (Virgil)
quot homines tot sententiae: so many men, so many opinions (Terence)
quot servi tot hostes: so many servants, so many enemies

R

radit usque ad cutem: he shaves down to the skin
radix omnium malorum est cupiditas: the love of money is a root to all evil
raram facit misturam cum sapientia forma: rarely are beauty and wisdom found together
rari nantes [swimming here and there]: one here and another there (Virgil)
ratio est legis anima: reason is the spirit and soul of the law
ratio est radius divini luminis: reason is a ray of divine light
recte et suaviter: justly and mildly
redintegratio amoris: the renewal of love
redire ad nuces [to return to the nuts]: resume childish interests

redolet lucerna or **redolet lucernam:** it smells of the lamp (a reference to a literary work whose labor was great)

regnant populi: the people rule (motto of Arkansas)

relata refero: I tell it as it was told to me

rem acu tetigisti [you have touched the thing with a needle]: you have hit the nail on the head

remis velisque [with oars and sails]: with all one's might

renovate animos: renew your courage

rerum cognoscere causas: to understand the cause of all things (motto of the London School of Economics and Political Science)

res accedent luminis rebus: one light shines upon others

res age, tute eris: be busy and you will be safe (Ovid)

res angusta domi: in straitened circumstances at home (Juvenal)

res est ingeniosa dare: giving requires good sense (Ovid)

res est sacra miser: (fig.) a person in misery is a sacred matter

res est solliciti plena timoris amor: love is full of anxious fears (Ovid)

res in cardine est [the matter is on the hinge]: the matter is hanging in the balances

res integra est: the matter is still undecided

res ipsa loquitur: the thing speaks for itself

res mihi integra est [I have not decided the matter]: I am still undecided

res mihi probatur: it meets my approval

res non posse creari de nilo: it is not possible to create matter from nothing

res perit suo domino: (leg.) the loss falls upon its owner

respice, adspice, prospice: examine the past, examine the present, examine the future (motto of the City University of New York)

respice finem [look to the end]: consider the result

respondeat superior [let the superior answer]: (leg.) let the principal answer for the actions of his agent

revocate animos: recover your courage (Virgil)

rex bibendi [king of drinkers]: king of the revelers

rex non potest peccare: the king can do no wrong

rex nunquam moritur: the king never dies

rex regnat sed non gubernat: the king reigns but does no govern

ride si sapis: laugh, if you are wise

ridentem dicere verum quid vetat?: what prevents a person from speaking the truth while laughing? (Horace)

ridere in stomacho [to laugh inwardly]: to laugh up one's sleeve

ridiculus mus: a ridiculous mouse (Horace)

risum teneatis, amici?: could you help laughing, friends? (Horace)

rixatur de lana saepe caprina [he often quarrels about goat's wool]: he argues about everything, whether right or wrong (Horace)

ruat caelum [though the heavens fall]: let the heavens fall!

S

saepe stilum vertas [often turn the stylus]: correct freely, if you want to write anything of merit
saeva indignatio: fierce wrath (Virgil)
saevus tranquillus in undis: calm amid the raging waters
sal sapit omnia: salt seasons everything
salus per Christum Redemptorem: salvation through Christ the Redeemer
salus populi est suprema lex: the welfare of the people is the supreme law
salus populi suprema lex esto: let the welfare of the people be the supreme law (motto of Missouri)
salus ubi multi consiliarii: there is safety in many advisors
salva conscientia [the conscience being preserved]: without compromising one's conscience
salva dignitate: without compromising one's dignity
salva fide: without compromising one's word
salva res est: the matter is safe (Terence)
salvam fac reginam, O Domine: God save the queen
salvum fac regem, O Domine: God save the king
sancte et sapienter: with holiness and wisdom
sapere aude: dare to be wise (Horace)
sapiens dominabitur astris: the wise will rule the stars
Sartor Resartus: the tailor retailored (title of a book by Thomas Carlyle)
sat cito, si sat bene: soon enough, if but well enough (Cato)
sat pulchra, si sat bona [beautiful enough, if she is good enough]: beauty is as beauty does
satis eloquentiae, sapientiae parum: enough eloquence but too little wisdom
satis quod sufficit: what suffices is enough
satis superque [enough and too much]: enough and some to spare
satis verborum [enough of words]: enough said
scientia est potentia: knowledge is power
scio enim cui credidi: I know in whom I have believed (2 Timothy 1:12)
scribere est agere: to write is to act
scribere jussit amor: love bade me write (Ovid)
scribimus indocti doctique: learned and unlearned, we all write (Horace)
scuto amoris Divini: with the shield of divine love
scuto bonae voluntatis tuae coronasti nos: with the shield of Thy good will you have surrounded us
securus judicat orbis terrarum: the whole earth judges in safety (i.e., unswayed by fear; St Augustine)
sed haec hactenus: but so much for this
seditio civium hostium est occasio: the dissatisfaction of the citizenry gives occasion to the enemy
semel abbas, semper abbas: once an abbot, always an abbot

semel et simul: once and together
semel insanivimus omnes: we have all been mad once
semper ad eventum festinat: he always hastens to the crisis (Horace)
semper avarus eget: the greedy are always in need
semper eadem: always the same (motto of Queen Elizabeth I)
semper et ubique: always and everywhere
semper felix [always happy]: ever fortunate
semper fidelis (pl. **semper fideles**): always faithful (motto of the U.S. Marine Corps)
semper idem: always the same
semper paratus: always ready
semper timidum scelus: crime is always fearful
semper vivit in armis: he lives ever in arms
senex bis puer: an old man is twice a boy
sequiturque patrem non passibus aequis: he follows his father but not with equal steps
sequor non inferior: I follow, but I am not inferior
sero sapiunt Phryges: the Phrygians became wise, but too late
sero sed serio: late, but in earnest
sero venientibus ossa [only bones for all those who come late]: first come, first served
serus in caelum redeas [late may you return to heaven]: long may you live
serva jugum [preserve the yoke]: preserve the bond of love
servabo fidem: I will keep faith
servata fides cineri: faithful to the memory of my ancestors
si componere magnis parva mihi fas est: if I may be allowed to compare small things with great (Ovid)
si Deus nobiscum, quis contra nos?: if God be with us, who shall be against us?
si Deus pro nobis, quis contra nos?: if God is for us, who is against us? (Romans 8:31)
si dis placet or **si diis placet:** if it pleases the gods
si fallor, sum: if I am deceived, then I exist (St. Augustine's refutation of skepticism through one's self-awareness of deception)
si fecisti nega: if you did it, deny it
si finis bonus est, totum bonum erit: if the end is good, all will be good
si fortuna juvat: if fortune favors
si monumentum requiris, circumspice: if you seek his monument, look around you (epitaph of Sir Christopher Wren, architect of London)
si parva licet componere magnis: if it be allowable to compare small things to great (Virgil)
si peccavi, insciens feci: if I have sinned, I have done so unknowingly (Terence)
si post fata venit gloria, non propero: if glory comes after death, then I am in no hurry
si quaeris peninsulam amoenam, circumspice: if you seek a pleasant peninsula, look around you (motto of Michigan)
si sic omnes!: if all did thus!
si sit prudentia: if there be prudence

si vis amari ama: if you want to be loved, then love (Seneca)
si vis pacem para bellum: if you desire peace, then prepare for war
sic eunt fata hominum: so go the destinies of men
sic itur ad astra [thus is the way to the stars]: such is the way to immortal fame
sic me servavit Apollo: thus Apollo preserved me (Horace)
sic semper tyrannis: thus always to tyrants (motto of Virginia)
sic transit gloria mundi: thus passes away the glory of the world
sic volo sic jubeo: thus I will, thus I command (Juvenal)
sic vos non vobis [thus do ye, but not for yourselves]: you do the work, another takes the credit (Virgil, as a challenge to Bathyllus who claimed authorship of a set of verses that Virgil himself had composed)
sicut meus est mos: as is my habit (Horace)
sicut patribus, sit Deus nobis: as with our fathers, may God also be with us (motto of Boston)
sile et philosophus esto: be silent and you will pass for a philosopher
silent leges inter arma: the laws are silent during war
similia similibus curantur: like cures like
simplex munditiis: elegant in simplicity (Horace)
sine cruce, sine luce: without the Cross, without light
sine ira et studio: without anger and without partiality
sis pacem, para bellum: if you want peace, then prepare for war
siste, viator!: stop, traveler!
sit pro ratione voluntas: let goodwill stand for reason
sit tibi terra levis: may the earth lie lightly upon you
sit ut est, aut non sit: let it be as it is, or let it not be
sit venia verbis: pardon my words
sol lucet omnibus: the sun shines on all
sola juvat virtus: virtue alone assists
sola nobilitas virtus: virtue alone is true nobility
sola salus servire Deo: our only salvation is in serving God
sola virtus invicta: virtue alone is invincible
solem quis dicere falsum audeat?: who would dare to call the sun a liar? (Virgil)
soli Deo gloria: to God alone be glory
solitudinem faciunt, pacem appellant [they make a solitude and call it peace]: they crush a rebellion by killing the population (Tacitus)
solventur risu tabulae [the indictments are dismissed with a laugh]: the case breaks down and you are laughed out of court (Horace)
solvitur ambulando [it is solved by walking]: the problem is solved by action (i.e., the theory is solved by practice)
spargere voces in vulgam ambiguas: spreading ambiguous rumors among the common crowd (Virgil)
spectemur agendo: let us be judged by our actions
spem pretio non emo: I do not give money for mere hopes (Terence)
sperat infestis, metuit secundis: he hopes in adversity and fears in prosperity (Horace)

spero meliora: I hope for better things (Cicero)
spes bona: good hope (motto of Cape Colony)
spes gregis: the hope of the flock or the common herd (Virgil)
spes mea Christus: my hope is in Christ
spes mea in Deo: my hope is in God
spes sibi quisque [let each be a hope unto himself]: each must rely on him/herself alone
spes tutissima coelis: the safest hope is in heaven
Spiritus Sanctus in corde: the Holy Spirit in the heart
splendide mendax [nobly mendacious]: untruthful for a good purpose (Horace)
spretae injuria formae: the insult to her slighted beauty (Virgil)
sta, viator, heroem calcas: stop, traveler, you trample upon a hero
stare super antiquas vias: to stand on the old ways
stat fortuna domus virtute: the fortune of the household stands by its virtue
stat magni nominis umbra: he stands, the shadow of a great name
stat pro ratione voluntas: goodwill stands for reason
stat promissa fides: the promised faith remains
stemmata quid faciunt: what do pedigrees matter? (Juvenal)
stet fortuna domus: may the fortune of the house endure
stet pro ratione voluntas: let my goodwill stand for reason
stillicidi casus lapidem cavat: a constant drip hollows a stone
strenua inertia: energetic idleness (Horace)
studiis et rebus honestis: by honorable pursuits and studies (motto of the University of Vermont)
studium immane loquendi: an insatiable desire for talking (Ovid)
sua cuique sunt vitia: everyone has his or her own vices
sua cuique utilitas: to everything its own use (Tacitus)
sua cuique voluptas: everyone has his or her own pleasures
sua munera mittit cum hamo: he sends his gift with a hook attached
suave mari magno: how pleasant when on a great sea (Lucretius)
suaviter et fortiter: gently and firmly
suaviter in modo, fortiter in re: gentle in manner, resolute in deed
sub cruce candida: under the pure white Cross
sub cruce salus: salvation under the Cross
sub hoc signo vinces: under this sign you will conquer (variation of **in hoc signo vinces**)
sub lege libertas: liberty under the law
sub specie aeternitatis: under the aspect of eternity (Spinoza)
sub tegmine fagi: beneath the canopy of the spreading beech (Virgil)
sublata causa, tollitur effectus: when the cause is removed, the effect ceases
sublato fundamento cadit opus: remove the foundation and the structure falls
sublimi feriam sidera vertice: with head lifted, I shall strike the stars (Horace)
suis stat viribus: he stands by his own strength
summa petit livor: it is the highest things that envy attacks

summa sedes non capit duos: the highest seat does not hold two

summo studio: with the greatest zeal (Cicero)

summum jus, summa injuria [extreme law, extreme injury]: (fig.) the law, strictly interpreted, may be the greatest of injustices (Cicero)

sumptus censum ne superet: let not your spending exceed your income

superstitio mentes occupavit: superstition has taken hold of their minds

superstitione tollenda religio non tollitur: religion is not abolished by abolishing superstition (Cicero)

suppressio veri suggestio falsi: suppression of the truth is the suggestion of falsehood

surgit amari aliquid [something bitter rises]: no joy without alloy (Lucretius)

sursum corda: lift up your heads

suspendens omnia naso: turning up one's nose at everything (Horace)

suspiria de profundis: sighs from the depths of the soul

sutor, ne supra crepidam [cobbler, stick to your last sandal]: mind your own business

suum cuique pulchrum: to each one's own beauty

suus cuique mos [everyone has his/her own custom]: different strokes for different folks

T

tacent satis laudant: their silence is praise enough

tacitum vivit sub pectore vulnus: the unuttered wound lies deep within the breast (Virgil)

taedet me: I am bored

tam facti quam animi: as much in action as in intention

tam Marte quam Minerva [as much by Mars as by Minerva]: as much by war as by wisdom

tandem fit surculus arbor: a shoot at length becomes a tree

tantae molis erat [so vast a work it was]: so great was the difficulty of the undertaking

tantaene animis caelestibus irae?: can so great a wrath abide in celestial minds?

tantas componere lites: to settle such great disputes

tantus amor scribendi: so great a passion for writing (Horace)

tarde venientibus ossa [to all that come late go the bones]: first come, first served

te hominem esse memento: remember that you are a man

te nosce: know thyself

telum imbelle sine ictu [a feeble spear thrown to no effect]: a weak and ineffectual argument (Virgil)

templa quam dilecta!: how lovely are Thy temples!

tempora mutantur, nos et mutamur in illis: times change and we change with them

tempori parendum: one must move with the times

temporis ars medicina fere est: time is the best of the healing arts
tempus abire tibi est: it is time for you to depart (Horace)
tempus anima rei: time is the essence of the contract
tempus edax rerum: time, the devourer of all things (Ovid)
tempus fugit: time flies
tempus omnia revelat: time reveals all things
tempus rerum imperator: time is sovereign over all things
tenax et fideles: steadfast and faithful
tenere lupum auribus [to hold a wolf by the ears]: to take the bull by the horns
tentanda via est: the way must be tried (Virgil)
ter quaterque beatus: thrice and four times blest (Virgil)
teres atque rotundus [smooth, polished, and rounded]: a polished and complete person (Horace)
terra es, terram ibis: you are dust, and to dust you will return (Genesis 3:19)
tetigisti acu [you have touched it with a needle]: you have hit the nail on the head (Plautus)
tibi seris, tibi metis [you sow for yourself, you reap for yourself]: as you sow, so shall you reap (Cicero)
time Deum, cole regem: fear God, honor the king
timeo Danaos et dona ferentes: I fear the Greeks, even when they bear gifts (Virgil)
timeo hominem unius libri: I fear the man of one book (St. Aquinas)
timet pudorem: he fears shame
timor addidit alas: fear gave him wings (Virgil)
timor mortis morte pejor: the fear of death is worse than death
tot homines quot sententiae: so many men, so many opinions (after Terence)
totum in eo est: all depends on this
totus in toto, et totus in qualibet parte: wholly complete and complete in every part (i.e., the human heart)
totus teres atque rotundus [entire, smooth, and round]: complete in itself
trahit sua quemque voluptas [each one is drawn by his own delight]: each is led by his or her own tastes (Virgil)
transeat in exemplum: let it become an example or a precedent
tria juncta in uno: three joined in one (motto of the Order of the Bath)
tristis eris si solus eris: (fig.) you will be sad if you keep company with only yourself (Ovid)
triumpho morte tam vita: I triumph in death as in life
Troja fuit: Troy was
truditur dies die: one day is urged on by another day
Tu solus sanctus: Thou alone art holy
tu est Christus, filius Dei vivi: you are the Christ, the son of the living God (St. Matthew 16:16)
tu ne cede malis, sed contra audentior ito: do not surrender to evil but go boldly against it (Virgil)
tu, Domine, gloria mea: Thou, O Lord, are my glory

U

ubi amici, ibi opes: where there are friends, there is wealth
ubi bene, ibi patria: where it is well with me, there is my country
ubi homines sunt, modi sunt: where there are persons, there are manners
ubi jus ibi remedium: where there is law there is remedy
ubi jus incertum, ibi jus nullum: where the law is uncertain, there is no law
ubi lapsus? quid feci?: where have I fallen into error? what have I done?
ubi libertas, ibi patria: where there is liberty, there is my country
ubi mel, ibi apes: where there is honey, there are bees
ubi sunt qui ante nos fuerunt? (or **ubi sunt?**): where are those who lived before us?
ubique patriam reminisci: everywhere to remember our country
ultra posse nemo obligatur: no one is obligated to do more than he or she is able
una et eadem persona: one and the same person
unguibus et rostro [with claws and beak]: tooth and nail
unguis in ulcere [a claw in the wound]: a knife in the wound
uni aequus virtuti, atque ejus amicis: equally a friend to virtue and to the friends of virtue
unica virtus necessaria: virtue is the only thing necessary
unius dementia dementes efficit multos: the madness of one makes many mad
unus vir, nullus vir [one man, no man]: two are better than one
urbem latericiam invenit, marmoream reliquit: he found the city brick and left it marble (Suetonius, referring to the emperor Augustus)
urbs in horto: a city in a garden (motto of the city of Chicago)
usus est optimum magister: experience is the best teacher
usus est tyrannus: custom is a tyrant
usus me docuit: experience has taught me
usus promptos facit: use makes one ready
ut ameris, amabilis esto: to receive love, be lovable (Ovid)
ut amnis vita labitur: like a brook, life flows away
ut apes geometriam: as bees practice geometry
ut homo est, ita morem geras: as the man is, thus adapt your conduct (Terence)
ut mos est: as the custom is (Juvenal)
ut nunc res se habet [as things are now]: as things stand
ut pictura poesis: poetry is like a painting (Horace)
ut quocunque paratus: prepared on every side
utcumque placuerit Deo: as it shall please God
uti non abuti: to use, not to abuse
utile dulci: the useful with the delightful (Horace)
utinam noster esset: would that he were ours
utrum horum mavis accipe: take whichever you prefer

V

vacuus cantat coram latrone viator: the traveler who has nothing sings before the robber
vade in pacem: go in peace
vade post me, satana: Get thee behind me, you satan! (St. Matthew 16:23)
vade retro me, Satana: Get thee behind me, Satan
vae soli: woe to the solitary person (Ecclesiastes 4:10)
vae victis: woe to the conquered
valeat quantum valere potest: let it pass for what it is worth
valet ancora virtus: virtue is a strong anchor
valete ac plaudite: farewell and applaud (the final line given by Roman actors at the end of a performance)
vanitas vanitatum, omnia vanitas: vanity of vanities, all is vanity (Ecclesiastes 1:2)
varium et mutabile semper femina: a woman is ever a fickle and changeable thing (Virgil)
vectigalia nervos esse rei publicae: taxes are essential to the strength of the republic (Cicero)
vehimur in altum: we are carried out into the depths
vel caeco appareat: it would be obvious to the blind
vel prece vel pretio [with either prayer or price]: for either love or for money
velis et remis [with sails and oars]: with all possible strength
velut aegri somnia: like the dreams of the sick (Horace)
veluti in speculum: even as in a mirror
venalis populus venalis curia patrum [the people and the senators are equally venal]: everyone has his or her price
vendidit hic auro patriam: this man sold his country for gold
venenum in auro bibitur: poison is drunk from a golden cup (Seneca)
veni, vidi, vici: I came, I saw, I conquered (Julius Caesar's message to the Roman Senate declaring his victory over the king of Pontus in Asia Minor)
venia necessitati datur: (fig.) necessity knows no law
venienti occurrite morbo: (fig.) prevention is better than cure
ventis secundis [winds aft]: with favorable winds
vento intermisso: the wind having died down
verba volant, scripta manent: spoken words fly away, written ones remain
verbera, sed audi: whip me, but hear me
verbis ad verbera: from words to blows
verbum sapienti (verb. sap.): a word to the wise
verbum sat sapienti (verb. sat.): a word to the wise is sufficient
veritas nihil veretur nisi abscondi: truth fears nothing save concealment
veritas nimium altercando amittitur: truth is lost through too much altercation
veritas nunquam perit: truth never dies
veritas odium parit: truth begats hatred

veritas omnia vincit: truth conquers all things
veritas praevalebit: truth will prevail
veritas temporis filia: truth is the daughter of time
veritas victrix: truth the conqueror
veritas vincit: truth conquers
veritas vos liberabit: the truth shall make you free (motto of Johns Hopkins University)
veritatem dies aperit: time reveals the truth
veritatis simplex oratio est: the language of truth is simple (Seneca)
vestigia morientis libertatis: the footsteps of dying liberty
vestigia nulla retrorsum: no footsteps backward (i.e., no retreat)
vestigia terrent: the footprints frightened me (Horace)
veteris vestigia flammae: the traces of my former flame (Virgil)
vi et armis [by strength and by arms]: by force of arms
via crucis, via lucis: the way of the Cross is the way of light
via trita est tutissima: the beaten path is the safest one
via trita, via tuta: the beaten path, the safe path
vicarius non habet vicarium: a vicar cannot have a vicar
vicisti, Galilaee: You have conquered, O Galilean (the dying words of Julian the Apostate)
victi vicimus: conquered, we conquer
victis honor: honor to the vanquished
victoria concordia crescit: victory is increased by concord
victoriae gloria merces: glory is the reward of victory
victrix fortunae sapientia: wisdom is the victor over fortune
vide et crede: see and believe
video meliora proboque deteriora sequor: I see and approve the better things but I follow the worse things
vidit et erubit lympha pudica Deum: the modest water saw God and blushed (a reference to Christ's first miracle of turning water into wine, St. John 2: 1–11)
vigilate et orate: watch and pray
vilius argentum est auro, virtutibus aurum: as silver is cheaper than gold, so gold than virtue
vincam aut moriar: I will conquer or die
vincere aut mori: to conquer or die
vincit amor patriae [love of homeland conquers]: (fig.) in the end, love of country wins out
vincit omnia veritas: truth conquers all things
vincit qui patitur: he conquers who endures
vincit qui se vincit: he conquers who conquers himself
vincit veritas: truth conquers
vino tortus et ira: tormented by wine and anger
vir sapit qui pauca loquitur: wise is the person who talks little
vires acquirit eundo: it gathers strength as it goes along (i.e., fame; Virgil)
virescit vulnere virtus: virtue flourished from a wound
viret in aeternum: it flourishes forever

Virgilium vidi tantum: so far I have only seen Virgil (Ovid)
viri infelicis procul amici: friends stay far away from an unfortunate person
virtus ariete fortior: virtue is stronger than a battering ram
virtus est militis decus: valor is the soldier's honor
virtus in actione consistit: virtue consists in action
virtus in arduis: virtue in difficulties
virtus incendit vires: virtue kindles one's strength
virtus laudatur et alget: virtue is praised and is left out to freeze
virtus millia scuta: virtue is a thousand shields (also **virtus milia scuta**)
virtus nobilitat: virtue ennobles
virtus non stemma: virtue, not pedigree
virtus post nummas: virtue after money
virtus probata florescit: virtue flourishes in trial
virtus semper viridis [virtue is always green]: virtue never fades
virtus sola nobilitat: virtue alone can ennoble
virtus vincit invidium: virtue overcomes envy
virtute et armis: by valor and arms (motto of Mississippi)
virtute et fide: by virtue and faith
virtute et labore: by virtue and toil
virtute et opera: by virtue and hard work
virtute fideque: by virtue and faith
virtute officii: by virtue of office
virtute quies: by virtue there is tranquility
virtute securus: secure through virtue
virtute, non astutia: by virtue, not by craft
virtute, non verbis: by virtue, not by mere words
virtute, non viris: by virtue, not by men
virtuti nihil obstat et armis: nothing can stand against valor and arms
virtuti non armis fido: I trust to virtue not to arms
virtutis amore: from love of virtue
virtutis avorum praemium: the reward of the valor of my ancestors
virtutis fortuna comes: fortune is the companion of valor (motto of the Duke of Wellington)
virum volitare per ora [to fly through the mouths of men]: to spread like wildfire
vis consilii expers mole ruit sua: force lacking judgment collapses under its own weight (Horace)
vis unita fortior: union is strength
vita brevis, ars longa: life is short, art is long
vita sine litteris mors est: life without literature is death
vitae via virtus: virtue is the way of life
vitam impendere vero: to risk one's life for the truth (Juvenal)
vitiis nemo sine nascitur: no one is born without faults
viva vox: living voice (the "still small voice" of 1 Kings 19:12)

vivamus atque amemus: let us live and love one another
vivant rex et regina: long live the king and queen
vivat regina: long live the queen
vivat respublica: long live the republic
vivat rex: long live the king
vive hodie: live for today
vive memor leti: live mindful of death (Persius)
vive ut vivas: live that you may truly live
vive, vale: long life to you, farewell (Horace)
vivere est cogitare: to live is to think (Cicero)
vivere sat vincere: to conquer is to live enough
vivit post funera virtus: virtue lives on after the grave (Tiberias Caesar)
vix ea nostra voco: with difficulty do I call these things ours
vixere fortes ante Agamemnona: there lived great men before Agamemnon (Horace)
volat hora per orbem: time flies through the world
volens et potens: willing and able
volens et valens: willing and able
volente Deo: God willing
volenti non fit injuria: (leg.) one cannot claim injury for an act that is willingly done
volo, non valeo: I am willing but unable
voluntas habetur pro facto: the will is taken for the deed
volventibus annis [with revolving years]: as the years roll on
vota vita mea: my life is devoted
vox audita perit, litera scripta manet: the voice that is heard perishes, the letter that is written remains
vox clamantis in deserto: the voice of one crying in the desert (St. John 1:23)
vox et praeterea nihil [a voice and nothing more]: sound without sense
vox faucibus haesit [the voice stuck in throat]: dumbfounded
vox populi, vox Dei: the voice of the people is the voice of God
vulgus amicitias utilitate probat: the common crowd seeks friendships for their usefulness
vulneratus non victus: wounded but not conquered
vultus est index animi: the face is the index of the soul

Z

zonam perdidit [he has lost his moneybelt]: he is ruined (Horace)

ABBREVIATIONS

A

A.B. or **B.A.** [Artium Baccalaureus]: Bachelor of Arts
ab init. [ab initio]: from the beginning
abs. re. [absente reo]: (leg.) the defendant being absent
A.C. [ante Christum]: before Christ
a.c. [ante cibum]: (med.) before meals
A.Ch.N. [ante Christum natum]: before Christ's birth
A.D. [anno Domini]: in the year of our Lord
a.d. [ante diem]: before the day
ad (med.): up to; so as to make
adi. or **adj.** [adiectivum]: adjective
add. [adde]: (med.) let there be added (i.e., add)
ad eund. [ad eundem (gradum)]: to the same (degree or standing)
ad fin. [ad finem]: finally
ad inf. or **ad infin.** [ad infinitum]: to infinity (i.e., forever)
ad init. [ad initium]: at the beginning
ad int. [ad interim]: in the meantime; meanwhile; temporarily
ad loc. [ad locum]: to or at the place
ad lib. [ad libitum]: at will (i.e., improvise)
ads. [ad sectam]: (leg.) at the suit of
ad us. [ad usum]: according to usage
adv. [adversus]: against
ad val. [ad valorem]: according to value
A.E.I.O.U. [Austriae est imperare orbi universo]: all the world is to be ruled by Austria
aet. or **aetat.** [aetatis; anno aetatis suae]: of the age; in his/her lifetime
ag. [argentum]: silver
agit. [agita]: (med.) shake
A.H. [anno Hebraico]: in the Hebrew year (see also **A.M.**)
A.H. [anno Hegirae]: in the year of the Hegira (Muhammad's sacred flight to Medina)
a.h.l. [ad hunc locum]: at this place
A.H.S. [anno humanae salutis]: in the year of humanity's redemption
a.h.v. [ad hanc vocem]: at this word
A.M. [anno mundi]: in the year of the world since its creation
A.M. or **a.m.** [ante meridiem]: before noon
A.M. or **M.A.** [Artium Magister]: Master of Arts

A.M.D.G. [ad majorem Dei gloriam]: to the greater glory of God (motto of the Jesuits)
A.P.C.N. [anno post Christum natum]: in the year after the birth of Christ
A.P.R.C. [anno post Roman conditam]: in the year after the building of Rome (ca. 753 B.C.E.)
aq. [aqua]: water
aq. bull. [aqua bulliens]: boiling water
aq. dest. [aqua destillata]: distilled water
A.R. [anno regni]: in the year of the reign
A.S. [aetatis suae]: of his/her age or lifetime
A.S. [anno salutis]: in the year of redemption
A.A.S. [anno aetatis suae]: in the year of his/her age
au. [aurum]: gold
a.u.c. [ab urbe condita]: from the founding of the city
A.U.C. [anno urbis conditae]: in the year or from the time of the founded city (Rome, founded about 753 B.C.E.)
a.v. [ad valorem]: according to the value
a.v. [annos vixit]: he/she lived (so many years)

B

b.i.d. [bis in die]: (med.) twice a day
B.M. [beatae memoriae]: of blessed memory
B.M. or **B.V.** [Beata Maria or Beata Virgo]: the Blessed Virgin (also **B.V.M.**: the Blessed Virgin Mary)
b.p. [bonum publicum]: the common good
b.v. [bene vale]: farewell

C

c̄ [cum]: (med.) with
c. [congius]: (med.) gallon
c. or **ca.** [circa]: about
c. or **circ.** [circiter]: about
c. or **circ.** [circum]: about
Cantab. [Cantabrigiensis]: of Cambridge
cap. [capiat]: (med.) take
c.a.v. [curia advisari vult]: the court wishes to be advised or to consider
cent. [centum]: hundred
cet. par. [ceteris paribus]: other things being equal
cf. [confer]: compare
coch. [cochleare]: (med.) a spoonful

coch. mag. [cochleare magnum]: a tablespoonful
coch. parv. [cochleare parvum]: a teaspoonful
con. [conjunx]: wife
con. [contra]: against
cont. bon. mor. [contra bonos mores]: contrary to good manners
C.R. [custos rotulorum]: the principle justice of the peace in an English county
cuj. [cuius or cujus]: of which
cur. adv. vult [curia advisari vult]: the court wishes to be advised or to consider
c.v. [curriculum vitae]: a résumé

D

d. [da]: (med.) give
d. [decretum]: a decree or an ordinance
D.B. [Divinitatis Baccalaureus]: Bachelor of Divinity
D.D. [Divinitatis Doctor]: Doctor of Divinity (an honorary degree)
d.d. [dono dedit]: given as a gift
de d. in d. [de die in diem]: from day to day
del. [delineavit]: he/she drew it
dil. [dilue]: (med.) dilute or dissolve
D.O.M. [Deo, Optimo, Maximo]: to God, the Best, the Greatest
D.O.M. [Domino, Optimo, Maximo]: the Lord, the Best, the Greatest
D.P. or **Dom. Proc.** [Domus Procerum]: the House of Lords
dram. pers. [dramatis personae]: the cast of characters in a play
d.s.p. [decessit sine prole]: died without issue
D.T. [delirium tremens]: an acute delirium caused by alcohol poisoning
D.V. or **d.v.** [Deo Volente]: God willing

E

e.g. [exempli gratia]: for example
e.o. [ex officio]: by virtue of office
et al. [et alibi]: and elsewhere
et al. [et alii or et aliae]: and others
etc. [et cetera]: and so forth
et conj. [et conjunx]: and spouse (either husband or wife)
et seq. [et sequens]: and the following
et seq. [et sequentes]: and what follows
et ux. [et uxor]: and wife
exc. [excudit]: he/she fashioned it
ex. gr. [exempli gratia]: for example

F

f. [femininum]: feminine
F.D. [fidei defensor]: Defender of the Faith
fe. [ferrum]: iron
fec. [fecit]: he/she made or did it
ff. [fecerunt]: they made or did it
fict. [fictilis]: made of potter's clay
fid. def. [fidei defensor]: Defender of the Faith
fi. fa. [fieri facias]: cause it to be done
fl. [flores]: flowers
fl. or **flor.** [floruit]: flourished
fldxt. [fluidum extractum]: (med.) fluid extract
f.r. [folio recto]: on the front of the page (i.e., the right-hand page)
ft. [fiat]: (med.) let it be made
ft. haust. [fiat haustus]: let a draught be made
ft. mist. [fiat mistura]: let a mixture be made
ft. pulv. [fiat pulvis]: let a powder be made
f.v. [folio verso]: on the back of the page (i.e., the left-hand page)

G

gr. [granum]: (med.) a grain
gtt. [guttae]: (med.) drops

H

H. [hora]: (med.) hour
h.a. [hoc anno]: in this year
hab. corp.: (leg.) a writ of habeas corpus
haust. [haustus]: (med.) a draught
her. [heres]: heir
H.I. [hic iacet or hic jacet]: here lies
H.I.S. [hic iacet sepultus]: here lies buried
h.l. [hoc loco]: in this place
h.m. [hoc mense]: in this month
H.M.P. [hoc monumentum posuit]: he/she erected this monument
hor. decub. [hora decubitus]: (med.) at bedtime
h.q. [hoc quaere]: look for this
H.S. [hic sepultus]: here [lies] buried
h.s. [hoc sensu]: in this sense

h.t. [hoc tempore]: at this time
h.t. [hoc titulo]: under this title

I

i.a. [in absentia]: in absence
ib. or **ibid.** [ibidem]: in the same place (e.g., in a book)
id. [idem]: the same as above
i.e. [id est]: that is
ign. [ignotus] : unknown
in d. [in dies]: (med.) daily
inf. [infra]: below
infra dig. [infra dignitatem]: beneath one's dignity
init. [initio]: in or at the beginning (referring to a passage in a book)
in lim. [in limine]: in the beginning
in pr. [in principio]: in the beginning
I.N.R.I. [Iesus Nazarenus Rex Iudaeorum]: the title placard appended to the Cross of Christ by Pontius Pilate at the Crucifixion (St. John 19:20)
in trans. [in transitu]: in transit; on the way
inv. [invenit]: he/she designed it
i.p.i. [in partibus infidelium]: a titular bishop whose title is that of an extinct Roman Catholic see
i.q. [idem quod]: the same as

J

J.D. [Juris or Jurum Doctor]: Doctor of Law (a professional degree)
J.U.D. [Juris Utriusque Doctor]: Doctor of both Canon and Civil laws

L

l. or **lib.** [libra; pl. libri]: a book
L.B. [lectori benevolo]: to the gentle reader
lb. [libra]: a pound in weight (also *libra pondo*)
l.c. [loco citato]: in the place cited
L.H.D. [Litterarum Humaniorum Doctor]: Doctor of Humanties
Lit. Hum. [Litterae Humaniores]: the Humanities (e.g., the ancient Classics)
Litt.D. [Litterarum Doctor]: Doctor of Letters
LL.B. [Legum Baccalaureus]: Bachelor of Laws
LL.D. [Legum Doctor]: Doctor of Laws
loc. cit. [loco citato]: in the place cited

loc. laud. [loco laudato]: in the place cited with approval
loq. [loquitur]: he/she speaks
lot. [lotio]: (med.) a lotion
L.S. [locus sigilli]: the place of the seal
l.s.c. [loco supra citato]: in the place cited before

M

m. [masculinum]: masculine
m. or **M.** [meridies]: noon
M.A. [Magister Artium]: Master of Arts
M.D. [Medicinae Doctor]: Doctor of Medicine
m.m. [mutatis mutandis]: with the necessary changes being made
mob. [mobile vulgus]: the fickle masses (i.e., the mob)
mod. praesc. [modo praescripto]: (med.) as prescribed or directed
MS [manuscriptus]: manuscript
MSS [manuscripta]: manuscripts

N

n. [natus]: born
n. [neutrum]: neuter
n. [nocte]: at night
N.B. or **n.b.** [nota bene]: note well
n.l. [non licet]: it is not permitted
n.l. [non liquet]: it is not clear; it is not proven
nol. pros. [nolle prosequi]: an entry into court records indicating a stay or discontinuance of proceedings, either wholly or in part
non obs. [non obstante]: notwithstanding
non pros. [non prosequitur]: a legal judgment where the plaintiff does not appear
non seq. [non sequitur]: it does not follow

O

o. [octarius]: (med.) a pint
ob. [obiit]: he/she died
ob. [obiter]: incidentally
ob.s.p. [obiit sine prole]: he/she died without issue
o.c. [opere citato]: in the work cited
o.d. [oculus dexter]: right eye

o.h. [omni hora]: every hour
ol. [oleum]: (med.) oil
o.n. [omni nocte]: every night
op. [opus]: a musical compostion
op. cit. [opere citato]: in the work cited
o.q.h. [omni quadranta hora]: every fifteen minutes
o.s. [oculus sinister]: left eye
Oxon. [Oxoniensis]: of Oxford

P

p. [partim]: in part
p.a. [per annum]: by the year
p.ae. [partes aequales]: equal parts
pass. [passim]: throughout; here and there
pb. [plumbum]: lead
p.c. [post cibum]: (med) after meals
P.Ch.N. [post Christum natum]: after Christ's birth
pct. [per centum]: by the hundred
per cent. or **p.c.** [per centum]: by the hundred
per. pro. [per procurationem]: by proxy; by the action of
p.g. [persona grata]: an acceptable or welcome person
Ph.B. [Philosophiae Baccalaureus]: Bachelor of Philosophy
Ph.D. [Philosophiae Doctor]: Doctor of Philosophy
pil. [pilula; pl. pilulae]: (med.) a pill
pinx. [pinxit]: he/she painted this
pl. [pluralis]: plural
p.m. [post meridiem]: after noon
P.M. [post mortem]: after death
p.n.g. [persona non grata]: an unacceptable or unwelcome person
p.o. [post office]: see above entry
p.p. [per procurationem]: by proxy; by the action of
PP.C. [patres conscripti]: a title of the Roman Senators
PPS [post postscriptum]: an additional postscript
p.r.n. [pro re nata]: (med) whenever necessary or as the situation demands
pro tem. [pro tempore]: temporarily
prox. [proximo]: of or in the following month
prox. acc. [proxime accessit]: he/she came very near (to winning)
prox. m. [proximo mense]: in the next month
PS [postscriptum]: a postscript
p.t. [pro tempore]: temporarily
ptc. [participium]: a participle

pulv. [pulvis]: (med.) a powder
pxt. [pinxit]: he/she painted this

Q

q.d. [quasi dicat]: as if one should say
q.d. [quasi dictum]: as if said
q.e. [quod est]: which is
Q.E.D. [quod erat demonstrandum]: which was to be demonstrated or proven
Q.E.F. [quod erat faciendum]: which was to be done
Q.H. [quaque hora]: every hour
q.i.d. [quater in die]: (med) four times a day
q.l. or **q.lib.** [quantum libet]: liberally
Q.M. [quaque mane]: every morning
q.p. or **q.pl.** [quantum placet]: as much as you please
qq.v. [quae vide]: (pl.) which see
q.s. or **quant. suff.** [quantum sufficit]: as much as suffices
qu. [quaere]: a question or query
q.v. [quantum vis]: as much as you will
q.v. [quod vide]: (sing.) which see

R

R. [regina]: queen
R. [rex]: king
rep. or **repet.** [repetatur]: let it be repeated
R.I.P. [requiescat in pace]: may he/she rest in peace
R.I.P. [requiescit in pace]: he/she rests in peace

S

S. [sepultus]: buried
S. or **Sig.** [signa]: (med.) that which is to be written on the label of a prescription
s [sine]: (med.) without
s. [sulfur]: sulfur
s.a. [sine anno]: without date
Sal. or **S.** [Salutem dicit!]: Greetings!
sc. [scilicet]: that is to say; namely
sc. or **sculpt.** [sculpsit]: he/she sculptured [it]

scan. mag. [scandalum magnatum; pl. or scandala magnatum]: the defamation of notables or of high ranking persons
sci. fa. [scire facias]: (leg.) a writ to enforce, annul, or vacate a judgment, patent, charter or other matter of record
s.d. [sine die]: indefinitely
sec. [secundum]: according to
sec. art. [secundem artem]: scientifically; artificially
sec. leg. [secundum legem]: according to law
sec. nat. [secundum naturam]: naturally
sec. reg. [secundum regulam]: according to rule
seq. [sequens]: (sing.) the following
seq. [sequitur]: it follows
seqq. [sequentia]: (pl.) the following [things]
sg. or **sing.** [singularis]: singular
s.l. [sine loco]: without place
s.l.a. [sine loco et anno]: without place and year
s.l.a.n. [sine loco, anno vel nomine]: without place, year, or name
s.l.p. [sine legitima prole]: without legitimate issue
s.m.p. [sine mascula prole]: without male issue
s.n. [sine nomine]: anonymous
sn. [stannum]: tin
sol. [solutio]: (med.) a solution
s.o.s. [si opus sit]: (med.) if necessary
s.p. [sine parole]: without issue
S.P.I. [Sacrum Romanum Imperium]: the Holy Roman Empire
S.P.Q.R. [Senatus Populusque Romanus]: The Senate and the People of Rome (motto of Rome)
s.p.s. [sine prole supersite]: without surviving issue
ss̄ [semis]: (med.) one half
stat. [statim]: immediately; on the spot
S.T.B. [Sacrae Theologiae Baccalaureus]: Bachelor of Sacred Theology
sub. [subaudi]: to read between the lines
sup. [supra]: above
sus. per col. [suspensio per collum]: execution by hanging
s.v. (pl., **s.vv.**) [sub verbo or sub voce]: look under the word

T

t. or **temp.** [tempore]: in the time of
tab. [tabella]: (med.) a tablet
text. rec. [textus receptus]: the received text
t.i.d. [ter in die]: (med) three times a day

U

ult. [ultimo]: last month
u.s. [ubi supra]: in the place mentioned above
ut dict. [ut dictum]: (med) as directed
ut inf. or **ut i.** [ut infra]: as stated or shown below
ut sup. or **u.s.** [ut supra]: as above
ux. [uxor]: wife

V

v. or **vo.** [verso]: reverse side
v. or **vs.** [versus]: against
v. [vide]: see
v.a. [vixit ... annos]: he lived ... years
V.D.M. [Verbi Dei Minister]: minister of the Word of God
verb. sap. [verbum sapienti]: a word to the wise
verb. sat. [verbum sat sapienti]: a word to the wise is sufficient
v.i. [vide infra]: see below
viz. [videlicet]: namely
v.s. [vide supra]: see above
V.V. or **v.v.:** [vice versa]: conversely

MISCELLANEOUS

THE CALENDAR YEAR
(mensis)

Januarius: January
Februarius: February
Martius: March
Aprilis: April
Maius: May
Iunius: June
Quinctilis or **Iulius** (after Julius Caesar): July
Sextilis or **Augustus** (after Augustus Caesar): August
September: September
October: October
November or **Novembris:** November
December: December

THE CALENDAR MONTH

Idus [the Ides]: the fifteenth day in March, May, July, and October; the thirteenth day in all other months
Kalendae or **Calendae** [the Calends]: the first day of a Roman month
Nonae [the Nones]: the seventh day in March, May, July, and October; the fifth day in all other months

THE DAYS OF THE WEEK
(dies)

Dominica: Sunday
Lunae: Monday
Martis: Tuesday
Mercurii: Wednesday
Iovis: Thursday
Veneris: Friday
Saturni: Saturday

PRIMARY AND SECONDARY COLORS

albus: white
caeruleus: blue
caesius: blue-grey
flavus: yellow
fulvus: brown
glaucus: green-grey
niger: black
puniceus: pink
purpureus: purple
ruber: red
viola: violet
viridis: green

THE SEVEN HILLS OF ROME

Collis Quirinalis
Collis Viminalis
Mons Aventinus
Mons Caelius
Mons Capitolinus
Mons Esquilinus
Mons Palatinus

COUNTRIES AND REGIONS

Aegyptus: Egypt
Aethiops: Ethiopia
Africa: north Africa
Alpes: the Alps
Ancyra: Ankara
Antipodes: the Antipodes
Aquincum: Budapest
Arelate: Arles
Augusta Treverorum: Trier
Augusta Vindelicorum: Augsburg
Augustodunum: Autun
Batavia: Holland
Bononia: Bologna
Britannia: Britain

MISCELLANEOUS

Countries and Regions

Burdigala: Bourdeaux
Caesar Augusta: Saragossa
Camulodunum: Colchester
Carthago: Carthage
Caledonia: Scotland
Carales: Cagliari
Colonia Agrippina: Cologne
Creta: the Island of Crete
Danuvius: the Danube river
Deva: Chester
Eboracum or **Eburacum:** York
Emerita Augusta: Merida
Etruria: Tuscany (i.e., the land of the Etruscans)
Florentia: Florence
Gades: Cadiz
Gallia: France
Genua: Genoa
Germania: Germany
Graecia: Greece
Helvetia: Switzerland
Hiberia: Spain
Hibernia: Ireland
Hispalis: Seville
Hispania: Spain
Ilium: Troy
Illyricum: the region of the former Yugoslavia
Italia: Italy
Iudea: Palestine
Lacus Lemannus: Lake Geneva
Latium: central Italy (i.e., Rome and it environs)
Lindum: Lincoln
Londinium: London
Lugdunum: Lyons
Lusitania: Portugal
Lugdunum Batavorum: Leiden
Lutetia: Paris
Malaca: Malaga
Mare Caspium: the Caspian Sea
Mare Inferum or **Mare Tyrrhenum:** the Tyrrhenian Sea
Mare Internum or **Mare Nostrum:** the Mediterranean Sea
Mare Superum or **Mare Adriaticum:** the Adriatic Sea
Massilia or **Massillia** or **Massuia:** Marseilles
Mazaca Caesarea: Kayseri

MISCELLANEOUS

Countries and Regions

Mediolanum: Milan
Melita: Malta
Moguntiacum: Mainz
Neapolis: Naples
Nemausus: Nimes
Nilus: the Nile
Oceanus Germanicus: The North Sea
Olisipo: Lisbon
Panormus: Palermo
Patavium: Padua
Pontus Euxinus: the Black Sea
Portus Dubris: Dover
Pygmaei: the Pygmies of Africa
Regiones Torrides: the Tropics
Rhenus: the Rhine river
Rhodanus: the Rhone river
Roma: Rome
Salmantica: Salamanca
Sarmatia: Russia
Scotia: Scotland
Sequana: the Seine
Seres: China (or the Chinese)
Sicilia: the Island of Sicily
Sinus Arabicus: the Red Sea
Tamesa or **Tamesis**: the Thames
Tanais: the Don river
Thessalonica: Salonika
Tiberis: the Tiber river
Tibur: Tivoli
Toletum: Toledo
Tolosa: Toulouse
Transalpinus: southern France
Trinacria: Sicily
Tridentum: Trent
Tros: a Trojan
Valentia: Valencia
Via Appia: the Appian Way
Vindobona: Vienna

ROMAN NUMERALS

CARDINALS
unus (I): one
duo (II): two
tres (III): three
quattuor (IV): four
quinque (V): five
sex (VI): six
septem (VII): seven
octo (VIII): eight
novem (IX): nine
decem (X): ten
undecim (XI): eleven
duodecim (XII): twelve
tredecim (XIII): thirteen
quattuordecim (XIV): fourteen
quindecim (XV): fifteen
sedecim (XVI): sixteen
septemdecim (XVII): seventeen
duodeviginti/octodecim (XVIII): eighteen
undeviginti/novemdecim (XIX): nineteen
viginti (XX): twenty
unus et viginti (XXI): twenty-one
duoetviginti (XXII): twenty-two
duodetriginta (XXVIII): twenty-eight
undetriginta (XXIX): twenty-nine
triginta (XXX): thirty
duodequadraginta (XXXVIII): thirty-eight
undequadraginta (XXXIX): thirty-nine
quadraginta (XL): forty
duodequinquaginta (XLVIII): forty-eight
undequinquaginta (XLIX): forty-nine
quinquaginta (L): fifty
sexaginta (LX): sixty
septuaginta (LXX): seventy

ORDINALS
primus: first
secundus: second
tertius: third
quartus: fourth
quintus: fifth
sextus: sixth
septimus: seventh
octavus: eighth
nonus: ninth
decimus/decumus: tenth
undecimus: eleventh
duodecimus: twelfth
tertius decimus: thirteenth
quartus decimus: fourteenth
quintus decimus: fifteenth
sextus decimus: sixteenth
septimus decimus: seventeenth
duodevicesimus/octavusdecimus: eighteenth
undevicesimus/novemdecimus: nineteenth
vicesimus: twentieth
unetvice(n)simus: twenty-first
duoetvice(n)simus: twenty-second
duodetriginta: twenty-eighth
undetrice(n)simus: twenty-nineth
trice(n)simus: thirtieth
duodequadrage(n)simus: thirty-eighth
undequadrage(n)simus: thirty-nineth
quadrage(n)simus: fortieth
duodequinquage(n)simus: forty-eighth
undequinquage(n)simus: forty-nine
quinquage(n)simus: fiftieth
sexage(n)simus: sixtieth
septuage(n)simus: seventieth

octoginta (LXXX): eighty
nonaginta (XC): ninety
centum (C): one hundred
centum (et) unus (CI):
  one hundred and one
ducenti (CC): two hundred
trecenti (CCC): three hundred
quadringenti (CD): four hundred

quingenti (D): five hundred
sescenti (DC): six hundred
septingenti (DCC): seven hundred

octingenti (DCCC): eight hundred

nongenti (DM): nine hundred
mille (M): one thousand
duo milia/millia (MM): two thousand

octoge(n)simus: eightieth
nonage(n)simus: ninetieth
centesimus: the hundredth
centesimus (et) primus:
  hundred and first
ducentesimus: two hundredth
trecente(n)simus: three hundredth
quadringente(n)simus:
  four hundredth
quingente(n)simus: five hundredth
sescente(n)simus: six hundredth
septingente(n)simus:
  seven hundredth
octingente(n)simus:
  eight hundredth
nongente(n)simus: nine hundredth
mille(n)simus: one thousandth
bis mille(n)simus: two thousandth

ENGLISH-LATIN INDEX

A

a nobody: **natus nemo**
a word to the wise is sufficient: **dictum sapienti sat (est)**
above: **supra**
absence of justice: **jus nullum**
absolute power: **imperium singulare**
absolutely: **in absoluto**
abuse does not take away use: **abusus non tollit usum**
acceptable: **nihil obstat**
accomplice in the crime: **particeps criminis**
according to: **secundum**
according to circumstance: **pro re**
according to custom: **ad usum** or **ex more**
according to law: **secundum legem**
according to merit: **pro merito**
according to nature: **secundum naturam**
according to rule: **ad amussim** or **secundum regulam**
according to the law: **in jure**
according to the value: **ad valorem**
according to truth: **secundum veritatem**
according to usage: **secundum usum**
across: **in transversum** or **trans**
act of God: **actus Dei**
action: **actus**
add: **adde**
add fuel to the flame: **oleum addere camino**
add to this: **adde huc**
adjourned indefinitely: **sine die**
afresh: **de integro**

after birth: **post partum**
after death: **post mortem** or **post obitum**
after dinner: **cenatus**
after litigation began: **post litem motam**
after meals: **post cibum**
after noon: **post meridiem**
after the appointed day: **post diem**
after the conclusion: **post terminum**
after the fact: **ex post facto**
after the fashion of: **ad instar**
after the manner of: **ad modum** or **more**
against: **adversus** or **contra** or **versus**
against my will: **me invito**
against the peace: **contra pacem**
against the stream: **adverso flumine**
against the world: **contra mundum**
aged: **grandis natu**
agreement: **consensus**
alcohol: **aqua vitae**
all is well: **recte est**
all kidding aside: **extra jocum** or **sine joco**
all right: **bene habet**
all that sort: **id genus omne**
all things being equal: **caeteris paribus** or **ceteris paribus**
all thumbs: **asinus ad lyram**
all-powerful: **omnipotens**
almighty God: **omnipotentia Dei**
alone: **solus**
aloud: **magna voce**
already enough: **jam satis**
also: **et**
alternately: **alternus** or **in vicem** or **in vices**

altogether: **in toto**
always: **semper**
among equals: **inter pares**
among other persons: **inter alios**
among other things: **inter alia**
among the goods: **in bonis**
among the living: **inter vivos**
among us: **inter nos**
and: **et**
and elsewhere: **et alibi**
and from the Son: **filioque**
and husband: **et vir**
and others: **et alii**
and so forth: **et cetera**
and spouse: **et conjunx**
and the following: **et sequens**
and the like: **et similia**
and what follows: **et sequentes** or **et sequentia**
and wife: **et uxor**
anew: **ab integro** or **de novo**
annually: **anniversarius** or **per annum**
annuity: **annua pecunia**
anonymous: **sine nomine**
archer: **sagittarius**
aristocratic: **optimas**
armed: **cum telo**
around: **circa**
art of love: **ars amandi**
as: **qua**
as a matter of form: **pro forma**
as a matter of law: **ex lege**
as a token of friendship: **ut pignus amicitiae**
as a warning: **in terrorem**
as above: **ut supra**
as directed: **more dicto** or **ut dictum**
as far as I know: **quantum scio** or **quod sciam**
as far as in me lies: **quantum in me est**
as far as possible: **in toto caelo** or **quam celerrime**
as if confessed: **pro confesso**

as if said: **quasi dictum**
as is impossible: **per impossibile**
as is usual: **ut adsolet**
as it were: **quasi**
as matters stand: **e re nata**
as much as is sufficient: **quantum satis**
as much as it is worth: **quantum valebat**
as much as it may be worth: **quantum valeat**
as much as possible: **quam maxime**
as much as required: **tantum quantum**
as much as suffices: **quantum sufficit**
as much as you please: **quam libet** or **quamlibet** or **quantum placet**
as much as you will: **quantum vis**
as nearly as possible: **quam proxime**
as regards the past: **quoad ultra**
as soon as possible: **quam primum** or **quamprimum**
as stated below: **ut infra**
as to the lesser matter: **quoad minus**
as usual: **ut solet**
as well as can be done: **pro viribus**
ashore: **in litus** or **in litore**
asleep: **in somno** or **per somnum**
at: **ad**
at a high price: **magna pretio** or **magni pretii**
at a moment's notice: **in promptu**
at bedtime: **hora decubitus**
at chambers: **in camera**
at dead of night: **nocte intempesta**
at first glance: **primo intuiti**
at first light: **prima luce**
at frequent intervals: **haud longis intervallis**
at full length: **in extenso**
at hand: **ad manum**
at high tide: **aestu incitato**
at home: **domi**
at its own time: **suo tempore**
at leisure: **otiosus**
at length: **per extensum** or **tandem**

at my own risk: **meo periculo**
at night: **nocte**
at nightfall: **sub noctem**
at once: **simul**
at one blow: **uno ictu**
at one's own peril: **suo periculo**
at our own risk: **nostro periculo**
at pleasure: **a bene placito** or **ad libitum**
at present: **hodie**
at that time: **id temporis**
at the agreed hour: **ad horam compositam**
at the beginning: **ad initium** or **initio** or **sub initio**
at the beginning of the year: **initio anni**
at the critical moment: **in ipso periculi discrimine**
at the end of the book: **in extremo libro**
at the foot of the mountain: **infimus mons**
at the man: **ad hominem**
at the marriage: **ad ostium ecclesiae**
at the mercy of fate: **ut fata trahunt**
at the opportune time: **in tempore opportuno**
at the outbreak of war: **in limine belli**
at the place: **ad locum**
at the point of death: **in articulo mortis** or **in extremis**
at the present time: **in praesenti**
at the public expense: **sumptibus publicis** or **sumptu publico**
at the right moment: **in tempore**
at the right time: **justo tempore**
at the same time: **simul** or **uno tempore**
at the suit of: **ad sectam**
at the turning point: **in discrimine rerum**
at the very instant: **in tempore ipso**
at this place: **ad hunc locum**
at this time: **hoc tempore**
at this word: **ad hanc vocem**

at what price fame?: **quanti fama?**
at will: **ad arbitrium**
at your instigation: **impulsu tuo**
attentive: **auritus**
augar: **auspex**

B

backwards: **retro**
backwards and forwards: **sursum deorsum**
bad conscience: **conscientia mala**
bad money: **nummi adulterini**
bald: **calvus**
banquet: **convivium**
barefoot: **pedibus nudis**
bastard child: **filius populi**
battlefield: **locus pugnae**
beast of burden: **jumentum**
because he fears: **quia timet**
before: **ante** or **pro**
before all things: **ante omnia**
before childbirth: **ante partum**
before daybreak: **ante lucem**
before death: **ante mortem**
before its time: **ante tempus**
before meals: **ante cibum**
before noon: **ante meridiem** or **ante meridianus**
before the court: **in facie curiae**
before the judge: **sub judice**
before the war: **ante bellum**
beggar: **mendicus**
beginning: **genesis**
behind: **a tergo**
Behold the Lamb of God!: **Ecce Agnus Dei**
Behold the Man!: **Ecce Homo**
below: **infra**
beneath one's dignity: **infra dignitatem**
beside oneself: **mente captus** or **sui impotens**
beside the point: **nihil ad rem**

best friend: **alter ego**
between: **inter**
between a rock and a hard place: **a fronte praecipitium a tergo lupi**
between hope and fear: **inter spem et metum**
between the hammer and the anvil: **inter malleum et incudem**
between two reigns: **interregnum**
between us: **inter nos**
beware of danger: **in cauda venenum**
beware of dog: **cave canem**
beyond: **ultra**
beyond measure: **extra modum**
beyond one's power: **ultra vires** or **supra vires**
beyond the legal limit: **ultra licitum**
beyond the value: **ultra valorem**
beyond the walls: **extra muros**
Big Dipper: **Ursa Major**
bird: **avis**
birthday: **dies natalis** or **genitalis dies**
bishop: **episcopus**
bit by bit: **frustillatim**
blacksmith: **faber ferrarius**
blameless: **rectus in curia**
blank slate: **tabula rasa**
bless you!: **benedicite!**
blessed are the peacemakers: **beati pacifici**
blessed are the poor in spirit: **beati pauperes spiritu**
blood: **sanguis**
blood relative: **consanguinitas**
bodily strength: **vires corporis**
body: **corpus**
body of Christ: **Corpus Christi**
body of law: **corpus juris**
body of the crime: **corpus delicti**
boiling water: **aqua bulliens**
bond of marriage: **vinculum matrimonii**
book: **codex** or **liber**
bookseller: **bibliopola**

bookworm: **helluo librorum**
born: **natus**
born to glory: **natus ad gloriam**
both: **ambo**
bottom of the sea: **imum mare**
braggert: **homo gloriosus**
brain: **cerebrum**
bread: **panis**
breakfast: **ientaculum**
bridge: **pons**
bringing back: **redux**
British peace: **Pax Britannica**
brother: **frater**
bull: **taurus**
burden of proof: **onus probandi**
buried: **sepultus**
busy: **occupatus**
butterfly: **papilio**
buyer: **emptor**
by a leap: **per saltum**
by accident: **per accidens** or **per infortunium**
by birth: **natu**
by chance: **per accidens**
by command: **iussu** or **jussu**
by common consent: **communi consensu**
by courage and faith: **animo et fide**
by craft: **per dolum**
by day: **interdius**
by degrees: **gradatim** or **tractim**
by design: **ex proposito**
by divine right: **jure divino**
by fair means or foul: **per fas et nefas**
by families: **per stirpes**
by favor: **de gratia**
by force: **manu forti**
by heart: **ex memoria** or **memoriter**
by implication: **implicite**
by invitation: **invitatu**
by its own motion: **suo motu**
by its own power: **proprio vigore**
by itself: **per se**

by Jove: **per Jovem**
by land: **pedibus**
by law: **jure**
by marital law: **jure mariti**
by means of: **per**
by moonlight: **ad lunam**
by mouth: **per os**
by my advice: **me auctore**
by my fault: **mea culpa**
by night: **noctu** or **nocturnus**
by no means: **nullo modo** or **nullo pacto**
by oneself: **solus**
by one's own prowess: **suo Marte**
by one's peers: **per pares**
by order: **iussu** or **jussu**
by permission: **permissu**
by perservering: **perserverando**
by proxy: **per procurationem**
by reason of domicile: **ratione domicilii**
by reason of soil: **ratione soli**
by retaliation: **per vices**
by right: **de jure** or **jure**
by right of blood: **jure sanguinis**
by right of crown: **jure coronae**
by right of relationship: **jure propinquitatis**
by right, not by gift: **jure non dono**
by sea and by land: **per mare per terram**
by special favor: **speciali gratia**
by that very fact: **ipso facto**
by the court: **per curiam**
by the day: **per diem**
by the entire court: **per totam curiam**
by the gift of God: **ex dono Dei**
by the favor of God: **Deo favente**
by the grace of God: **Dei gratia**
by the hundred: **per centum**
by the judge: **per eundem**
by the law itself: **ipso jure**
by the light of day: **de claro die**

by the living voice: **per vivam vocem**
by the month: **per mensem** or **per mese**
by the roots: **radicitus**
by the straight road: **per vias rectas**
by the thousand: **per mille**
by the way: **obiter**
by the way of sorrows: **per viam dolorosam**
by the wayside: **in itinere**
by the will of the people: **jure humano**
by this sign conquer: **in hoc signo vinces**
by threats: **per minas**
by virtue of one's office: **ex officio**
by way of: **per viam**
by what means?: **quo modo?** or **quomodo?**
by what right?: **quo jure?**
by which: **per quod**
by word of mouth: **ore tenus**
by your leave: **pace tua**
bygone years: **praeteriti anni**

C

calendar of events: **fasti**
cancellation of debts: **novae tabulae**
canon law: **jus canonicum**
cardinal point: **cardo duplex**
cast of characters: **dramatis personae**
cattle market: **forum bovarium** or **boarium**
cause it to be done: **fieri facias**
celebrity: **vir insignis**
celestial mysteries: **arcana caelestia**
censor of morals: **censor morum**
century: **centum anni**
children's paradise: **limbus puerorum**
Christian: **Christianus**
church: **ecclesia**
circular reasoning: **circulus vitiosus**
citizen of the world: **mundanus**

City of God: **Civitas Dei**
city center: **media urbs**
civil law: **jus civile**
civil war: **bellum civile** or **bellum domesticum** or **bellum intestinum**
close by: **juxta**
close formation: **phalanx**
coffin: **sarcophagus**
coined money: **aes signatum**
coined silver: **argentum signatum**
college: **collegium**
comic genius: **vis comica**
comity of nations: **comitas inter gentes**
common bread: **panis cibarius**
common folk: **plebs**
common good: **bonum publicum** or **commune bonum**
common law: **jus commune** or **lex non scripta**
common rabble: **faex populi** or **profanum vulgus**
commonwealth: **res publica** or **respublica**
communion of the saints: **communio sanctorum**
community: **communitas**
companion volume: **vade mecum**
compare: **confer**
comparison: **parabola**
compassion: **misericordia**
completely: **funditus**
compulsory: **in invitum**
concerning: **in re** or **re**
conditions of peace: **legis pacis**
confidentially: **sub rosa**
confused: **in nubibus**
connectedness: **nexus**
consider the outcome: **finem respice**
constellation: **astrum**
contemplation of flight: **meditatio fugae**
contract: **pactum**
contradiction in terms: **contradictio in adjecto**

contrary to good manners: **contra bonos mores**
contrary to nature: **opposuit natura**
conversely: **vice versa**
corpse: **cadaver**
corrections: **corrigenda**
costly: **magno pretio**
cottage: **casa**
court action: **querela**
crab: **cancer**
credits: **accepta**
creed: **credo**
crescent moon: **crescens luna** or **luna crescens**
crime: **delictum**
criminal act: **actus reus**
crocodile tears: **lacrimae simulatae**
cross: **crux**
crown: **corona**
cure-all: **panacea**
cursing: **maledictum**
custodian of morals: **custos morum**
customs: **mores**

D

daily: **in dies**
daily bread: **victus cotidianus**
dandy: **homo elegans**
dare to be wise: **aude sapere** or **sapere aude**
daughter: **filia**
dawn: **aurora**
Day of Judgment: **Dies Irae**
day is breaking: **lucescit**
day's journey: **iter unius diei**
daybreak: **diluculum**
daytime: **dies**
dead: **ad patres** or **mortuus**
dead men tell no tales: **motui non mordant**
dead of the night: **concubia nocte** or **intempesta nox**

debt: **aes alienum** or **debitum** or **res alienae**
deceased: **demortuus**
decided case: **res judicata**
decree: **edictum**
deed: **factum**
deeds not words: **facta non verba**
deep calls unto deep: **abyssus abyssum invocat**
deep silence: **altum silentium** or **silentium altum**
defendant being absent: **absente reo**
Defender of the Faith: **fidei defensor**
defense of one's life conduct: **apologia pro vita sua**
definitely: **in terminis**
deification: **apotheosis**
delight of battle: **gaudium certaminis**
den of iniquity: **colluvies vitiorum**
deputy: **locum tenens**
deservedly: **pro meritis**
desire: **libido**
desirous of praise: **laudis cupidus**
dessert: **mensa secunda** or **secunda mensa**
devil: **diabolus**
Devil's advocate: **advocatus diaboli**
diametrically opposite: **toto caelo**
diary: **adversaria** or **commentarii diurni**
dictum: **ipse dixit**
died: **obiit**
died without issue: **obiit sine prole**
different kind: **alieni generis**
digression: **excursus**
diplomatic agreement: **pacta conventa**
directly: **per vias rectas**
divide and rule: **divide et impera**
divination: **divinatus**
divine food: **ambrosia**
divine law: **jus divinum**
divine soul: **anima divina**
dizziness: **vertigo**
do not admit: **ne admittas**

do unto another as to thyself: **alteri sic tibi**
dog in a manger: **canis in praesepi**
door to door: **ostiatim**
double: **duplex**
double jeopardy: **non bis in idem**
downstream: **secundo flumine**
dozen: **duodecim**
draught: **haustus**
drop by drop: **guttatim**
drops: **guttae**
drunkard: **homo ebriosus**
during absence: **durante absentia**
during dinner: **inter cenam**
during hostilities: **flagrante bello**
during life: **durante vita**
during the trial: **lite pendente**

E

each day: **per diem**
ear: **auris**
early in the morning: **multo mane**
earth: **terra**
Earthly City: **Civitas Terrena**
earthquake: **terrae motus**
easily the first: **facile princeps**
ebb and flow: **accessus et recessus**
echo: **vocis imago**
eclipse of the sun: **labores solis**
egg: **ovum**
eldest child: **maximus natu**
empty threat: **brutum fulmen**
enemy: **hospes hostis**
enough: **satis**
equal: **par**
equal parts: **partes aequales**
equal to the task: **par oneri**
equally: **juxta**
equally at fault: **in pari delicto**
equals with equals: **pares cum paribus**
error: **erratum**

especially: **in primis**
essentially: **per essentiam**
eternal darkness: **tenebrae aeternae**
eulogy: **laudatio funebris**
Evening Star: **Hesperus**
evening of life: **vita occidens**
everlasting: **aere perennius**
everlasting glory: **sempiterna gloria**
every hour: **omni hora** or **quaque hora**
every morning: **quaque mane**
every night: **omni nocte**
every other day: **alternis diebus**
every other year: **alternis annis**
everyone: **nemo non**
everything: **nihil non**
everywhere: **ubique**
evil: **malum**
evil omen: **omen infaustum** or **omen sinistrum**
evil person: **homo nefarius**
evolution: **rerum progressio**
exactly: **verbatim et literatim**
exceedingly: **sane quam**
excellent!: **bene!**
excessive: **immodicus**
exempt: **immunis**
eye: **oculus**
eyewash: **collyrium**

F

fable: **fabella**
face to face: **coram**
faith alone: **sola fide**
faithful to the end: **ad finem fidelis**
faithfully: **fideliter**
fallacy of cause and effect: **post hoc ergo propter hoc**
false modesty: **malus pudor**
false reading: **falsa lectio**
farce: **fabula**
farewell: **bene vale** or **vale** or **valete**

farewell forever: **aeternum vale**
farthest point: **nil ultra**
father: **pater**
favorable omen: **omen faustum**
fellowship: **communitas**
festival: **dies festus**
fig: **ficus**
finally: **ad finem**
finishing point: **terminus ad quem**
fire: **ignis**
firm of purpose: **propositi tenax**
first: **primo**
first act: **actus primus**
first among equals: **prima inter pares**
first among his equals: **primus inter pares**
first come, first served: **prior tempore, prior jure**
first impression: **prima facie**
first light: **prima lux**
first mover: **primum mobile**
first name: **praenomen**
fish: **piscis**
fish market: **forum piscarium** or **piscatorium**
Five Ways: **Quinque Viae**
flood: **diluvium**
flourished: **floruit**
flowing free: **fusus crines**
fluid: **fluidus**
following: **in sequens**
food for Acheron: **Acheruntis pabulum**
food of the soul: **pabulum animi**
fool: **homo stultus**
foot-washing: **pedilavium**
for a few days: **ad paucos dies**
for a memorial: **pro memoria**
for a short time: **ad exiguum tempus**
for a time: **in tempus**
for all time: **ad vitam aeternam** or **in omne tempus**
for an indefinite period: **in incertum**
for and against: **pro et contra**

for better or for worse: **de bono et malo**
for bravery: **fortitudini**
for each individual: **per capita**
for each month: **per mensem**
for example: **exempli gratia**
for glory: **ad gloriam**
for instance: **exempli causa** or **verbi causa**
for life: **ad vitam**
for many years: **ad multus annos**
for my part: **pro mea parte**
for my sake: **mea gratia**
for now: **pro nunc**
for political reasons: **rei publicae causa**
for reference: **ad referendum**
for sure: **pro certo**
for the first time: **primitus**
for the future: **in futurum** or **in posterum**
for the last time: **ad postremum**
for the moment: **in praesens** or **pro tempore**
for the most part: **maximam partem**
for the present: **de praesenti** or **impraesentiarum** or **in praesentia**
for the present time: **in praesens tempus**
for the public good: **pro bono publico**
for the sake of gain: **lucri causa**
for the sake of honor: **honoris causa**
for the sake of piety: **pietatis causa**
for the sake of the joke: **joci causa**
for the second time: **iterum**
for the third time: **tertium**
for the time being: **pro tempore**
for the winter: **hibernus**
forbidden: **impermissus**
forefathers: **patres**
forever: **ad infinitum** or **ad perpetuitatem** or **in aeternum** or **in perpetuum**
forever and ever: **in saecula saeculorum**

formerly: **quondam**
fortunate fault: **felix culpa**
fortune favors the bold: **audentes fortuna juvet** or **audaces fortuna juvet**
fortune favors the strong: **fortes fortuna [ad]juvat**
forward and backward: **per recto et recto**
four times: **quater**
four times a day: **quater in die** or **quater die**
freak of nature: **lusus naturae**
free time: **otium**
free will: **liberum arbitrium**
friend and foe: **aequi iniqui**
friend of the court: **amicus curiae**
friendship without deceit: **amicitia sine fraude**
from: **ab**
from a distance: **e longinquo** or **ex longinquo**
from anger: **ab irato**
from bed and board: **mensa et toro**
from beginning to end: **ab ovo usque ad mala**
from boyhood: **a pueris** or **a puero**
from cause to effect: **a priori**
from childhood: **a teneris annis** or **ab incunabulis**
from date: **a dato**
from day to day: **de die in diem** or **diem ex die** or **in dies singulos**
from door to door: **ostiatim**
from effect to cause: **a posteriori**
from every perspective: **omni ex parte**
from head to toe: **a capite ad calcem**
from home: **domo**
from one to all: **ab uno ad omnes**
from possibility to reality: **a posse ad esse**
from table and bed: **a mensa et toro**
from tender years: **a teneris annis**
from that day: **a die**
from the absurd: **ab absurdo**

from the beginning: **a principio** or **ab initio** or **ab origine** or **ab ovo**
from the beginning of time: **ab aeterno**
from the bonds of marriage: **a vinculo matrimonii**
from the bottom: **funditus**
from the bottom of the heart: **ab imo pectore** or **imo pectore**
from the first: **a primo**
from the founding of the city: **ab urbe condita**
from the greatest to the least: **a maximis ad minima**
from the heart: **ex animo**
from the high mountain: **de monte alto**
from the inconvenience involved: **ab inconvenienti**
from the inside: **intus**
from the lesser to the greater: **a minori ad majus**
from the library of: **ex libris** or **e libris**
from the outside: **ab extra**
from the side: **a latere**
from the spear a crown: **a cuspide corona**
from which: **a quo**
from within: **ab intra**
from words to blows: **a verbis ad verbera**
from youth: **a teneris annis**
gap: **lacuna**
gentle reader: **lector benevole**
give: **da**
Glory be to God Most High: **Gloria in Excelsis Deo**
Glory be to the Father: **Gloria Patri**
glory: **gloria**
go in peace: **vade in pacem**
goat: **capricornus**
God be with you: **Deus vobiscum**
God forbid!: **quod abominor!** or **quod avertat Deus!**
God is the greatest good: **Deus est summum bonum**

God save the king: **salvum fac regem, O Domine**
God save the queen: **salvam fac reginam, O Domine**
God willing: **Deo volente** or **volente Deo**
god: **deus**
God's speed!: **salve!**
goddess: **dea**
going step by step: **gradarius**
gold: **aurum**
good: **bene**
good conscience: **conscientia recta**
good deeds: **bene facta**
good fortune: **fortuna prospera** or **fortuna secunda**
good luck: **bene vale vobis** or **macte!**
good-will: **benevolentia**
goods: **bona**
goose bumps: **cutis anserina**
Gospel: **evangelium**
gout: **dolor artuum**
grace alone: **sola gratia**
gradually: **minutatim**
Grant Us Peace: **Dona Nobis Pacem**
grass: **herba**
gratitude: **gratus animus**
gravity: **nutus et pondus**
Great Mother: **Magna Mater**
great good: **magnum bonum**
great unwashed: **ignobile vulgus**
great year: **annus magnus**
greatly: **magno opere**
Greetings!: **Salutem dicit!** or **ave**
gross negligence: **culpa lata**
guardian deity: **genius loci**
guest: **hospes**
guild: **conlegium**
guilty person: **homo reus**
guily intent: **mens rea**

H

habitually: **de more**
Hail!: **ave!**
Hail Mary: **Ave Maria**
half: **semis**
half a pint: **hemina**
hallucination: **aegri somnia**
handful: **manipulus**
happily: **feliciter**
happiness: **beata vita** or **vita beata**
hare: **lepus**
harmony: **concordia**
having resigned from office: **functus officio**
he is hit: **habet!** or **hoc habet!**
he owes nothing: **nihil debet**
he says nothing: **nihil dicit** or **nil dicit**
head: **caput**
healing power: **vis medicatrix**
healing power of nature: **vis medicatrix naturae**
heart: **cor**
heartbroken: **animo fractus**
height of glory: **summa gloria**
held in trust: **in commendam**
hello!: **heus** or **hui**
here!: **adsum**
here and everywhere: **hic et ubique**
here and now: **hic et nunc**
here and there: **passim** or **sic passim**
here begins: **incipit**
here lies: **hic iacet** or **hic jacet**
here lies buried: **hic iacet sepultus** or **hic sepultus**
here lies . . . : **hic situs est . . .**
heroine: **virago**
heyday: **flos aetatis**
hidden: **occultus**
High Mass: **Missa solemnis**
high priest: **Pontifex Maximus**
high treason: **laesa majestas**
highest evil: **extremum malorum**
highest good: **extremum bonorum** or **summum bonum**
highest law: **summum jus**
highest point: **ne plus ultra**
hither and thither: **huc et illuc** or **ultro et citro**
Holy Roman Empire: **Sacrum Romanum Imperium**
holy deeds: **acta sanctorum**
holy of holies: **sanctum sanctorum**
holy place: **fanum**
homeless: **homo sine censu**
honorable mention: **accessit**
honorary: **honoris gratia**
hope: **spes**
horn of plenty: **cornu copiae**
horse: **equus**
horse track: **hippodromos**
hot: **calidus**
hour: **hora**
hourly: **in horas**
House of Lords: **Domus Procerum**
house: **domicilium** or **domus**
house-arrest: **custodia libera**
household: **familia**
how do you do?: **quid agis?**
human being: **homo**
human body: **corpus humanum**
human soul: **anima humana**
humanity: **humanitas**
hundred: **centum**
husband: **vir**
husband and wife: **vir et uxor**

I

I: **ego**
I absolve: **absolvo**
I am a man: **homo sum**
I am ashamed: **pudet me**
I came, I saw, I conquered: **veni, vidi, vici**
I have sinned: **peccavi**

I hope in the Cross: **in cruce spero**
I know not what: **nescio quid**
I love as I find: **amo ut invenio**
I myself: **ego ipse**
I think I can: **posse videor**
I think, therefore I am: **cogito ergo sum**
I'm sorry: **me paenitet**
if necessary: **si opus sit**
ignorance of the law does not excuse: **ignorantia juris non excusat**
Iliad of woes: **Ilias malorum**
ill-will: **malevolentia**
illegal: **inlicitus**
illegally: **contra leges**
illegitimate son: **filius nullius** or **nullius filius**
image of God: **imago Dei**
imbecile: **impos animi**
immediately: **ilicet**
immoral life: **vita turpis**
impartial judge: **judex incorruptus**
impasse: **pari ratione**
implicit trust: **uberrima fides**
important witness: **testis gravis**
in a bad sense: **in malum partem** or **sensu malo**
in a broad sense: **lato sensu**
in a domestic court: **in foro domestico**
in a dream: **in somnis** or **per somnum**
in a folio volume: **in folio**
in a friendly way: **amiciter** or **via amicabili**
in a good sense: **sensu bono**
in a heap: **in cumulo**
in a nutshell: **in nuce**
in a safe place: **in tuto esse**
in a series: **seriatim**
in a single bound: **per saltum** or **uno saltu**
in a state of doubt: **in tenebris**
in a state of nature: **in naturalibus**
in a straight line: **ad lineam** or **ad perpendiculum** or **in directum**
in a strict sense: **stricto sensu**
in a test tube: **in vitro**
in a vacuum: **in vacuo** or **vacuo**
in a word: **uno verbo**
in absence: **in absentia**
in all directions: **in omnes partes**
in all respects: **in omnibus**
in all things love: **in omnibus caritas**
in an analogous case: **in pari materia**
in an equal cause: **in pari causa**
in an evil manner: **malo modo**
in an instant: **puncto temporis**
in an opposite direction: **in contrarium**
in an orderly manner: **secundum ordinem**
in an outward direction: **ad extra**
in another place: **in alio loco**
in another way: **alio pacto**
in bad faith: **mala fide**
in being: **in esse**
in body: **in corpore**
in both cases: **in utraque re**
in brief: **ne multa**
in Christ's name: **in Christi nomine**
in close order: **grege facto**
in confidence: **sub rosa**
in confusion: **nec caput nec pedes**
in contemplation of flight: **in meditatione fugae**
in contempt of court: **in contumaciam**
in darkness: **in tenebris**
in default: **in mora**
in different ways: **alius aliter**
in doubt: **in ambiguo** or **in dubio**
in droves: **gregatim**
in due time: **ad tempus**
in each month: **in singulos menses**
in episcopal robes: **in pontificalibus**
in equilibrium: **in equilibrio**
in error: **frustra**
in everlasting remembrance: **memoria in aeterna**
in every respect: **omnibus rebus**

in fact: **de facto**
in few words: **paucis verbis**
in French: **Gallice**
in full: **in pleno**
in full court: **in banco**
in full leaf: **comata silva**
in full measure: **pleno modio**
in fun: **per ludibrium**
in general: **ad summam**
in happier times: **melioribus annis**
in his own way: **more suo**
in ill-will: **in invidiam**
in intention and fact: **animo et facto**
in inverse order: **inverso ordine**
in Italian: **Italice**
in its place: **in situ**
in its proper place: **suo loco**
in itself: **in se** or **per se**
in jest: **per jocum**
in kind: **in genere**
in like manner: **similiter**
in many respects: **in rebus multis**
in many ways: **multimodis**
in memory: **in memoriam**
in mourning: **atra cura**
in my absence: **me absente**
in my judgment: **meo judicio**
in my lifetime: **me vivo**
in my opinion: **me judice**
in my own way: **more meo**
in name only: **verbo**
in one place: **in unum**
in one's own person: **in propria persona**
in one's own right: **suo jure**
in open court: **in curia**
in opposition: **ex adverso**
in part: **ex parte**
in passing: **obiter**
in peace: **in pace**
in perpetual remembrance: **in perpetuam rei memoriam**
in person: **in persona**

in plain words: **nudis verbis**
in pledge: **in vadio**
in prison: **in carcerem** or **in custodiam**
in private: **in privato**
in private life: **privatim**
in prospect: **in prospectu**
in public: **in propatulo** or **in publico**
in public view: **in oculis civium**
in readiness: **in promptu**
in reality: **in actu**
in reserve: **in pectore**
in respect of: **intuitu**
in secret: **in pectore** or **januis clausis**
in short: **ad summam**
in silence: **sub silentio**
in smoke: **in fumo**
in so many words: **in totidem verbis** or **totidem verbis**
in sport: **per ludibrium**
in substance: **in corpore**
in the abstract: **in abstracto**
in the back: **in dorso**
in the beginning: **in limine** or **in principio**
in the clouds: **in nubibus**
in the course of the year: **anno vertente**
in the court of conscience: **in foro conscientiae**
in the custody of the law: **in custodia legis**
in the egg: **in ovo**
in the end: **tandem denique**
in the English fashion: **more Anglico**
in the evening: **vesperi**
in the first place: **ante omnia** or **imprimis**
in the following month: **proximo** or **proximo mense**
in the future: **in futuro**
in the Golden Age: **in illo tempore**
in the highest: **in excelsis**
in the Irish fashion: **more Hibernico**
in the Italian manner: **Italice**

in the Latin manner: **Latine**
in the living organism: **in vivo**
in the meantime: **ad interim** or **per interim**
in the middle: **in medio**
in the midst of the work: **opere in medio**
in the midst of things: **in mediis rebus**
in the mind: **in intellectu**
in the name of: **in nomine**
in the name of the Father, the Son, and the Holy Spirit: **in nomine Patris et Filii et Spiritus Sancti**
in the name of the Lord: **in nomine Domini**
in the nature of things: **in rerum natura**
in the nick of time: **in ipso articulo temporis**
in the notes: **in notis**
in the nude: **in naturalibus**
in the open air: **sub dio** or **sub divo** or **sub Jove**
in the original state: **in statu quo**
in the past year: **praeterito anno**
in the place: **loco**
in the place cited: **in loco citato** or **loco citato**
in the place mentioned above: **ubi supra**
in the place of a parent: **in loco parentis**
in the proper place: **in loco**
in the rear: **a tergo**
in the same place: **ibidem**
in the silence of night: **silentio noctis**
in the south: **in meridiem**
in the usual manner: **more solito**
in the very act: **in actu**
in the very act of crime: **in flagrante delicto**
in the very words: **ipsissimis verbis**
in the womb: **in utero** or **in ventre**
in the work cited: **opere citato**
in the year of our Lord: **anno Domini**
in the year of the reign: **anno regni**
in the year of the world since the creation: **anno mundi**
in this direction: **horsum**
in this month: **hoc mense**
in this place: **hoc loco**
in this sense: **hoc sensu**
in this year: **hoc anno**
in time of war: **in bello**
in transit: **in transitu**
in truth: **re vera** or **revera**
in turn: **in vicem** or **in vices**
in unison: **in concordia vocum**
in use: **in usu**
in vain: **frustra** or **in cassum**
in various directions: **alius alio**
in whatever manner: **quovis modo**
in witness: **in testimonium**
in your judgment: **te judice**
indirectly: **per ambages**
indiscriminately: **per saturam**
indispensible condition: **causa sine qua non** or **conditio sine qua non** or **sine qua non**
indisputably: **sine controversia**
individuality: **propria natura**
individually: **viritim**
inherently evil: **mala in se**
inherited property: **patrimonium**
inland: **mediterraneus**
innate goodness: **naturae bonitas**
innermost thoughts: **penetralia mentis**
insanity: **dementia**
inside: **intra**
instead of: **ad vicem**
intelligible world: **mundus intelligibilis**
intentionally: **de industria**
intermarriage: **connubium**
internal witness: **testimonium internum**
international law: **jus gentium**
interwoven: **intertextus**
into the heart of the matter: **in medias res**
intrinsically: **per se**

188

invalid law: **lex irrita est**
inward teacher: **magister internus**
inwards: **intro**
iron: **ferrum**
island: **insula**
it does not follow: **non sequitur**
it happens: **usu venit**
it has been proven: **probatum est**
it is all over: **actum est**
it is day: **lucet**
it is done: **factum est**
it is finished: **consummatum est**
it is fraud to conceal fraud: **fraus est celare fraudem**
it is lawful: **fas est**
it is legal: **licet**
it is pointless: **nihil attinet**
it is proper: **oportet**
it is rumored: **fama est**
it is so: **ita res est** or **ita est**
it is the third hour: **tertia hora est**
it is useful: **res expedit**
it seems: **videtur**
itch for writing: **cacoëthes scribendi**
jealousy: **zelotypus**

J

Jew: **Iudaeus**
jointly: **in solidum** or **in solido**
journal: **adversaria**
judge: **judex**
judgement of God: **Dei judicium** or **judicium Dei**

K

keen wit: **sal Atticum**
kinetic energy: **vis viva**
king: **rex**
king of kings: **rex regum**

king's peace: **pax regis**
kiss of peace: **osculum pacis**
know thyself: **nosce te ipsum** or **nosce teipsum**
knowledge is power: **scientia est potentia**
known: **cognitus**

L

laboratory: **officina**
laboratory of the nations: **officina gentium**
Lamb of God: **Agnus Dei**
last farewell: **ultimum vale**
last of the heirs: **ultimus haeres**
last of the kings: **ultimus regum**
last year: **priore anno**
late at night: **multa de nocte** or **multa nocte**
late night study: **lucubratus**
law: **lex** or **jus**
law of consanguinity: **jus sanguinis**
law of nations: **jus gentium**
law of retaliation: **lex talionis**
law of the land: **lex terrae**
law of the place: **lex loci**
law of the soil: **jus soli**
law of the sword: **jus gladii**
lawless: **inlex**
lawlessness: **leges nullae**
leader of the pack: **dux gregis**
leaf: **folium**
leap-year: **annus bisextus**
learned: **literatus** or **litteratus**
learned class: **literati** or **litterati**
least: **minimus**
leave well enough alone: **actum ne agas**
left: **sinister**
left eye: **oculus sinister**
left-hand page (the backside): **folio verso**
left-hand page of a book: **verso folio**
legal detention: **habeas corpus**

legal right: **jus**
leisure: **otium**
length-wise: **in longitudinem**
lest ye forget: **ne obliviscaris**
let it be so!: **fiat**
let me know: **fac sciam**
let the buyer beware: **caveat emptor**
let there be light: **fiat lux**
let us be joyful (while we are young): **gaudeamus igitur (juvenes dum sumus)**
letter: **epistula**
letter of the law: **strictum jus**
liberally: **quantum libet**
liberty: **libertas**
library: **bibliotheca**
life: **vita**
life span: **vitae summa**
lifelike: **ad vivum**
light: **lux**
light of faith: **lumen fidei**
light of grace: **lumen gratiae**
light of nature: **lumen naturale**
light of the world: **lux mundi**
like father, like son: **patris est filius** or **qualis pater, talis filius**
likeness of God: **similitudo Dei**
likewise: **item** or **itidem**
limb by limb: **membratim**
lion: **leo**
liquid: **fluidus**
literally: **ad litteram** or **ad verbum** or **e verbo** or **literatim** or **litteratim** or **pro verbo**
Little Dipper: **Ursa Minor**
little by little: **unciatim**
live for today: **vive hodie**
loan: **pecunia mutua**
long conversation: **multus sermo**
long live the king: **vivat rex**
long live the king and queen: **vivant rex et regina**
long live the queen: **vivat regina**
long live the republic: **vivat respublica**

look for this: **hoc quaere**
loophole: **fenestra**
Lord have mercy: **Kyrie eleison**
Lord's Day: **dies dominicus**
Lord's Prayer: **Paternoster** or **Pater Noster**
Lord's Supper: **Cena Domini**
loss: **damnum**
lost: **adiratum**
love: **amor** or **caritas**
love begets love: **amor gignit amorem**
love conquers all things: **amor vincit omnia** or **omnia vincit amor**
love of country: **amor patriae**
love of money: **amor nummi**
love of money is a root to all evil: **radix omnium malorum est cupiditas**
love of one's neighbor: **amor proximi**
love of self: **amor sui**
love potion: **philtrum**
love sick: **aeger amore** or **aegra amans**
lovers' quarrels: **amantium irae**
Low Mass: **Missa bassa**
lower class: **proletarius**
lucky and unlucky days: **fasti et nefasti dies**
lucky day: **dies faustus**
lukewarm: **tepidus**
lunar eclipse: **defectio lunae**
lunch: **prandium**

M

made of pottery: **fictilis**
magical: **Hecatean**
magician: **magus**
maiden: **virgo**
majority: **major pars**
make it so: **fieri facias**
Maker of the World: **Orbis Factor**
malpractice: **mala praxis**
man: **homo** or **vir**

man is a wolf to man: **homo homini lupus** or **lupus est homo homini**
man is the measure of all things: **homo mensura**
man of letters: **homo doctus** or **vir literatus** or **vir litteratus**
man of the people: **homo plebeius**
manner of living: **modus vivendi**
many times: **multis partibus**
many-headed snake: **Hydra**
market: **emporium**
married: **nupta**
Mass: **Missa**
Mass of the faithful: **Missa fidelium**
master: **magister**
master of ceremonies: **magister ceremoniarum**
masterpiece: **magnum opus** or **opus magnum**
may it flourish: **floreat**
may the omen augur no evil: **absit omen**
meanwhile: **interim**
memorandum: **notandum**
men of straw: **faeneus homines**
mercantile law: **lex mercatoria** or **mercatorum**
mercury: **argentum vivum**
mere assertion: **gratis dictum**
mere word: **flatus vocis**
meritorious: **bonae notae**
middle of the road: **media via** or **via media**
middle way: **media via** or **via media**
middling: **mediocris**
midnight: **media nox**
milk: **lac**
Milky Way: **lacteus orbis** or **via Lactea**
mine and thine: **meum et tuum**
minister of the Word of God: **Verbi Dei Minister**
miscarriage of justice: **judicium perversum**
misfortune: **fortuna adversa** or **infelicitas** or **res adversae**

mix: **misce**
mob: **mobile vulgus**
mode of operating: **modus operandi**
money does not smell: **pecunia non olet**
month: **mensis**
monthly: **menstruus** or **per mensem**
moon: **luna** or **noctiluca**
moonlight: **lunae lumen**
more lasting than bronze: **aere perennius**
more than usual: **plus solito**
morning star: **lucifer**
most excellent: **optime**
mother: **mater**
mountain: **mons**
mountain air: **afflatus montium**
much in little: **multa paucis** or **multum in parvo**
much later: **multo post**
much obliged: **bene facis**
murder: **homicidium**
music of the spheres: **vox stellarum**
mutual consent: **assensio mentium** or **mutuus consensus**
mutually: **inter nos**
mystical union: **unio mystica**
mythical creature: **chimaera**

N

naked body: **nudatum corpus**
naked truth: **nuda veritas**
name having been changed: **mutato nomine**
namely: **scilicet** or **videlicet**
narrow-minded: **animus angustus**
national hero: **pater patriae**
native soil: **natale solum**
natural advantages: **naturae bona**
natural intelligence: **lumen naturale**
natural law: **jus naturae**
natural world: **rerum natura**

nature abhors a vacuum: **natura abhorret a vacuo**
near: **circa**
near at hand: **inibi**
necessary changes being made: **mutatis mutandis**
necessity is the mother of invention: **mater artium necessitas**
necessity knows no law: **necessitas non habet legem**
needle: **acus**
negative vote: **non placet**
neither: **neuter**
neither delay nor rest: **nec more nec requies**
neither desire nor fear: **nec cupias nec metuas**
neither head nor foot: **nec caput nec pedes**
new king, new law: **novus rex, nova lex**
new moon: **nova luna**
night: **nox**
nightlong: **pernox**
no: **non**
no contest: **nolo contendere**
no offense intended: **absit invidia**
no one else: **nemo alius**
no sooner said than done: **dictum ac factum**
noble class: **optimates**
non agreement: **res discrepat**
nonexistence: **non esse**
nonsense!: **fabulae!**
noon: **meridies**
North Pole: **polus glacialis**
north wind: **Boreas**
not a doubt: **haud dubie**
not in the least: **nihil omnino**
not of sound mind: **non compos mentis**
not particularly: **non ita**
not permitted: **non licet**
not pleasing: **non libet**
not sacred: **profanus**
not too much: **ne nimium**
note well: **nota bene**
nothing: **nihil**
nothing new under the sun: **nihil sub sole novum**
notwithstanding: **non obstante**
notwithstanding these things: **his non obstantibus**
now: **nunc**
now and always: **et nunc et semper**
now and later: **alius alias**
now and then: **interdum**
now or never: **nunc aut nunquam**

O

O Come, All Ye Faithful: **Adeste Fideles**
of his own right: **proprio jure**
of low birth: **filius terrae**
of one mind or spirit: **unanimus**
of one's own accord: **ex proprio motu** or **motu proprio**
of that age: **id aetatis**
of the faith: **de fide**
of the lower world: **infernus**
of the people: **plebeius**
off the record: **obiter dictum**
officially: **ex cathedra**
oil: **oleum**
old age: **fessa aetas**
older child: **major natu**
on a level surface: **in plano**
on alert: **arrectus auribus**
on deposit: **in deposito**
on equal terms: **ex aequo** or **in aequo**
on foot: **pedibus**
on hand: **in manibus**
on my account: **mea de causa** or **meo nomine**
on my behalf: **nomine meo**
on my word of honor: **fide mea**

on purpose: **ex industria**
on the back: **in dorso**
on the contrary: **e contrario** or **ex contrario** or **per contra**
on the ground: **humi**
on the left: **a sinistra**
on the other hand: **e contra**
on the right: **a dextra**
on the spot: **ilico**
on the spur of the moment: **ex tempore** or **temporis causa**
on the way: **in transitu** or **obiter**
on the whole: **ad summam** or **ex toto** or **in toto**
on tiptoe: **suspenso gradu**
once for all: **semel pro semper**
one by one: **membratim**
one of a kind: **sui generis**
one of two: **alteruter**
one or two: **unus et alter**
one quarter: **quarta pars**
one thing after another: **aliud ex alio**
one witness is no witness: **testis unus, testis nullus**
one-sided: **iniquus**
only-begotten: **unigena**
opposite: **contra**
optical illusion: **deceptio visus**
orally: **viva voce**
oratory: **ars dicendi**
origins: **primordium**
our light comes from God: **a Deo lux nostra**
our people: **nostri**
out of court: **ex curia**
out of date: **obsoletus**
out of sight, out of mind: **absens haeres non erit**
out of the depths: **de profundis**
out of tune: **absonus**
over: **super**
over a glass: **inter pocula**

P

pain: **dolor**
pain of judgment: **poena sensus**
pain of the damned: **poena damni**
painless: **sine dolore**
painted by: **pinxit**
painter: **pictor**
pair of scales: **libra**
pair of scissors: **forfex**
pair of tongs: **forceps**
pale Death: **pallida mors**
pale with rage: **pallidus irae**
palimpsest: **codex rescriptus**
panel of jurors: **judicis**
papal encyclical: **bulla**
part for the whole: **pars pro toto**
partially: **per studium**
partnership: **consortium**
party: **convivium**
passion for writing: **furor scribendi**
patriot: **civis bonus**
Peace of God: **Pax Dei**
Peace of the Church: **Pax Ecclesiae**
peace: **pax**
peace be with you: **pax vobiscum**
peace in war: **pax in bello**
pearls before swine: **margaritas ante porcos**
pending: **in fieri**
pending lawsuit: **lis pendens**
pending the suit: **pendente lite**
perennials: **semper florens**
perfectly: **ad unguem** or **in unguem**
perforce: **nolens volens**
perpendicularly: **ad lineam**
perpetual motion: **mobile perpetuum** or **perpetuum mobile**
person of full legal rights: **legalis homo**
petition: **libellus**
philosopher's stone: **lapis philosophorum**
physician, heal thyself: **medice, cura te ipsum**

pilgrimage: **peregrinatio sacra**
pint: **octarius**
pious fraud: **fraus pia**
place of the seal: **locus sigilli**
please: **amabo te** or **amabo** or **si placet**
poetic genius: **vis poetica**
poetic inspiration: **furor poeticus**
poetic license: **licentia vatum**
point for point: **punctatim**
point of time: **punctum temporis**
political revolution: **novae res**
posse: **posse comitatus**
postscript: **postscriptum**
potentially: **in posse** or **in potentia**
poverty: **impotentia**
power: **vis**
power of inertia: **vis inertiae**
pray for the soul of . . . : **orate pro anima**
pray for us: **ora pro nobis**
prepared for all things: **in omnia paratus**
prepared for either event: **in utrumque paratus**
prepared for the worst: **ad utrumque paratus**
presence of mind: **praesentia animi**
pretty: **bellus**
prevenient grace: **gratia praeveniens**
priest: **pontifex**
principle elements: **principia rerum**
private life: **vita privata**
private person: **vir privatus**
privately: **privatim** or **sub silentio**
pro and con: **in utramque partem**
probable: **veri similis**
procedural law: **ordinandi lex**
prodigy: **niger cycnus** or **rara avis**
prohibition: **interdictum**
promise of protection: **fides publica**
promoter of the faith: **promotor fidei**
property: **bona**
proportionally: **pro rata**

providential intervention: **deus ex machina**
public affairs: **negotia publica**
public archives: **tabulae publicae**
public enemy: **inimicus**
public inscription: **aes publicum**
public land: **ager publicus**
public life: **respublica forum**
public opinion: **vulgi opinio**
public place: **locus communis**
public square: **forum**
pure act: **actus purus**
puzzle: **crux**

Q

Queen of Heaven: **Regina Caeli**
queen: **regina**
quota: **numerus clasus**

R

race track: **hippodromos**
rain clouds: **cumulus nimbus**
rainbow: **arcus pluvius**
ram: **aries**
raw: **incoctus**
read between the lines: **sub audi**
ready for battle: **in procinctu**
really?: **ita?**
rear guard: **agmen novissimum** or **agmen extremum**
received text: **textus receptus**
reciprocally: **inter se**
recitation: **recitatio**
recluse: **homo solitarius**
records: **annales**
red-handed: **flagrante delicto**
redundant act: **actum agere**
reference volume: **vade mecum**
regarding: **re**

regent: **interrex**
rejoice in God: **Jubilate Deo**
reluctantly: **gravatim**
renown: **ad astra**
repeatedly: **identidem** or **toties quoties**
republic: **res publica** or **respublica**
rest in peace: **requiescat in pace**
restored to life: **redivivus**
reverse side: **verso** or **verso folio**
résumé: **curriculum vitae** or **vitae curriculum**
riddle: **aenigma**
right: **jus**
right eye: **oculus dexter**
right hand: **dextra**
right of pledge: **jus pignoris**
right of possession: **jus possessionis**
right of property: **jus proprietatis**
right of royalty: **jus regium**
right of the first night: **jus primae noctis**
right of the widow: **jus relicti**
right-hand page (the front side): **folio recto**
right-hand page of a book: **recto** or **recto folio**
robber: **raptor**
Roman mile: **mille passuum**
Roman peace: **Pax Romana**
room for doubt: **ambigendi locus**
rub well: **tere bene**
rumor: **fama clamosa**
runner-up: **proxime accessit**
rural: **paganus**

S

said and done: **dictum factum**
salient point: **punctum saliens**
salt seasons everything: **sal sapit omnia**
salvation is by the Cross: **a cruce salus**
same old thing: **crambe repetita**
scandal: **fama clamosa**

scene of the crime: **locus criminis** or **locus delicti**
scholar: **vir doctus**
science: **scientia**
scorpion: **scorpio**
scripture alone: **sola scriptura**
sculptured by: **sculpsit**
seasoning: **condimentum**
second self: **alter idem**
second to none: **nulli secundus**
secret teaching: **disciplina arcana**
secretarial matters: **ab epistulis**
see: **vide**
see above: **vide supra**
see after this: **vide post**
see before: **vide ante**
see below: **vide infra**
see the above comment: **vide ut supra**
seize the day: **carpe diem**
self-confidence: **fiducia sui**
sense of duty: **officium**
sensible world: **mundus sensibilis**
sensual pleasures: **voluptates corporis**
sentimental value: **pretium affectionis**
series of calamities: **Ilias malorum**
serious: **gravitas**
severely wounded: **graviter ictus**
sex drive: **libido**
shade: **umbra**
shake: **agita**
short cut: **via compendiaria**
siblings: **fratres**
sick: **aeger**
sickly: **infirmus**
sideways: **in obliquum**
siege machines: **moles belli**
sieve: **cribrum**
silent: **tacitus**
silent actor: **persona muta**
silver: **argentum**
sincerely: **bona fide**
sinew of proof: **nervus probandi**
sinew of things: **nervus rerum**

sing unto the Lord: **cantate Domino**
sister: **soror**
sketch: **adumbratio**
sleep on it: **in nocte consilium**
sleepless: **ex somnis** or **insomnis**
slip of the memory: **lapsus memoriae**
slip of the pen: **lapsus calami**
slip of the tongue: **lapsus linguae**
smell of profit: **odor lucri**
snake in the grass: **anguis in herba**
so far: **pro tanto**
so help me God!: **medius fidius!**
so ordered: **ordinatum est**
social life: **vitae societas**
solar eclipse: **defectio solis**
sole heir: **heres ex asse**
solid earth: **terra firma**
someone significant: **aliquid**
something significant: **aliquid**
son: **filius**
son of the earth: **terrae filius**
soon: **mox**
sorcery: **ars magica**
sorrow: **dolor**
soul: **anima** or **animus**
sound of mind: **compos mentis**
sounding alike: **idem sonans**
source of evils: **fons malorum**
source of life: **vivendi causa**
south: **australis**
southward: **ad meridiem**
southwest wind: **ventus Africus**
speak of the devil: **lupus in fabula**
speech impediment: **haesitantia linguae**
speechless: **bos in lingua**
spirit: **numen**
spirit of the law: **mens legis** or **sententia legis** or **voluntas legis**
spirits of the dead: **manes**
spoken in Latin: **Latine dictum**
sponsorship: **aegis**
spontaneously: **de proprio motu** or **proprio motu**

spoonful: **cochleare**
spouse: **conjunx** or **conjux**
SPQR (the Senate and the People of Rome): **Senatus Populusque Romanus**
Spring: **ver**
spring water: **aqua fontana**
star: **astrum**
stark naked: **in puris naturalibus**
starting point: **terminus a quo**
state secrets: **arcana imperii**
statute law: **lex scripta**
step by step: **gradatim** or **per gradus**
still water runs deep: **aqua profunda est quieta**
stone: **lapis** or **saxum**
straight ahead: **recta via**
straight line: **recta linea**
stranger: **hospes hostis**
strength: **vis**
struck by lightning: **fulmine ictus**
such as it is: **talis qualis**
suicide: **felo-de-se**
sum of all things: **summa summarum**
summarily: **acervatim**
Summer: **aestas**
sunflower: **heliotropium**
sunny: **apricus**
superior force: **vis major**
supreme achievement: **spolia opima**
supreme jurisdiction: **jus gladii**
surname: **cognomen**
syphilis: **lues venerea**

T

table salt: **sal culinarius**
take courage!: **macte animo!**
take notice: **nota bene**
task-master: **operis exactor**
tasteless: **sine sapore**
teacher: **magister**

tear of Christ: **lacrima Christi**
tell me: **fac ut sciam**
temperate zone: **orbis medius**
temporarily: **in tempus** or **pro tempore**
Ten Commandments: **Decalogus**
tendency to find fault: **cacoëthes carpendi**
tendency to talk: **cacoëthes loquendi**
thank you: **benigne dicis** or **gratias tibi ago**
thankfulness: **animus gratus**
thankless: **ingratus**
thanks be to God: **Dei gratias** or **Deo gratias**
thanks to me: **opera mea**
that and that alone: **id demum**
that is: **id est**
that is to say: **id est**
the cure is worse than the disease: **aegrescit medendo**
the die is cast: **alea jacta est** or **jacta est alea** or **jacta alea est**
the end: **explicit** or **finis**
the finding of the jury: **sententiae judicum**
the following: **sequens**
the following things: **sequentia**
the many: **multi**
the master has spoken it: **magister dixit**
the play is over: **acta est fabula**
the question is settled: **res confecta est**
the same: **idem**
the same as: **idem quod**
the time for play: **tempus ludendi**
the Virgin: **Virgo**
the whole: **totum**
there is need: **opus est**
therefore: **ergo**
they leave the stage: **exeunt**
thigh: **femur**
third choice: **tertium quid**
this day: **hodie**
this do: **hoc age**

this for that: **quid pro quo**
this is my body: **hoc est corpus meum**
this pleases me: **hoc mihi placet**
thoughtful of the future: **prudens futuri**
thread by thread: **filatim**
three times: **ter**
three times a day: **ter in die**
thrice holy: **Tersanctus** or **Trisagion**
through carelessness: **per incuriam**
throughout: **passim**
thumb's down: **pollice verso**
thus: **sic**
time: **tempus**
time flies: **tempus fugit**
time reveals all things: **tempus omnia revelat**
time reveals the truth: **veritatem dies aperit**
tit for tat: **par pari refero** or **quid pro quo**
to: **ad**
to a great extent: **magna ex parte**
to a higher degree: **in majus**
to and fro: **ultro citroque**
to call into question: **in dubium vocare**
to descend into the lower world: **ad inferos descendere**
to die: **abiit ad plures** or **ad majores**
to each his/her own: **cuique suum** or **suum cuique**
to err is human: **errare humanum est** or **hominis est errare** or **humanum est errare**
to feed the flame: **alere flammam**
to give thanks: **gratias agere**
to go by foot: **iter pedestre**
to go by land: **iter terrestre**
to hang by a thread: **pendere filo**
to infinity: **in infinitum**
to live for the moment: **in horam vivere**
to live for today: **in diem vivere**
to my house: **ad me**
to one's advantage: **in rem**
to one's taste: **ad gustum**
to remain on stage: **manet**

to rush to arms: **ad arma concurrere**
to swear an oath: **facere sacramentum**
to take a turn for the better: **in melius mutari**
to that extent: **pro tanto**
to the best of one's ability: **pro sua parte** or **pro virili parte**
to the center of the road: **ad filum viae**
to the center of the stream: **ad filum aquae**
to the extreme: **ad extremum**
to the gentle reader: **lectori benevolo**
to the greater glory of God: **ad majorem Dei gloriam**
to the highest authority: **ad limina apostolorum** or **ad limina**
to the highest point: **ad summum**
to the last: **ad ultimum**
to the light of day: **superas ad auras**
to the matter: **ad rem**
to the people: **ad populum**
to the place: **ad locum**
to the point of disgust: **usque ad nauseum** or **ad nauseam**
to the point of extermination: **ad internecionem**
to the same degree: **ad eundem gradum**
to the same point: **ad idem**
to this: **ad hoc**
to what end?: **cui bono?**
to your disadvantage: **incommodo tuo**
toastmaster: **arbiter bibendi**
today: **hodie**
tomorrow: **cras**
tomorrow evening: **cras vespere**
tomorrow morning: **cras mane**
tomorrow night: **cras nocte**
tongue: **lingua**
tonight: **hoc nocte**
touch of bitterness: **amari aliquid**
tragic farce: **flebile ludibrium**
travel weary: **fessus de via**

traveling day and night: **itinera diurna nocturnaque**
trial by ordeal: **Dei judicium**
triple brass defense: **aes triplex**
truism: **dictum**
trust God: **crede Deo**
trust not to appearances: **ne fronti crede**
truth: **veritas**
truth conquers all things: **vincit omnia veritas**
truth will prevail: **veritas praevalebit**
turn of phrase: **genus dicendi**
turning point: **magni momenti**
twice a day: **bis in die**
twice as much: **alterum tantum**
twilight: **crepusculum**
twins: **gemini**
two: **duo**
two pairs: **bis bina**

U

unabridged: **in extenso**
unaided: **sine auxilio**
unanimously: **ad unum omnes** or **per totam curiam** or **una voce** or **uno animo** or **uno consensu** or **uno ore**
unbeaten: **invictus**
unbelief: **impietas**
unborn: **nondum natus**
unburied: **inhumatus** or **insepultus** or **intumulatus**
unchanged: **status quo**
uncle: **avunculus** or **patruus**
unconstitutional: **non legitimus**
unconventionally wise: **abnormis sapiens**
uncooked: **incoctus**
under: **sub**
under arms: **in armis**
under bad auspices: **malis avibus**
under my direction: **me duce**
under penalty: **sub poena**
under the influence of wine: **sub vino**

under the protection of the law: **in gremio legis**
under the skin: **intercus**
under this title: **hoc titulo**
underground: **subterraneus**
undeveloped: **in ovo**
undomesticated: **ferae naturae**
unfaithful: **infidelis**
union is strength: **vis unita fortior**
unique: **sui generis**
universal consent: **consensus omnium**
universal peace: **pax orbis terrarum**
universally: **in universum**
universe: **mundi universitas**
unknown: **ignotus**
unknown land: **terra incognita**
unknown painter: **pictor ignotus**
unknown person: **quidam**
unlucky: **infaustus**
unlucky day: **dies infaustus** or **nefasti dies**
unmarried: **innuba** or **innupta**
unprepared: **illotis manibus**
unprovoked: **non laccessitus**
unpublished: **nondum editus**
unrestrained: **impotens sui**
unsatisfactorily: **minus bene**
unsolicited: **sponte sua** or **sua sponte**
unthankful: **male gratus**
until late at night: **ad multam noctem**
until late in the day: **ad multum diem**
unwelcome person: **persona non grata**
unwillingly: **ab invito**
up and down: **sursum deorsum**
up the mountain: **in adversum montem**
up to: **ad**
up to this point: **hactenus**
uphill: **adverso colle** or **adversus collem**
upside down: **inversus**
upstart: **novus homo**
useful: **ex usu**
useless: **inutilis**

V

valid law: **lex rata est**
vanguard: **agmen primum**
variant reading: **varia lectio**
vegetable market: **forum holitorium**
venal throng: **grex venalium**
very little: **minimum**
very much: **impendio**
vestal virgin: **virgo vestalis**
veteran: **emeritus**
vexing question: **quaestio vexata**
victim: **hostia**
virtuous life: **vita honesta**
vital force: **vis vitae**
vital principle: **nisus formativus**
voice of one crying in the desert: **vox clamantis in deserto**
voice of the people: **vox populi**

W

war-cry: **clamor bellicus**
war horse: **equus bellator**
warning: **caveat**
watch and pray: **vigilate et orate**
water: **aqua**
water-carrier: **aquarius**
way of sorrows: **Via Dolorosa**
We praise Thee, O God: **Te Deum, Laudamus**
we cannot: **non possumus**
we have a pope!: **habemus papa!**
weariness of life: **taedium vitae**
weary traveler: **fessus viator**
weighty: **gravitas**
well-being: **bene esse**
well-read: **literatus** or **litteratus**
western: **Hesperius**
westward: **ad occasum** or **ad occidentem**

what does this mean?: **quid hoc sibi vult?**
what is to be done?: **quid faciendum?**
what is truth?: **quid est veritas?**
what now?: **quid nunc?**
what time is it?: **hora quota est?**
what's new?: **quid novi?**
whenever necessary: **pro re nata**
where are you going?: **quo tendis?**
where in the world?: **ubi gentium?**
wherever the book opens: **ad aperturam libri**
wherever you like: **qualibet**
which is: **quod est**
which is the same: **quae est eadem**
which see (pl.): **quae vide**
which see (sing.): **quod vide**
while feasting: **inter epulas**
while still day: **de die**
while still night: **de nocte**
while unmarried: **dum sola**
whirlpool: **vortex**
whisper: **vox clandestina**
whither goest thou?: **quo vadis?**
why do you laugh?: **quid rides?**
why not?: **quid ni?**
wife: **uxor**
wild: **ferus**
will of heaven: **numen divinum**
willy-nilly: **nolens volens**
winter solstice: **bruma**
wisdom: **sapientia**
with: **cum**
with a grain of salt: **cum grano salis**
with advancing years: **aetate progrediente**
with advantage: **ob rem**
with all one's might: **totis viribus** or **viribus totis**
with ease: **de plano**
with envy: **aegris oculis**
with equal pace: **pari passu**
with evil intent: **malo animo**

with favorable omens: **faustis ominibus**
with few words: **paucis verbis**
with full right: **optimo jure** or **pleno jure**
with good reason: **non sine causa**
with great loss (of life): **magno cum detrimento**
with great praise: **magna cum laude**
with greater force: **a fortiori**
with highest honors: **summa cum laude**
with limitations: **secundum quid**
with many tears: **magno cum fletu** or **multis cum lacrimis**
with my pleasure: **me libente**
with praise: **cum laude**
with regard to rank: **salvo ordine**
with the left hand: **sinistra manu**
with the stream: **flumine secundo**
with the teeth: **mordicus**
with the utmost accuracy: **verbatim et literatim et punctatim**
with this proviso: **hac lege**
with tossled hair: **passis crinibus**
with unequal steps: **haud passibus aequis**
with united strength: **viribus unitis**
with unwashed hands: **illotis manibus**
with what intent?: **quo animo?**
within: **intra**
within range: **intra jactum**
within the walls: **intra muros**
without: **sine**
without a blow: **sine ictu**
without anger: **sine ira**
without any danger: **sine omni periculo**
without care: **sine cura**
without charge: **pro bono publico**
without cost: **gratuitus**
without date: **sine anno**
without deceit: **sine fraude**
without delay: **sine mora**
without doubt: **sine dubio**
without envy: **sine invidia**
without hatred: **sine odio**

without help: **sine ope**
without issue: **sine prole**
without jesting: **sine joco**
without legitimate issue: **sine legitima prole**
without male issue: **sine mascula prole**
without objection: **nihil obstat**
without offending modesty: **salvo pudore**
without partiality: **pari passu**
without place: **sine loco**
without prejudice: **salvo jure** or **sine praejudicio**
without pretense: **sine fuco**
without reservation: **simpliciter**
without smell: **inolens**
without stain: **sine maculis**
without strength: **sine nervis**
without surviving issue: **sine prole supersite**
without this: **absque hoc**
without violating sense: **salvo sensu**
witness to a will: **obsignator**
woman: **femina**
wonderful year: **annus mirabilis**
word for word: **ad verbum** or **de verbo**
wordy: **verbosus**
work of art: **opus**

world: **mundus** or **orbis terrae** or **orbis terrarum**
world of images: **mundus imaginalis**
world soul: **anima mundi**
worse: **peior** or **pejor**
worst: **pessimus**
worthy of note: **notatu dignum**
wow!: **hui**
wrath of god: **ira deorum**
writer's cramp: **chorea scriptorum**
written by: **scripsit**

Y

year: **annus**
year from now: **ad annum**
yearlong: **perennis**
yes: **certo** or **etiam** or **ita**
yesterday: **heri** or **hesternus**
yield not to misfortunes: **nec cede malis**
younger: **junior** or **minor natu**
youth: **bona aetas**

Z

Zodiac: **orbis signifer**